35

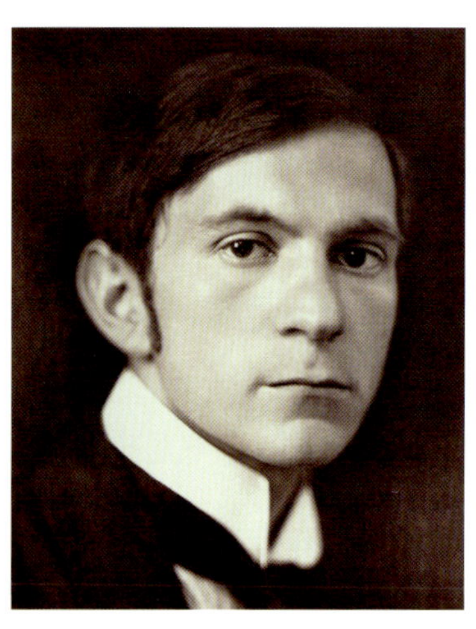

ANTONÍN DUFEK

Vladimír Jindřich **Bufka**

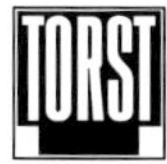

Kniha byla vydána ve spolupráci s Moravskou galerií v Brně (www.moravska-galerie.cz) při příležitosti konání výstavy „Vladimír J. Bufka", pořádané 11. listopadu 2010–13. února 2011.

Kniha byla vydána s podporou Ministerstva kultury ČR.

Oponentní posudky: Prof. PhDr. Petr Wittlich, CSc, Pavel Scheufler.

Autor děkuje za pomoc při přípravě knihy Janě Effenbergerové, Monice Faber, Astrid Mahler, Lucii Horákové, Petře Trnkové, Veronice Jičínské, Pavle Vrbové, Olze Vrkoslavové, Jindřichu Bubeníkovi, Zbyňku Heřmánkovi, Martinu Hrubešovi, Petru Klimentovi, Martinu Krummholzovi, Janu Mlčochovi, Danielu Müllerovi, Derku Patonovi, Pavlu Scheuflerovi, Miloši Šejnovi a Liboru Vykoupilovi.

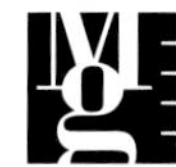

Vladimír Jindřich Bufka, Pioneering Fine Art Photography in Prague

The 1890s were a watershed period for Czech culture and European culture in general. In many countries at the time the first modern movements emerged. In this period, known as the *Fin de siècle*, the Secession movement emerged in central Europe. Not limiting themselves to sculpture and painting, these movements also transformed architecture, design, costume, and ways of life in general. In Paris, Alphonse Mucha began to set the tone. In Prague, "The Manifesto of Czech Modernism" (Manifest České moderny), signed, for instance, by the writers J. S. Machar, Antonín Sova, and F. X. Šalda, was published in 1895, and was soon having an impact on all the arts, not just literature. Of no less importance was the founding of the Mánes Fine Arts Society (Spolek výtvarných umělců Mánes) even earlier, in 1887. The importance of Prague as a European metropolis grew. Art went beyond national boundaries and important exhibitions of artists, including Rodin (1902) and Munch (1905), were held in Prague.

In photography, always dependent on scientific discoveries and technical improvements, the boom in the arts could now draw on a new, technical basis. The greatest innovation since 1860, when the photographic "carte de visite" and the "cabinet card" were beginning to spread rapidly, was the invention of the "dry plate" (or gelatin process) and the advent of the mass production of gelatin-on-glass negatives (and then, later, mostly celluloid), which freed photography from the hands of the professional. Portable and hand-held cameras began to be manufactured. The number of people who began to take up photography as a hobby increased many fold. They were often from the better situated social strata, which were typically not only wealthy but also educated and had, moreover, sufficient leisure time. In the history of photography a new phenomenon appeared, the amateur photographic movement. After nondescript beginnings, the movement soon aimed above all to use photography to make art, an ambition that has endured to this day.

These amateurs of the first mechanical medium of depiction were soon making increasingly sophisticated works, gradually leaving behind the Sunday photographers, for whom photography was primarily a private matter, seeing themselves as treasurers of immortalized memories. In addition to professionals for whom photography was business, amateur photographers began to make "art prints." These enthusiasts wanted to devote their leisure time to the most noble of aims, art. But can photography, this work of optics, mechanics, and chemistry, be art? According to the contemporaneous aesthetic canons some degree of art could be attributed to arranging the subject matter in front of the camera. This was the domain of professional photographers, from whom the amateurs wished to distinguish themselves as much as possible. They therefore chose a difficult path, which the recently simplified technologies had made more complicated: when making prints they began to use laborious chemical processes based on light-sensitive substances other than silver salts. These substances made possible the manipulation of the original negative and, in addition, their resistance to light was verified (art, after all, had to last for ages), whereas the experience with silver compounds had been too short. Consequently, apart from the earlier carbon print, the gum bichromate and tri-color gum bichromate prints, the oil print, bromoil print, and other nineteenth-century photochemical fine-art printing processes began to be employed.[1]

Although the generation of photographers active in the 1890s had already shown their work in public at the grand Bohemian Jubilee Exhibition in Prague in 1891, there were still no artistic aims to speak of here. It took a few more years before the ideas of Impressionism and Art Nouveau made themselves felt in photography. The first Czech amateur photographers' club was established in 1889 to mark the fiftieth anniversary of the publishing of the invention of the daguerreotype. For a long time it provided a reliable basis for future work.[2] In 1893 the club began to publish the periodical *Fotografický obzor* (The Photographic Review). In the course of a few years other amateur photographic clubs were established in the country, Czech and German. Among their first successful photographers were Ludvík Pinka of Kukleny, Bohuslav Mayer of Libochovice, and Otto Šetele of Prague. Another photographer who began as an amateur was Vladimír Jindřich Bufka (1887–1916).

Bufka's forgotten works and life were again made part of the lively continuity of Czech photography by Rudolf Skopec, one of the first collectors of photographs and first historians of the medium.[3] For his research he had access to Bufka's estate, which was kept by Bufka's widow, Marie, who also provided Skopec with additional information. In about 1960, when Bufka's autochrome plates were still kept in a cabinet,[4] Skopec presented a proposal for the publication of a Bufka monograph in the now famous Umělecké fotografie (Art Photography) series (which the Fototorst series follows on from). The editorial board rejected the proposal (which is no surprise, when one recalls the attitude to Art Nouveau, but it is odd that it has taken so long since then to publish anything substantial about Bufka and his work). Skopec's efforts came to fruition only in the form of a short article in a periodical. He also included Bufka in his *Dějiny fotografie v obrazech* (A History of Photography in Pictures) and other articles and also in an exhibition on the history of photography.[5] Skopec saw in Bufka's work the influence of Hermann Clemens Kosel, Edward Steichen, Rudolf Dührkoop, and Nicola Perscheid. He pointed out that the studio in the Lucerna building, in Prague, had been a center of artistic activity.

The pivotal event in making Bufka's work visible was the important exhibition, "Czech Photographic Modernism" (Česká fotografická moderna), which was held at the Museum of Decorative Arts in Prague, in 1989, before moving on, in a modified form, to the Museum of Modern Art in Vienna and other institutions abroad in 1991–92. The already famous work of František Drtikol was juxtaposed with less well-known, and sometimes completely unknown, works by Vladimír J. Bufka, Karel Novák, Josef Anton Trčka, and a smaller number of comparable prints by other photographers. The project was conceived by Josef Kroutvor, who adopted the term "Modernism" from "Manifesto of Czech Modernism." He included photographs which stylistically were between Pictorialism and the Avantgarde, between Art Nouveau and the period after the First World War.[6] Kroutvor sees Czech photographic Modernism as an interlude on the borderline between two eras, and has convincingly found points in common between the Czech poetry of the generation of the 1890s and exhibition prints that we associate with the Art Nouveau style and art photography. This includes, for example, subject matter such as the surface of water and reflections, which appear in the works of both the poet Antonín Sova and Vladimír J. Bufka (not to mention a considerable number of photographers, such as Edward Steichen, Josef Sudek, and Erwin Raupp). Kroutvor also aptly characterized one of the areas of Art Nouveau photography as the development of Romanticism and melancholy at the end of the century.[7] Including Bufka in the context of photography, Kroutvor writes: "If we wish to find works with which to compare Bufka's photographs, then we would say his urban scenes are closest to those of the American photographer Alfred Stieglitz."[8] The term "Czech Photographic Modernism" did not take hold, however, and it is complicated by the already unstandardized terminology used so far. Monika Faber, in the German catalogue to the exhibition, points mainly to how photographers sought stylistically to link up with the current styles of painting and sculpture – Bufka and Drtikol to Symbolism and Post-Impressionism, Novák and Trčka to Art Nouveau and Art Deco.[9]

The first breakthrough that brought together art photographs by many well-known Czechs photographers, but also some nearly unknown ones, both amateurs and professionals, including Bufka, was the "Czech Pictorialism, 1895–1928" exhibition in 1999 and 2000.[10]

Pavel Scheufler, in his writing, has mainly emphasized Bufka's role in popularizing the autochrome. New information about Bufka, discovered in archives and contemporaneous periodicals and also in the photography collection of the Moravian Gallery in Brno, is provided by the photographer Martin Hrubeš in his dissertation for the School of Film and Television of the Academy of Performing Arts (FAMU), Prague.[11]

Jaroslav Anděl and Anne Tucker first included works of all the important Czech photographers, including Bufka, in the context of modern Czech art.[12] Elizabeth Clegg consummated the process of assessing Bufka's works by including him in the first publication on central European art from around 1900. (And a crop of one of Bufka's color gum bichromate prints of night-time Prague is reproduced on the cover of her book.[13]) It was probably his inclusion in a comprehensive exhibition on Art Nouveau photography in 2005 that placed Bufka definitively in the context of European photography probably.[14]

Many gaps remain in our knowledge of this extraordinary man, who was granted only 29 years of life. A short, hitherto unknown recollection by his mother, Karla, is therefore worth quoting almost in its entirety:

"I suffered ill fortune. In less than ten years, death prematurely cut short the life of my husband, Vilibald Absolon, M.D., who died in 1882, a universally loved, respected, and mourned man, leaving me with two small children, Olga and Karel.

Saddened, I returned to my father's home. When my father went into retirement and moved to Olomouc, I married again, five years later, so that my children would have a father – Eduard Bufka [...] The only son of that second marriage, Vladimír, died five years before his father, in the twenty-ninth year of his life. He had studied chemistry at the polytechnic in Prague, was a pupil

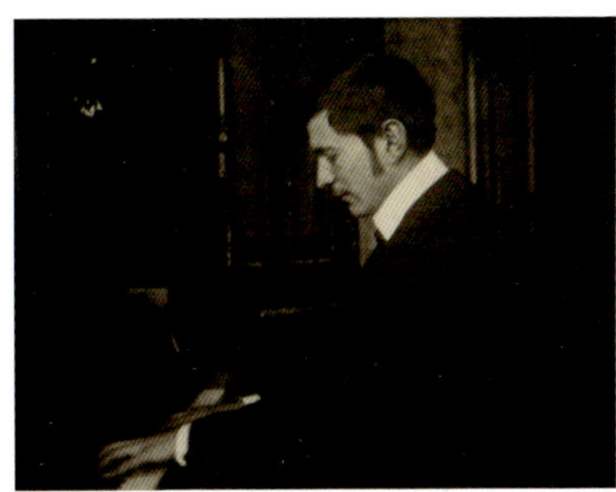

V. J. Bufka at the piano / V. J. Bufka u klavíru, c. 1911

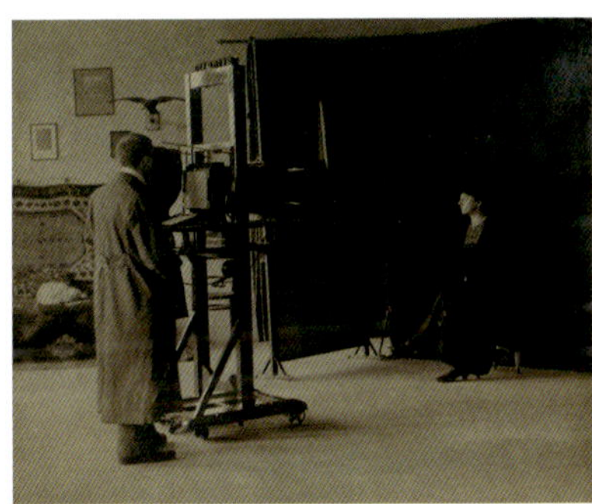

V. J. Bufka in his studio / V. J. Bufka při práci v ateliéru, c. 1911

of the Lumière brothers in Lyon and of the master photographer Kozel [*sic*], a photographer appointed to the royal and imperial court in Vienna. For the Neubert company, which sent him to Russia and Poland, he made color photographs of paintings of the Napoleonic Wars. He spoke six languages as fluently as his mother tongue. He was diligent and of an artistic disposition. He wrote about photography. He went in for art photography, which he wanted to take to a higher level of excellence. His pictures are deposited in the photography department of the Prague Polytechnic."[15]

Bufka was probably not well enough situated socially to remain an amateur photographer. He wanted to make a living with photography. He also studied chemistry at the Prague Polytechnic. It was there that he most probably met Karel Kruis, a professor of zymurgy (chemistry concerned with fermentation processes) and photography, who established a photography studio at the polytechnic in 1899.[16] For many years after his death, in 1917, Kruis's department remained the center of photographic expertise in Prague. Before Czechoslovak independence in October 1918, it was probably the best-equipped Czech photography studio in the country. Kruis's specialty was microphotography and it is not surprising that Bufka devoted himself to microphotography as well. In 1908 Kruis was also interested in the autochrome and it is possible that it was from Kruis that he became acquainted with this method, though only Karel Šmirous, one of the inventers of color photography, is listed as Kruis's pupil.[17] The second likely consultant on the matter of autochromes may have been Jaroslav Husník, who had worked with this innovation since 1908. Being

9

a polyglot, Bufka was probably familiar with the literature and surely needed no help from Husník. Bufka may have worked with Kruis in another area of specialization too, the reproduction of works of art, which Kruis devoted himself to intensively. The landscape photographs that Kruis made for his own pleasure are much like Bufka's photos from the Kladno area, but similar landscapes and snapshots depicting workers in the fields, old cottages, and so on were common in the period of trying out various handheld cameras.

What we know about the relations between Bufka and the now famous painter and print-maker Josef Váchal (1884–1969) comes only from Váchal's biographical notes.[18] From these we learn that Bufka bought wood engravings and "carved figures" from him, and also had portrayed Váchal,[19] including a wedding photograph of him and his wife, Máša (Marie Pešulová). And with friends Váchal celebrated New Year's Eve in Bufka's Lucerna studio in 1911. Váchal and Bufka also performed in Antonín Pech's silent film, *Zub za zub* (A Tooth for a Tooth, 1913).[20] Váchal was, moreover, the artist of the wood-engraved lantern emblem of Bufka's Lucerna studio. It is possible that this artist of color wood engravings helped Bufka to master the difficult technique of color gum bichromate (although the photographs by Váchal that we know so far are black-and-white and technically simple). A connection between Váchal's and Bufka's works is hard to establish, which is surprising, since we know that Bufka used to buy Váchal's works for himself. Could he have perhaps admired them as a mystical and inimitable counterpart to the precision of his own medium? At least one preserved photograph resonates with Váchal's world – *At the Chuchle Cemetery* (color gum bichromate, 1913), a night-time photo with a little glowing lantern, similar to the one from Bufka's Lucerna studio logo.

Another person with whom Bufka undoubtedly used to associate was his contemporary, Jaroslav Petrák (1883–1917), a photographer and writer who also died before his time. His book, *Žeň světla a stínu* (A Harvest of Light and Shadow, 1910), published when he was 27 years old, provided the first comprehensive Czech survey of the international art photography movement. Here we read: "A special place of honor in Czech amateur photography is held by J. V. [*sic*] Bufka, an artist-photographer of dreamy evening and night-time atmospheres. His exquisite works in this field are certainly well known from numerous shop windows in Prague. He has achieved particularly fine results, perhaps unique in this country, in color autochrome photography" (p. 78). Bufka was granted the unique privilege of being able to comment on his own photographs in this publication: "When the February sun sets behind Petřín Hill [Prague], and the grey fog rising from the cold waters of the River Vltava drives out the last pink tinge of evening, many charming lamps glow on Charles Bridge, bringing to life the ancient, blessed scenery. The searcher has found what he has dreamt of. A feeling leads him to these places. And he has set himself the task, by a purely mechanical way, of achieving a picture in which airiness, coolness, and the charm of moods can be concentrated."

In three sentences the twenty-three-year-old Bufka has sketched out a strategy for the subjectivization of his medium, which is generally considered a passive reflection of material things. The way to the photograph begins in the soul, in a picture that the artist has dreamt up. A feeling then leads him, not to the thing, but to a momentary "atmosphere" bringing to life the character of the ancient place. The result is not a superficial imitation of something, but rather the evocation of a mood. Though the picture still comes from a machine called a camera, it is subordinated to the will of the artist. It was therefore a new conception of a work of art, based on the psychological theory of empathy. The most influential theorist writing in German, and read by Czechs, was the psychologically oriented Willi Warstat. Jaroslav Petrák, for example, was dependent on Warstat's views. The theory of empathy dominated photography until the 1930s, when "pure," unmanipulated photography, which we now usually call "modern," became fully accepted. The evocation of a mood was one of the key strategies with which photography freed itself from "mere" description, and approached high art. According to the esteemed art historian V. V. Štech (1885–1974), the evocation of moods was the most that photography could achieve but that was not enough for photography to be awarded the status of high art.[21] In the late Art Nouveau period and afterwards, mood or atmospheric pictures made with a wide variety of media were appropriated by kitsch. But at the time of the birth and development of art photography, these pictures played an important role in the photographic works of almost all members of this movement. Bufka's interpretation of his own work is a unique and important example not only of his theoretic views, but also of a probe into the aesthetic thinking of the time.

Whereas his previous works did not break with convention, the evening and night photos of Prague established Bufka's fame. Some of them were made using double-exposures with time lapse, so that the night-time illumination glows and yet the depicted segment is visible. Considering the low sensitivity of negative stock in those days, the photographer has presented a small miracle to his colleagues, which, when asked, he willingly explained in an article entitled "Fotografie za noci" (Photography at Night).[22] The article is a textbook example of Bufka's writing. He begins with poetically expressed admiration for Prague, followed by confident advice, which demonstrates his expert knowledge, not only of the available techniques and materials but also of the kinds of city lighting used at the time. He then recommends the reader to take photographs of effects like reflections on water, snow, or shiny pavement after the rain. And he concludes by revealing that at the Dresden exhibition he was most fascinated by the Americans, whom he calls "born jugglers" (p. 137).

In addition to the three small illustrations to the article "Fotografie za noci," Bufka was granted the privilege of providing a loose plate supplement to the issue, printed with the best available technology of the day. It was made from the platinum print *Praga Caput Regni* (Prague, Capital of the Kingdom),[23] which Bufka had exhibited as the sole representative of Czech amateur photography at one of the largest exhibitions of art photography, in Dresden in 1909, when the movement was at its peak. (Czech professional photographers were represented there by Jan Langhans.) A reporter for *Fotografický obzor*, Karel Dvořák, was not, however, impressed:

"I walked three times around the hall where the picture was meant to be, and was three times drawn to a large picture by Gustav Mautner of Prague. It was called *Prague*, a view of St. Nicholas's Church from the Golden Well. But Mr. Bufka's picture was simply not to be found. Until finally, in the darkest corner of the whole room, one of the smallest pictures at the exhibition. As to its subject matter – well, you know it from the plate in the October issue of [*Fotografický*] *Obzor*, an almost full-size reproduction of the original. Nice work. Here, however, it is so small and inconsequential that it does not at all correspond to its grand title. Indeed it seems to me a real mockery among these grandly conceived pictures, a painful satire on the wretched role that amateur photography plays in this country in general. I can understand it when, on his own initiative and for the material reasons of an international exhibition, a businessman or industrialist participates; but at this high-quality assembly of amateurs of all nations we should have been represented either impressively or not at all."[24]

We may understand Dvořák's opinion better if we recall that he himself had exhibited his photographic print, *Prague of a Hundred Spires*, in Prague in 1903. Measuring 1×2.30 meters, it was, in its day, a truly monumental work.[25]

In May 1909, Bufka first gave a talk at the Czech Amateur Photographic Club in Prague ("Taking Night and Atmospheric Photographs") at which he also projected autochromes. In the course of one year he had thus attracted attention with innovations. It was a truly rapid start to his career in photography. In the following years he often gave talks and held courses, which were a source of income for him. At the age of twenty-two he had thus already influenced the field, particularly Czech photography. It is unclear what Bufka's autochromes were actually like. The autochrome, a colored slide on a glass plate, was the first wide-spread technique of color photography. It was right in the factory of the inventors of this technique (and indeed mainly of cinematography), the Brothers Lumière in Lyon, that Bufka became an expert in exploiting the potential of the autochrome. And he became its first popularizer in the Bohemian Lands. Stylization was, however, almost impossible with this method. The portrait reproduced in the book that he wrote about the autochrome adheres to the conventions of the commercial photography of those days.[26] Similarly, the series of postcards, printed from his own masterfully composed autochromes, presents a predictable picture of the beauties of ancient Prague.[27] Yet, as Skopec remarks: "On autochrome plates he then made his masterpieces in portraiture, the genre picture, and the landscape."[28] The autochrome genre in particular must have been interesting, and the portraits may have been of leading artists, scientists and scholars, and members of the aristocracy.

Bufka completed his training in photography at Hermann Clemens Kosel's prominent studio in Vienna, where he worked as an unpaid intern from 1 November 1910 to the spring of 1911. A native of Temný důl (Dunkelthal) in the Krkonoše mountains (Riesengebirge) of north Bohemia, Kosel was, in these years, at the peak of his career as a photographer of Viennese high society (including the heir to the throne, Franz Ferdinand and his family). Kosel's portraits are among the first, still unsurpassed, examples of "glamour" photography, which was later, and actually is to this day, linked mainly with alluring, flattering photographs of film stars. Kosel's portraits are also an incarnation of the idea of the Vienna of Strauss waltzes, Sacher torte, and the glitter of the Imperial court. They follow on from the painterly tradition of the flattering portrait miniature.

Many of Kosel's subtle approaches – for example, considerable retouching, a painted background, the setting of the figure and the head in an oval cut-out – later came in useful to Bufka. All commercial photographers, without exception, had to accommodate at least some of their clients' wishes to be made to look as good as possible in the photographs. (That is evident, for instance, from Bufka's portraits of the Schwarzenbergs.) None of the available portraits by Bufka, however, reduces the sitter to a merely attractive exterior without a personality.

At Kosel's, Bufka could also perfect the pigment print techniques, particularly the gum bichromate. Though he worked for Kosel without a wage, Bufka must have counted on this internship eventually paying off. After all, the previous training at the Lumière brothers was later a superb advertisement for him. Based on what we now know of Bufka's work, we admire mainly his outstanding photos from the center of Vienna, which were even published in specialist periodicals.

Bufka's prestige continued to grow rapidly. He was given the honor of writing an editorial to a new volume of the *Fotografický věstník* (Photographic Bulletin) in 1911. He ends the piece with the saying "Per aspera ad astra!" (Through adversity to the stars), and appears to have consistently applied this motto in practice. After his return from Vienna, he offered photography courses from 15 March 1911 onwards (see the Biographical Chronology), not wishing to keep the knowledge he had gained only to himself.

Then, in the spring, came "The Exhibition of the Czech Club of Amateur Photographers in Prague," held in the Lucerna building. It was, for the

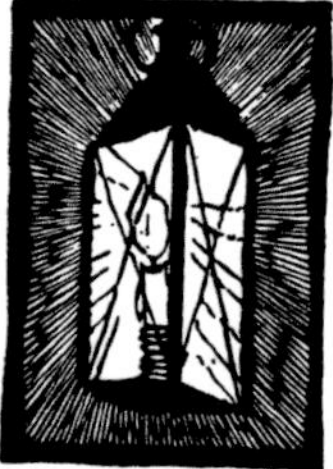

Josef Váchal: The logo of Bufka's studio in the Lucerna building / Josef Váchal: značka ateliéru V. J. Bufky v Lucerně, 1912

An advertisement for Bufka's studio /
Inzerát ateliéru V. J. Bufky

first time since 1903, now participated in by a number of other clubs, exhibiting more than three hundred works. Apart from Drtikol, it was Bufka who aroused the most interest in one reporter:

"The best works at the exhibition, without question, belong to Messrs. Bufka and Drtikol. With regard to subtlety, Bufka's *Urania* is unequalled at the exhibition. The foggy atmosphere of the rainy day has here been done justice to by his artistic eye and the execution is evidence of his absolute mastery of the platinum print. The portrait of H. C. Kosel is the best portrait at the exhibition and Kosel's pupil could surely not have rewarded his master in a better way than by exhibiting this superb portrait. The gum bichromate, *The Sculpture*, is a first-class achievement by Bufka in tones and light; though the manual work on the picture is in places somewhat more visible than one might have wished, the picture leaves a very good impression. Likewise, *Summer Evening on Kampa* and *The Last Rays* are evidence of Bufka's refined artistic taste and technical excellence. I hope, to the benefit of our amateurs, that Bufka becomes the teacher of everyone who wants to devote himself to art photography."[29]

Probably that summer Bufka left for St. Petersburg and Warsaw to make photographs of paintings for the Neubert printing house back in Prague. It is also likely that he was interested in the potential of the reproduction of photographs in print, particularly autochromes. After the color postcards of Prague, this was the second commission of which we know. In October, Bufka returned from his travels, got married, and opened a new studio in the renowned Lucerna building, which became a center of art activity. He worked together with the inventor Jaroslav Husník on an exhibition of amateur photography in the new Museum of Technology in Prague, and evidently also included his own work in it. His short life had probably reached its zenith at this point. For reasons unknown to us, he left the studio in the Lucerna the following year, and eventually settled down, in 1913, in another excellent spot in the center of Prague, in Jindřišská ulice, opposite the main post office. After that there is little news of him. In late 1914 he published a large collection of his own works, both commissions and photos made strictly for himself, at an exhibition of professional photographers, which was held in the most respected exhibition space in Prague, the Rudolfinum to mark the 75th anniversary of the public announcement of the daguerreotype. Most of the works were portraits; only some of them included the names of the sitters.[30] Of the other photographs, we have titles that match the preserved prints (gum bichromates combined with other processes) of *Evening Train, Chuchle Cemetery on All Souls' Day,* and perhaps also *Evening at Košíře Cemetery* and *On the River Vltava.* The section of the exhibition with photos by foreigners included works by some of the most respected art photographers, in particular Hugo Erfurth and Nicola Perscheid. Concerning Bufka's local competitors, apart from works by Drtikol the exhibition also showed photos by Schlosser & Wenisch and Vaněk & Kanderál. None of them had an easy time earning a living.

After Bufka's death in 1916, his widow, Marie, ran his studio until 1928. She even signed some of his prints "V. J. Bufka," either because she wanted to retain the name of the company or because she had made the prints or had ordered them made from her late husband's negatives.[31] It is not always possible to be certain on this point.[32] Some of the series of (self-)portraits of Marie Bufková was, to judge from the fashion of the clothing, made after her husband's death. (One of them is signed "Maňa," a familiar form of "Marie," and is dated "1919", another is signed "atelier Bufka 1914"). A portrait of the actress Anna Sedláčková, published in the periodical *Rozpravy Aventina* in 1927 and signed "M. Bufka," was made in a similar way.[33] The authorship of some undated photographs, for example Bufka's (self-)portrait , remains uncertain. On the other hand, it is safe to assume that Marie took part in the stylization of her husband's portraits of her.

Bufka's works can usefully be categorized into several groups. The first contains photos in the album of thirteen prints, which was published as *Večerní Praha (Prague in the Evening,* 1909). Five of them show Prague under snow with an ice-covered Vltava. (Snow, reflecting the light, enabled Bufka to photograph in the early evening, even with the low sensitivity of the negatives of those times.) On the white surfaces the silhouettes of people and things are delineated in sharp contrast; the photographic prints resemble engravings. In comparison with these, prints like *Praga Caput Regni* are completely covered by fine grey tones, which the platinum print was best able to achieve. Things are enveloped in semi-darkness, which blurs their boundaries; the silhouette of Prague Castle blends with the cloudy sky. In other photos the night-time illumination of the embankment predominates. The light or, more precisely, the transformation of visual reality by light, is what links all the prints in the album. *Prague in the Evening* is probably the first set in Czech art photography to have unified subject matter and method. Series were not supposed to become the order of the day until Modern photography (promoted mainly by one of its pioneers, László Moholy-Nagy) but series were actually not unusual in the art photography of the nineteenth century. The emergence of the set may have been inspired by the evening scenes that Jakub Schikaneder painted in the 1890s and 1900s."[34]

Light as a theme is developed further in Bufka's Vienna work. Here he photographed, on the one hand, using contrasting backlighting and, on the other, in fog, perhaps even rain. To photograph using backlighting is to this day a test of the photographer's mastery of light contrasts. With his photographs from the arcades of the Vienna Opera and Town Hall, Bufka provides the first, indeed textbook, examples, of the use of diagonal and frontal backlighting to compose a picture with cast shadows, whose blacks are often employed more in the texture or composition of the picture than in the objects that create the shadows (here, grey architectural elements). A striking graphic element (and thanks to the articulation of the architecture often also geometric) thus becomes part of the image. In Vienna Bufka also made *The Sculpture*, a photograph of dazzling white sculpture at the Museum of Decorative Arts, illuminated by the sun in front of the dark facade of the building. He thus created the extraordinarily effective addition to his works using light contrasts. Many of these photos were made as platinum prints and gum bichromate prints, but in them Bufka did not stray far from either the look or the potential of straight photography.

Similarly masterful are the photos of Vienna in fog. Bufka depicts the frequently photographed Urania building not only in the usual frontal view (with stunning staffage), but also in an unusual view from the Danube. The

Votive Church in the rain is reflected on the inundated pavement, and appears to be sailing over the surface of the water. Another outstanding photo is of St. Charles's Church with a landau, again close to Jakub Schikaneder and late nineteenth and early twentieth century genre painting. The affinity with Schikaneder is not only in the subject matter, but, as with the other misty and gloomy photographs, also in the blurry delineation of the boundaries between the atmosphere and the depicted objects, which, in black-and-white, look like shadows. It also brings to mind Monet's Impressionism and Seurat's Pointillism. We may then imagine the whole world as permeable, as thick or thin fog or as a cloud; the contrast between the sky and the earth is suppressed. Another surprise from the Vienna sojourn is the portrait of Kosel, delineated with similar softness, like the outdoor photos in the fog. Another, similar Bufka portrait has not been preserved. In this case the journeyman may have used some of the first soft-focus lenses that had belonged to his teacher, although blurriness could also be achieved by other means. A fine print, which can reasonably be considered an original, shows a face shimmering with light, as if observed through hot air. A group of photos, using light contrasts and the blurry delineation of visuality, declares its advocacy of Impressionism. In this sense, Bufka proposed the term "style photography" (*stylová fotografie*), instead of "art photography" (*umělecká fotografie*). But he did not limit himself to only one style.

In the context of photographic history, Bufka's photos are linked with the solution of lighting problems typical of early work with hand-held cameras. The new technology and techniques and

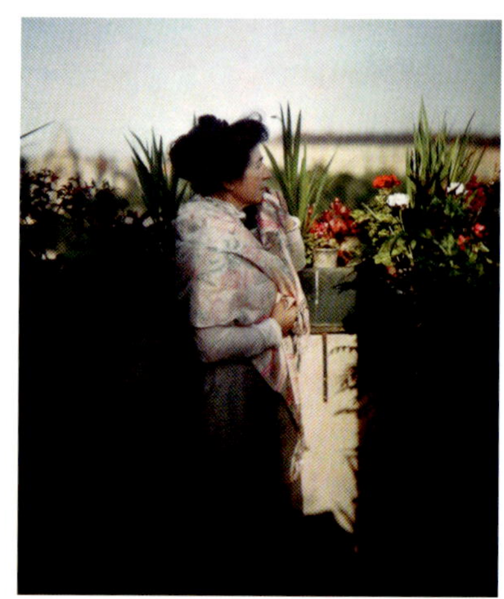

V. J. Bufka: Karla Bufková-Wanklová, autochrome / autochrom, c. 1915

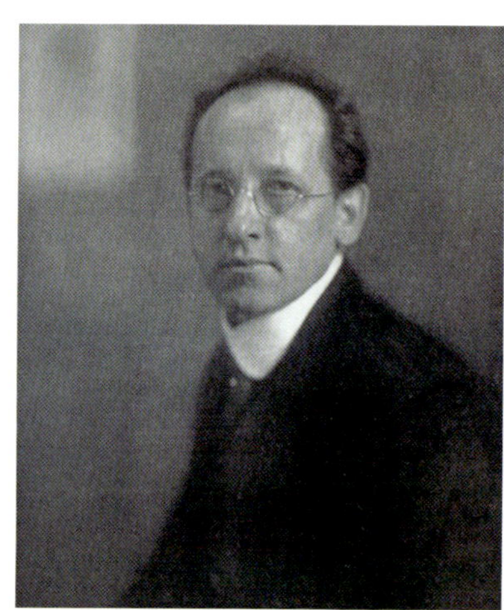

V. J. Bufka: Hermann C. Kosel, c. 1911

the new possibilities became a challenge to the thematization of the medium itself, to investigating its potential in comparison with manual techniques of depiction used in painting, drawing, and printing. Light, the main instrument of the photographer, necessarily had to interest him. Few photographers explored the extreme possibilities of their medium. With his photographs taken at night and in bad weather, Stieglitz was the one who initiated the task. Most photographers in Europe chose to work on the negative by means of the gum bichromate print and other processes that enabled them to influence the final result. Bufka, inspired perhaps by the Dresden exhibition of 1909, was in this respect exceptional. His works start from seeing, from original visual observations. Among the best examples of this is a miniature depiction of an ordinary street (perhaps in Prague) with a gleaming puddle. Were it not for the costumes of the figures, we might mistake this for a work by someone associated with the Skupina 42 (Group 42), whose main subject matter became the outskirts of Prague during the Second World War.

Bufka's most renowned photographs were, however, made with the gum bichromate technique. The chronology of when they were made is unclear. A number of them are undated and we know the dates of only a few important works. The prints were usually dated when they were made. The earliest gum bichromate print bears the date 1908, and probably depicts a sunset, the main subject of all atmospheric photographs. Part of the usual repertoire of Art Nouveau landscape art is photos with poplars and particularly well depicted birches, whereas the uncolored photos of snowy woods near the town of Říčany (1911) and the diagonally composed nocturne, *After Sunset* (1908)[35], are reminiscent, for example, of early works by Jaromír Funke, from about 1920. In the thematization of the medium of photography, Funke unconsciously followed on from Bufka.

Apart from the works by which he became ranked among the virtuoso interpreters of the requisite repertoire of Art Nouveau photography, Bufka also expanded the repertoire in an original way in terms of subject matter and style. The most surprising photo in this respect is the head of Marie Bufková in a Sioux head-dress (though the gum bichromate print is, unfortunately, untitled). It is presumably not meant as a portrait, because a head in a such a headdress would properly be a man's (since women's head ornaments were different). The profile of the head with the headdress must have been conceived as a symbol of magnanimity, probity, bravery, toughness, pride, and defiance – in other words, the values with which one still associates the original inhabitants of America. It is because of these values that the indigenous peoples surprisingly were a model of unyielding patriotism also in the Czech National Revival, as in Mikoláš Aleš's *The Elements* (1881). For Bufka, however, the link to indigenous peoples (albeit South American) was probably the Czech traveler Alberto Vojtěch Frič, whom he also portrayed. (Frič also took a member of the Chamacoco tribe, Chervuish, to Prague in order to diagnose of what was ailing him and to cure the whole tribe. Chervuish stayed in Prague in 1908–09, so the portrait of Frič may date from these years. The fact that Frič looks younger, may be because of retouching.) Bufka's gum bichromate print is conceived in dark (low-key) tones, from which emerges the noble profile of the head, on both the center of which and the side that is turned away light is falling (a "Rembrandt profile"). The hand at the chin and the downward gaze suggest contemplation, while the light from an unknown source may symbolize the dawn or point to the future.

The outbound evening train in a huge shroud of smoke, its red tail-lights lit in an otherwise black-and-white print, is in Bufka's work another textbook example of his conception of subject matter that would later become so popular. Bufka was not of course the first "railroad photographer." Here too he was preceded by Stieglitz, who, with characteristic eloquence, called his famous, dark photo of a train yard with a locomotive spewing a vertical column of smoke *The Hand of Man* (1902). Yet his and Bufka's are radically different works. It is fair to see Stieglitz's photo as a symbol of industrial civilization (though we today perceive the cloud of smoke with feelings opposite to those of a hundred years ago), whereas Bufka's train (surely an express) is speeding off into the distance (although at the moment of exposition it may be standing still) and is a romantic symbol of far away lands. The diagonal of the tracks along the ground and the diagonal of smoke along the sky meet somewhere in front of the visible end of the train, perhaps at infinity. The machine represents speed, as it does in Futurism

Bufka also photographed a cargo ship with Chuchle in the background and smoke rising above the town. This was his depiction of the industrial outskirts of Prague. His steamer sailing down the river has much in common with Schikaneder's steamers. His interest in technology and science, as well as the precision evident in all his writings, were, however, linked in his work with a sense of the irrational and subject matter from cemeteries. The night-time photos from the cemeteries in Chuchle and Smíchov (later part of Prague) are characteristic of Decadent art, whereas the photo from the town of Košíře (later also part of Prague) is Impressionistic. Although the gum bichromate versions of these works also enabled Bufka to make manual changes to the photos, here the specifically photographic quality is not being denied and can easily be perceived as a remarkable counterpart to handcrafted artworks with similar subject matter.

The unique still life with a vase and porcelain figurine (a gum bichromate print) is executed entirely in a blue tone, and demonstrates that Bufka allowed himself greater freedom in this genre. It is similar to the work of the Artěl arts and crafts cooperative and mainly to the nascent Art Deco style. Among his works most approaching abstraction is a sepia landscape. Visuality here takes the form of decorative print-like silhouettes, as in the gum bichromate print *At the Wonderful Old Smíchov Cemetery* (1914).

We do not know which of Bufka's photos is still missing, but if we consider the short period in which he worked, the missing ones would probably include the autochrome plates and of course most of the commissioned portraits; the photos published in the illustrated periodicals have not been taken into account. Bufka was also an outstanding writer on photography. His life remains, however, half concealed. Even though in his day almost every artist was considered a genius, Bufka probably truly merits the name. The cultural links of his photographic works are far more numerous and deeper than one can tell from this publication. He was the kind of artist who was independently able to contemplate the new potential of his medium, and was one of the first, or perhaps the first ever, to employ it and also to relate it to the topics of his day which appeared in the arts. He was a pioneer of straight art photography within pure photography and a superb stylist beyond it. He started from visual observations, and perhaps for that very reason often moved about on the boundaries of the visible, where the lack of light makes it difficult for forms to be captured, and instead accentuates the role of light in the appearance of reality and the importance of seeing. In this respect his photographs have something in common with the late work of Josef Sudek.[36] Bufka was not the kind of artist to be concerned only with expressing himself. Rather, it seems that he understood the times he lived in as a plurality of possibilities, including stylistic plurality, which even back then was striking. Impressionism, Post-Impressionism, Art Nouveau, Symbolism, Cubism, and Futurism to some extent coexisted side by side and Bufka's attitude to this plurality was almost postmodern. To make his photos he employed strategies based on an impressive knowledge and understanding of the possibilities and tasks of his day.

Notes

1   See Pavel Scheufler, *Historické fotografické techniky*, Prague and Pilsen: Ipos Artama and Společnost IF, 1993.

2   Josef Mühldorf and PavlaVrbová, *První klub fotografů amatérů v Čechách*, Prague: Národní informační a poradenské středisko pro kulturu, forthcoming, 2010.

3   Antonín Dufek, "Rudolf Skopec in Relation to Helmut Gernsheim," in *Helmut Gernsheim Reconsidered: The Proceedings of the Mannheim Symposium*. Edited by Anna Auer and Alistair Crawford, Passau: Dietmar Klinger, 2004, pp. 53–56; Antonín Dufek, "Rudolf Skopec, předseda poradního sboru fotografické sbírky Moravské galerie v Brně," 62. *Bulletin Moravské galerie v Brně*, 2006, pp. 29–32; Otakar Jiránek, "Život a dílo prof. Rudolfa Skopce." Extended essay, Department of Photography, FAMU, Prague, 1980.

4   Rudolf Skopec in a private interview.

5   – ec. [Rudolf Skopec], "V. J. Bufka," *Československá fotografie* 12 (1961), no. 4, pp. 58–59, with plates. At "The History of Photography II" exhibition he presented three loose plates from *Fotografický obzor*. The two plates in Rudolf Skopec, *Dějiny fotografie v obrazech od nejstarších dob k dnešku*, Prague: Orbis, 1963, were made from original negatives.

6   "Czech modern photography lasted from 1908 to 1926," claims Kroutvor. See Josef Kroutvor and Zdeněk Kirschner, *Česká fotografická moderna* (exh. cat.), Prague: Museum of Decorative Arts, 1989, no page numbers.

7   Josef Kroutvor, "Die tschechische Moderne," in Monika Faber and Josef Kroutvor (eds.), *Photographie der Moderne in Prag 1900–1925* (exh. cat.), Zurich: Edition Stemmle, 1995, pp. 6–13.

8   Kroutvor and Kirschner, *Česká fotografická moderna*, no page numbers.

9   Monika Faber, "Portraits zwischen Versunkenheit und Pose," in Faber (ed.) *Photographie der Moderne in Prag 1900–1925*, p. 103.

10 Jan Mlčoch and Pavel Scheufler (eds.), *Český piktorialismus 1895–1928*, Prague: Paideia, 1999.

11 Martin Hrubeš, "Vladimír Jindřich Bufka," B.A. essay, FAMU, Prague, 1994; Martin Hrubeš, "Vladimír Jindřich Bufka," M.A. extended essay, FAMU, Prague. 1998.

12 Jaroslav Anděl et al (eds.), *Czech Modernism 1900–1945*, New York and Houston: Bulfinch Press and The Museum of Fine Arts Houston, 1989, pp. 123–47. This is the catalogue to an exhibition held at the Museum of Fine Arts, Houston, 8 October 1989–7 January 1990. The exhibition then moved to the Akron Art Museum, the Brooklyn Museum, the International Center of Photography, and the Anthology Film Archives, New York, 2 March–13 May 1990.

13   Elizabeth Clegg, *Art, Design and Architecture in Central Europe 1890–1920*, New Haven and London: Yale UP, 2006. The volume mentions only a few photographers, including, from the Bohemian Lands, František Drtikol.

14   *La photographie pictorialiste en Europe 1888–1918* (exh. cat.), Rennes: Musée des Beaux-arts de Rennes, 2005; *Impressionist Camera: Pictorial Photography in Europe, 1888–1918* (exh. cat.), Edited by Patrick Daum, Frances Ribemont, and Phillip Prodger. London: Merrell, 2006; Clegg, *Art, Design & Architecture in Central Europe 1890–1920*.

15   Karla Bufková-Wanklová, "Vzpomínky," in Berthold Kladivo (ed.), *Zlatá rodina*. Blansko: Masarykova měšťanská škola, 1936, pp. 41–42. I am indebted to Petra Trnková for bringing this to my attention and lending it to me.

16   Miroslav Kotěšovec, *Karel Kruis: Fotografie z let 1882–1917 / Photographs from 1882–1917*. Trans. Karolina Hughes and Barbara Day, Prague: Libri, 2009.

17   Jiří Číp, Rudolf Jung, and Pavel Scheufler, *Karel Šmirous – výběr barevných fotografií z rastrových diapozitivů z let 1908–1955 / A Selection of Color Photographs from the Screened Positives from 1908–1955*, Prague: Národní technické muzeum, 1993.

18   *Paměti Josefa Váchala, dřevorytce*. Edited by Milan Drápala with an Afterword by Hana Klinková (MS, 1935), Prague: Prostor, 1995.

19   The portrait is published in Miloš Šejn, *Josef Váchal: Dílo* (exh. cat.), Roudnice nad Labem: Galerie výtvarného umění, 1984. According to Šejn, the two artists made each other's acquaintance in 1906.

20   Jaroslav Brož and Myrtil Frýda, *Historie československého filmu v obrazech*, Prague: Orbis, 1959. The information was compiled by Martin Hrubeš in his M.A. research.

21   V. V. Štech, "Estetika fotografie," *Fotografický obzor* 30 (1922), a series of articles running almost throughout the whole volume, adapted from lectures given in 1914.

22   V. J. Bufka, "Fotografie za noci," *Fotografický obzor* 17 (1909), no. 6, pp. 133–37.

23   "Praga caput regni" (apart from being medieval a motto from the city emblem) is a poem by Petr Bezruč from his *Slezské písně* (Silesian Songs), which were first published in 1903. With this title, Bufka is demonstrating his patriotism and, indirectly, his social compassion.

24   Karel Dvořák, "Jinde a u nás: 5. výstavní list drážďanský," *Fotografický obzor* 17 (1909), no. 12, pp. 182–83. Gustav Mautner was one of the most important members of the Club deutscher Amateurphotographen in Prag. His *Prague* dates from 1908.

25   See, for example, Jiří Jeníček, *Fotografie jako zření světa a života*, Prague: Československé filmové nakladatelství, 1947, p. 21.

26   V. J. Bufka, *O fotografii v barvách pomocí desky autochromové*, Prague: E. Weinfurter, 1910.

27   The postcards were published by Minerva, a Prague publisher of art, in 1910.

28   – ec. [Rudolf Skopec], "Mistři světové fotografie: Vladimír Jindřich Bufka," *Československá fotografie* 2 (1961), no. 4, p. 58.

29   V[ladimír] Fanderlík, "Jarní výstava klubová," *Fotografický obzor* 19 (1911), no. 5, p. 104.

30   František Kobliha, the editor Rydlo (perhaps Jaroslav Rydlo), Renata Tyršová, Professor Ostrčil (propably the composer-conductor Otakar Ostrčil [1879–1935]), Dr. Hartmann, the original, in the National Technical Museum, Prague, is signed "Atelier Bufka, P. (?) Hartman, and three portraits of Schwarzenbergs ("His Serene Highness Karl Fürst zu Schwarzenberg," "Portrait of

His Serene Highness Karl Fürst zu Schwarzenberg with His Little Son," "Portrait of Her Serene Highness Eleonora, Fürstin zu Schwarzenberg, with Her Little Son." The last two mentioned here are in the collection of the Moravian Gallery, Brno, together with three other Bufka portraits of Schwarzenbergs.

31 Evidence of that is an unsigned oil print (of birches at the edge of a forest), signed "V. J. Bufka 1921," which has been preserved also as a gum bichromate print signed "V. J. Bufka 1912."

32 Gabriela Kontra, "Fotografky v českých zemích 1839–1918," extended essay for a degree, FAMU, Prague, 2005.

33 *Rozpravy Aventina*, 1927–28, p. 33. It is this relationship between the signed portrait and the series of some portraits by Marie Bufková that justifies the assumption that this is a series of self-portraits. The signature alone, "Maňa 1919," is not enough, however, to justify its attribution to Marie.

34 In his referee's report on the manuscript of the current book, the art historian Petr Wittlich points out another connection to Bufka's works: "In particular, a comparison of Bufka's Prague photos and the subject matter of the paintings of Antonín Slavíček [1870–1910] would reveal interesting similarities and contrasts. It is probably here that one would locate the core question concerning the artistic value of Art Nouveau pictorialist photography employing this sort of subject matter."

35 The photo, a platinum print, may have been shown in 1911 under the name *The Last Rays* at "The Exhibition of the Czech Club of Amateur Photographers in Prague," cat. no. 29.

36 Bufka's *Evening Prague* has much in common also with Sudek's first set, *Praha: 10 náladových fotografií: Album fotografií* (Prague: Ten Atmospheric Photographs, an Album), Prague: Ústřední státní ústav grafický, [1922–24]. This set is available in UPM, Prague.

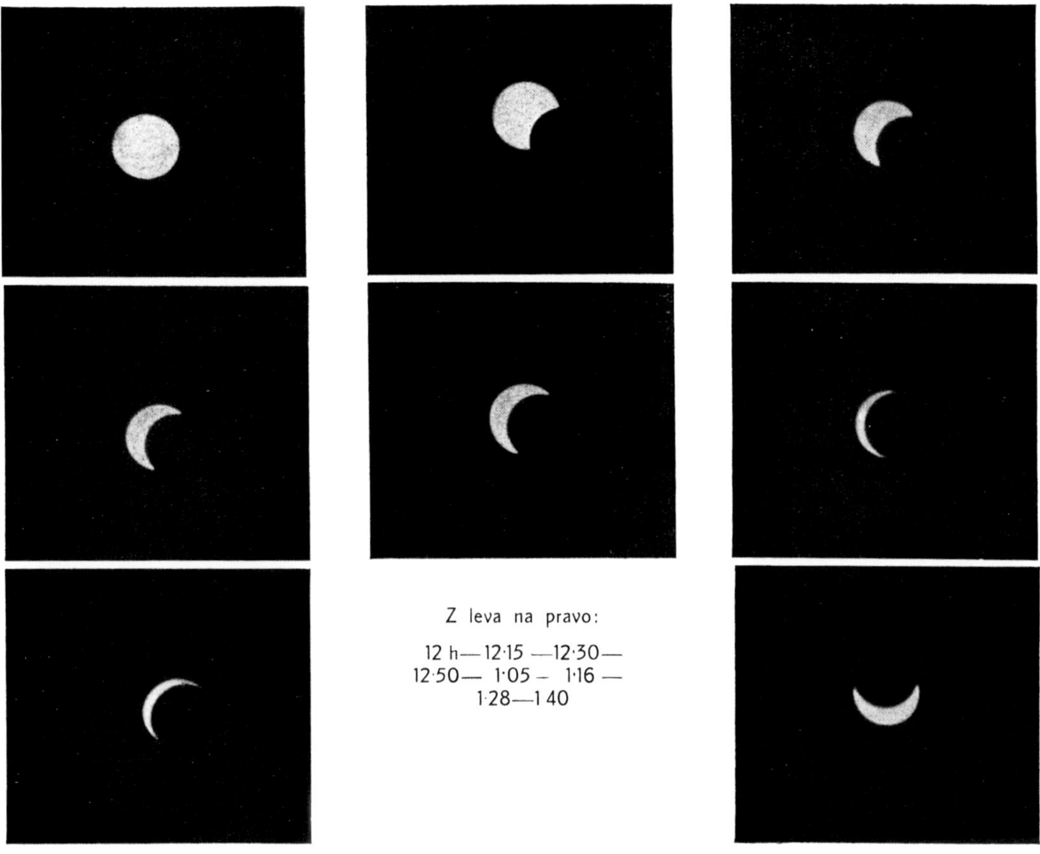

A table for an article by V. J. Bufka: This Year's Solar Eclipse / Tabulka ke článku V. J. Bufky Letošní zatmění slunce, 1912

Vladimír Jindřich Bufka, průkopník umělecké fotografie v Praze

Devadesátá léta 19. století byla přelomovým obdobím pro českou i evropskou kulturu. V mnohých zemích tehdy vznikla první moderní hnutí. V době označované jako *fin de siècle* se odtrhují od akademického umění secesní skupiny v některých evropských metropolích. Neomezují se jen na zobrazující umění, proměňují též architekturu, design, módu a životní styl. V Paříži začíná udávat tón Alfons Mucha. V Praze Manifest Česká moderna (1895), podepsaný literáty Josefem Svatoplukem Macharem, Antonínem Sovou, Františkem Xaverem Šaldou a dalšími, neměl význam jen pro literaturu, ale pro celou kulturu. Nemenší význam mělo založení Spolku výtvarných umělců Mánes (1887). Rostl význam Prahy jako významné evropské metropole, umění přesáhlo domácí poměry. Připomeňme si alespoň pražské výstavy Augusta Rodina roku 1902 a Edvarda Muncha roku 1905.

Ve fotografii, stále závislé na vědeckých objevech a technických zdokonaleních, se shodou okolností mohl kulturní rozmach opřít o novou technickou bázi. Uskutečnila se největší inovace od roku 1860, kdy se začaly lavinovitě šířit fotografické vizitky a později kabinetky. Vynález tzv. suchého procesu a tovární výroba skleněných (později většinou celuloidových) želatinových negativů osvobodily fotografii z rukou profesionálů. Začaly se vyrábět přenosné a příruční fotoaparáty. Mnohonásobně vzrostl počet osob, které se začaly věnovat fotografii jako svému koníčku. Rekrutovaly se často z vyšších společenských vrstev, k jejichž sociologickým charakteristikám patřily nejen movitost a vzdělání, ale i dostatek volného času. V dějinách fotografie se objevil nový fenomén, amatérské hnutí, které si po nevyhraněných začátcích stanovilo jako svůj nejvyšší cíl využít média fotografie k umělecké tvorbě. Cíl, který přetrvává dodnes.

Tvorba těchto milovníků prvního mechanického média zobrazování byla stále sofistikovanější a postupně se uzavírala před nedělními fotografy, pro něž byla fotografie především privátní záležitostí, pokladnicí zvěčnělých vzpomínek. Vedle řemeslných prací živnostníků se začaly objevovat umělecké „tisky" amatérských fotografů, kteří chtěli svůj volný čas věnovat nejušlechtilejšímu cíli, umění. Může však být uměním fotografie, toto dílo optiky, mechaniky a chemie? Podle tehdejších estetických kánonů bylo možno přiznat uměleckou úroveň aranžování před kamerou, což byla doména živnostenských fotografů, od nichž se amatéři chtěli co nejvíc odlišit. Zvolili si obtížnou cestu, jíž právě dosažená technická zjednodušení opět zkomplikovali: při vytváření pozitivů začali používat pracné chemické procesy, které byly založeny na jiných světlo-citlivých látkách, než na solích stříbra. Umožňovaly totiž manipulaci původní-ho negativu a kromě toho jejich stálost ke světlu byla prověřená (umění přece musí přetrvat věky), kdežto zkušenost se stříbrnými sloučeninami byla příliš krátká. Vedle staršího uhlotisku tak byly postupně aplikovány gumotisk a ba-revný gumotisk, olejotisk, bromolejotisk a další „ušlechtilé tisky".[1]

Fotografická generace devadesátých let se sice představila veřejnosti již roku 1891 na grandiózní Zemské jubilejní výstavě v Praze, o uměleckých cílech zde však nemohla být řeč. Trvalo ještě několik let, než se ve fotografii prosadi-ly ideje impresionismu a secesních hnutí. První český klub fotografů amatérů vznikl roku 1889 při příležitosti padesátého výročí zveřejnění vynálezu dague-rrotypie. Na dlouhou dobu poskytoval spolehlivou základnu dalšímu dění.[2] Roku 1893 začal klub vydávat časopis *Fotografický obzor*. Během několika let při-byly další německé a české kluby fotoamatérů, k prvním úspěšným českým au-torům patřili Ludvík Pinka z Kuklen (nyní část Hradce Králové), Bohuslav Mayer z Libochovic a Pražan Otto Šetele. Jako amatér začínal i Vladimír Jindřich Bufka.

Jeho zapomenuté dílo a osobnost vracel do kontextu živé kontinuity české fotografie Rudolf Skopec, jeden z prvních historiků a sběratelů fotografie.[3] Mohl těžit z pozůstalosti dochované u vdovy po autorovi Marie a z jejích infor-mací. Asi roku 1960, kdy ještě existovala skříň plná Bufkových autochromů,[4] podal návrh na vydání Bufkovy monografie v dnes již slavné edici Umělecká fo-tografie, na niž dnes navazuje edice Fototorst. Redakční rada návrh zamítla (což za tehdejšího vztahu k secesi nebylo nic překvapivého, nicméně Bufka měl smů-lu i po smrti) a Skopcovo úsilí se realizovalo jen v nevelkém časopiseckém textu. Zařadil Bufku do svých Dějin fotografie v obrazech a dalších textů a do výstavy o dějinách fotografie.[5] Rudolf Skopec spatřoval v Bufkově díle vlivy Hermanna Clemense Kosela, Edwarda Steichena, Rudolfa Dührkoopa a Nicoly Perscheida. Upozornil na to, že ateliér v Lucerně byl uměleckým střediskem.

Přelomovou událostí ve zviditelnění Bufkova díla byla významná vý-stava Uměleckoprůmys-lového muzea v Praze s názvem *Česká fotografická mo-derna* (1989), přenesená v pozměněné podobě do Muzea moderního umění ve

Vídni a dalších zahraničních institucí (1991–92). Tehdy již slavné dílo Františka Drtikola zde bylo konfrontováno s méně známými a zcela neznámými pracemi Vladimíra J. Bufky, Karla Nováka, Josefa Antona Trčky a menším počtem srovnatelných pozitivů od dalších autorů. Autor projektu výstavy Josef Kroutvor termín moderny odvodil z Manifestu české moderny (1895). Stylově situoval fotografickou modernu mezi piktorialismus a avantgardu, mezi secesi a dobu po první světové válce,[6] považoval ji za mezihru na hranici dvou epoch. Našel přesvědčivé vztahy mezi českou poezií generace devadesátých let a fotografiemi z uvedeného období, které spojujeme se secesním slohem a s uměleckou fotografií této doby. Jsou to například motivy vodních ploch a zrcadlení u básníka Antonína Sovy a Vladimíra J. Bufky (celou řadu dalších fotografů jako byli Edward Steichen, Josef Sudek nebo Erwin Raupp nepočítaje). Kroutvor také adekvátně charakterizoval jednu z poloh secesní fotografie jako rozvíjení romantismu a melancholických pocitů konce století.[7] Vyjádřil se i k zařazení Bufky do kontextu fotografie: „Pokud chceme Bufku srovnávat, pak jeho městské scenérie jsou nejbližší americkému fotografovi Alfredu Stieglitzovi.“[8] Návrh termínu Česká fotografická moderna se neprosadil, komplikuje beztak již nejednotné dosavadní názvosloví. Monika Faberová v německém katalogu výstavy upozornila především na to, jak se fotografové snažili stylově přičlenit k aktuálním stylům výtvarného umění: Bufka a Drtikol k symbolismu a postimpresionismu, Novák a Trčka k secesi a art deco.[9]

První objevný souhrn uměleckých fotografií mnoha známých i téměř neznámých českých amatérů i profesionálů včetně V. J. Bufky přinesla výstava Český piktorialismus 1895–1928.[10]

Pavel Scheufler ve svých pracích zdůraznil především Bufkovu roli v popularizaci autochromu. Nové poznatky o Bufkovi, zjištěné v archivech a dobových časopisech i ve fotografické sbírce Moravské galerie v Brně, přinesla magisterská teoretická práce fotografa Martina Hrubeše.[11]

Jaroslav Anděl a Anne Tuckerová poprvé vřadili díla všech významných fotografů včetně Bufky do kontextu moderního českého výtvarného umění,[12] Elizabeth Cleggová zatím dovršila proces zhodnocení Bufkova díla jeho zařazením do první publikace o středoevropském umění kolem roku 1900 (výřez Bufkova barevného gumotisku noční Prahy je reprodukován i na obálce její knihy).[13] Definitivní prosazení V. J. Bufky do kontextu evropské fotografie by mohlo znamenat jeho zařazení do shrnující výstavy a publikace o secesní fotografii.[14]

Naše vědomosti o Bufkově výjimečné osobnosti, jíž bylo dopřáno pouhých 29 let života, jsou stále ještě nedostatečné. Krátkou dosud neznámou vzpomínku jeho matky Karly zde přinášíme téměř v úplnosti: „Mne postihl záhy zlý osud. Za necelých deset let přervala smrt předčasně život mého chotě MUDr. Vilibalda Absolona, který zemřel roku 1882, všeobecně milován, vážen a oplakáván, zanechav mne s dvěma malými dětmi, Olgou a Karlem. Smutna vrátila jsem se do otcovského domu. Když otec odešel do penze a odstěhoval se do Olomouce, vdala jsem se po pěti letech znovu, abych dětem dala otce. Můj druhý muž, Eduard Bufka [...] Jediný syn z druhého manželství, Vladimír, předešel otce o pět let; zemřel v 29. roce svého věku. Studoval chemii na technice v Praze, stal se žákem bratří Lumièrových v Lyonu a mistra Kozla [sic], dvorního fotografa ve Vídni. Pro firmu Neubert, která ho vyslala do Ruska a Polska, zhotovil barevné fotografie obrazů napoleonských válek. Ovládal šest jazyků jako svou mateřštinu. Byl snaživý a umělecky založen. Napsal spisek o fotografii. Pěstoval uměleckou fotografii, kterou chtěl přivésti na vyšší stupeň dokonalosti. Jeho obrazy jsou umístěny v pražské technice, v oddělení pro fotografii.“[15] V několika větách matka načrtla portrét svého syna jako mimořádně nadané osobnosti.

Vladimír Jindřich Bufka zřejmě nebyl společensky situován tak, aby mohl zůstat fotoamatérem, chtěl se fotografováním živit. Studoval též chemii na Vysoké škole technické v Praze. Zde zřejmě musel potkat profesora kvasné chemie a fotografie Karla Kruise, který zde roku 1899 založil fotografický ateliér.[16] Kruisova katedra byla ještě dlouho po zakladatelově smrti (1917) centrem fotografické odbornosti v Praze a před vznikem Československa v roce 1918 byla pravděpodobně nejlépe vybaveným českým fotografickým pracovištěm na státní půdě. Specialitou jejího zakladatele byla mikrofotografie, jíž se asi ne náhodou věnoval i V. J. Bufka. Kruis se také roku 1908 zabýval autochromy a je možné, že se Bufka s autochromy seznámil právě u něj, i když jako Kruisův žák je uváděn jen Karel Šmirous, jeden z vynálezců barevné fotografie.[17] Druhým pravděpodobným konzultantem ohledně autochromů mohl být Jaroslav Husník, který se touto novinkou zabýval od roku 1908. Bufka, ovládající několik jazyků, byl pravděpodobně obeznámen s literaturou a nedá se předpokládat, že by potřeboval Husníkovu pomoc v pravém slova smyslu. S Kruisem mohl Bufka spolupracovat i v další specializaci, v reprodukování uměleckých děl, jímž se pražský profesor zabýval velmi intenzivně. Také Kruisovy volné fotografie z venkova jsou blízké Bufkovým snímkům z Kladenska, ale podobných krajin a momentek zobrazujících polní práce, staré chalupy a podobně bylo v době „testování" příručních kamer hodně. Pokud jde o Bufkovy vztahy ke Kruisovi a Husníkovi, pohybujeme se ve sféře dohadů.

O stycích V. J. Bufky s dnes slavným Josefem Váchalem (1884–1969) víme jen z Váchalovy strany, z biografických poznámek.[18] Dozvídáme se, že Bufka od něj kupoval dřevoryty a „řezané figurky", portrétoval ho[19] a vytvořil i svatební fotografii Váchala a jeho ženy Máši (Marie Pešulové), s přáteli slavil v Bufkově ateliéru v Lucerně Silvestra 1911. Váchal i Bufka účinkovali v němém filmu Antonína Pecha Zub za zub (1911).[20] Josef Váchal je také autorem dřevorytové značky ateliéru v Lucerně s motivem svítilny. Je možné, že proslavený tvůrce barevných dřevorytů pomohl Bufkovi zvládnout obtížnou techniku barevného gumotisku (dosud známé Váchalovy fotografie jsou ale černobílé a technicky jednoduché). Souvislost mezi Váchalovým a Bufkovým dílem lze jen těžko najít, což je překvapivé, když víme, že si Bufka Váchalova díla kupoval. Obdivoval je snad jako mystickou a nenapodobitelnou protiváhu k exaktnosti svého média? Alespoň jedna dochovaná fotografie s váchalovským světem souzní: Na chuchelském hřbitově (barevný gumotisk 1913), noční záběr se svítící lampičkou, podobnou té z Bufkovy značky pro ateliér v Lucerně.

Další osobností, s níž se V. J. Bufka nepochybně stýkal, byl jeho generační vrstevník Jaroslav Petrák (1883 – leden 1917), rovněž předčasně zesnulý fotograf a publicista. Jeho Žeň světla a stínu (1910) byla vydána, když mu bylo 27 let a přitom podala v češtině první celkový přehled o internacionálním hnutí umělecké fotografie. Zde se dočteme, že „Čestné, výlučné místo v české fotografii amatérské zaujímá J. V. [sic] Bufka, umělec-fotograf snivých nálad večerních a nočních, jehož ekskvisitní práce v tom oboru z četných výkladních skříní pražských jsou zajisté dobře známy. Zvláště skvělých výsledků, možno říci u nás ojedinělých, dosáhl v barevné fotografii autochromové." (s. 78). Bufkovi se zde dostalo jako jedinému výsady okomentovat svoji reprodukovanou fotografii: „Když únorové slunce zapadlo za Petřínem, a šedivá mlha, vystoupivší ze studených vod Vltavy, zahnala poslední růžový nádech večera, rozžata na Karlově mostě řada půvabných světel, oživujících starobylou a požehnanou scenerii. Hledající našel, co v duši se mu zdálo, cit vede jej na tato místa. I vytkl si za úkol: ryze mechanickou cestou získat obraz, v němž by byly soustředěny: vzdušnost, chlad a náladový půvab." Ve třech větách načrtl třiadvacetiletý mladík strategii subjektivizace svého média, všeobecně považovaného za pasivní odraz hmotných objektů. Cesta k fotografii začíná v duši, v obrazu, který si autor vysní („co v duši se mu zdálo"). Cit ho pak dovede ne k objektu, nýbrž k momentální „atmosféře" (růžový nádech, vzdušnost, chlad) oživující charakter starobylého místa. Výsledkem není plošná napodobenina objektu, nýbrž evokace nálady. Obraz sice stále pochází ze stroje – kamery, je ale podroben vůli umělce. Byla to tehdy nová koncepce tvorby, založená na psychologické teorii vcítění. Nejvlivnějším teoretikem německy psané literatury, sledované u nás, byl psychologizující autor Willi Warstat. Na jeho názorech byl závislý i Jaroslav Petrák. Teorie vcítění fotografii dominovala až do třicátých let minulého století, kdy se plně prosadila „čistá", nemanipulovaná fotografie, jíž dnes obvykle říkáme „moderní". Evokace nálady byla jednou z hlavních strategií, jimiž se fotografie odpoutávala od „pouhé" popisnosti a přibližovala se vysokému umění. Podle váženého historika umění V. V. Štecha (1885–1974) bylo vzbuzování nálad maximum, jehož může fotografie dosáhnout, k přiznání statutu vysokého umění to však nestačí.[21] V doznívající secesi a později si náladové obrazy vznikající prostřednictvím všech médií přivlastnil kýč, v době zrodu a rozvoje umělecké fotografie ale sehrály významnou roli v díle téměř všech reprezentantů tohoto hnutí. Bufkova autointerpretace jediného vlastního díla je velmi ojedinělou a významnou ukázkou nejen teoretické koncepce autora, ale i zcela konkrétní sondou do tehdejšího estetického myšlení.

Zatímco předešlé Bufkovy snímky se nevymykaly konvencím, večerní a noční snímky Prahy založily Bufkovu slávu. Některé z nich vznikly dvojexpozicí s časovým odstupem, takže svítí noční osvětlení, a přesto je zobrazený výsek viditelný. Při tehdejší malé světlocitlivosti negativů autor předvedl svým kolegům malý zázrak, který ovšem na požádání ochotně vysvětlil v článku *Fotografie za noci*.[22] Text je vzorovou ukázkou Bufkovy publicistiky. Začíná poeticky formulovaným obdivem k Praze, po němž následují suverénní rady svědčící o výborných znalostech dostupné techniky a materiálů, ale také druhů tehdy používaného městského osvětlení, dále doporučení fotografovat efekty, jako jsou odlesky ve vodě, sníh nebo lesknoucí se dlažba po dešti. Na závěr pisatel prozrazuje, že ho na drážďanské výstavě nejvíc zaujali Američané, „rození žongléři!" (s. 137)

Vedle tří malých ilustrací textu *Fotografie za noci* dostalo se Bufkovi výsady přílohy čísla, tištěné nejlepší dostupnou tiskařskou technikou. Předlohou se stal platinotisk Praga caput regni (Praha hlava království),[23] vystavený jako jediný reprezentant české amatérské fotografie (z profesionálů vystavoval Jan Langhans) na jedné z největších přehlídek umělecké fotografie v Drážďanech roku 1909, kdy hnutí dosáhlo svého zenitu. Referent *Fotografického obzoru* ministerský rada Karel Dvořák nebyl nadšen. „Třikrát jsem obešel sál, kde se přece obraz měl nacházeti a třikrát mne přivábil velký obraz Gustava Mautnera z Prahy – nazvaný Prag, jenž podával pohled na Sv. Mikuláše od Zlaté studně – ale obraz páně Bufkův ne a ne k nalezení. Až konečně! V nejtemnějším koutku celé místnosti, jeden z nejmenších obrazů výstavy a co do motivu – vždyť znáte jej z reprodukce v říjnovém sešitě *Obzoru*, která podává jej téměř ve velikosti originálu. Pěkná práce – ale tak drobounká a bezvýznamná, že nikterak neodpovídá honosnému titulu svému. Ba zdá se mně uprostřed těch obrazů vskutku velkolepé koncepce jako výsměch, jako bolestná satyra [sic] na ubohou úlohu, již u nás hraje amatérská fotografie vůbec. Pochopuji to, když se obchodní nebo průmyslník súčastní [sic] sám a sám na svou pěst z hmotných důvodů mezinárodní výstavy, ale na tomto representativním shodu [sic] amatérstva všech národů měli jsme býti zastoupeni buď imposantně aneb vůbec ne.“[24] Dvořákův názor pochopíme lépe, připomeneme-li si, že on sám vystavil v Praze roku 1903 fotografii Praha stověžatá, velikou 1 x 2,30 m. To bylo na tehdejší dobu skutečně monumentální dílo.[25]

V květnu roku 1909 Bufka poprvé přednášel v Českém klubu fotografů amatérů v Praze „O fotografování nočních a náladových snímků“ a promítal také autochromy. Během jednoho roku na sebe tedy dvakrát upozornil novinkami, byl to raketový start jeho fotografické dráhy. V dalších letech často přednášel a pořádal fotografické kurzy, které byly jedním ze zdrojů jeho příjmu, ve svých 22 letech již zřetelně ovlivňoval především českou fotografii.

Autochrom, barevný diapozitiv na skleněné desce, byl první široce rozšířenou technikou barevné fotografie. Bufka se ve využívání možností autochromu zdokonalil přímo v továrně vynálezců této techniky (a předtím kinematografu) bratří Lumièrů v Lyonu. Byl prvním popularizátorem autochromů u nás. Stylizace byla v případě autochromu téměř nemožná. Portrét reprodukovaný v knize, kterou o autochromu napsal, nepřesahuje konvence tehdejší živnostenské fotografie.[26] Také série pohlednic, vytištěná podle jeho mistrně komponovaných autochromů, podává očekávaný obraz krásné a starobylé Prahy.[27] Je však nutno vzít v úvahu svědectví Rudolfa Skopce: „Na autochromových deskách pak vytvořil mistrovská díla portrétní, žánrová i krajinářská.“[28] Zvláště žánrové autochromy

nemohly být nezajímavé, portréty mohly zobrazovat
přední umělce, vědce, šlechtice...

Své fotografické vzdělání dokončil Bufka
v prominentním ateliéru Hermanna Clemense
Kosela ve Vídni, kde pracoval jako volontér od
1. 11. 1910 do jara roku 1911. Kosel, rodák z Temného
dolu v Krkonoších, byl tehdy na vrcholu své kariéry
fotografa vídeňské společenské smetánky (včetně
následníka trůnu Franze Ferdinanda s rodinou).
Jeho portréty patří k prvním a nepřekonatelným
příkladům „glamour" (půvabné, lichotivé) fotografie, později a vlastně až dodnes spjaté především
se snímky filmových hvězd. Koselovy podobizny
byly i inkarnací představy Vídně Straussových val-
číků, Sacherových dortů a lesku císařského dvora.
Navazovaly na malířskou tradici lichotivých por-
trétních miniatur. Bufkovi se mnohé z Koselových
fines v budoucnu hodily, například silná retuš, ma-
lířská pozadí, zasazování postav a hlav do oválných
výřezů a podobně. Všichni živnostenští fotografové
bez výjimky museli alespoň trochu vycházet vstříc
touze svých zákazníků, aby na fotografiích vypadali
co nejlépe (platí to například pro Bufkovy portréty
Schwarzenbergů). Žádná z dostupných Bufkových
podobizen však neredukuje portrétované na odo-
sobněné líbivé zevnějšky.

U Kosela se Bufka mohl zdokonalit také
v ušlechtilých tiscích, především v gumotisku.
Přestože byl Bufka u Kosela jako volontér, musel
počítat s tím, že se mu tento pobyt zúročí. Ostatně
i předchozí pobyt v továrně bratří Lumièrů v Lyonu
byl pro něj výbornou reklamou. Podle dnešních
znalostí Bufkova díla musíme obdivovat především
vynikající snímky z centra Vídně, které našly své
místo i na stránkách odborných časopisů.

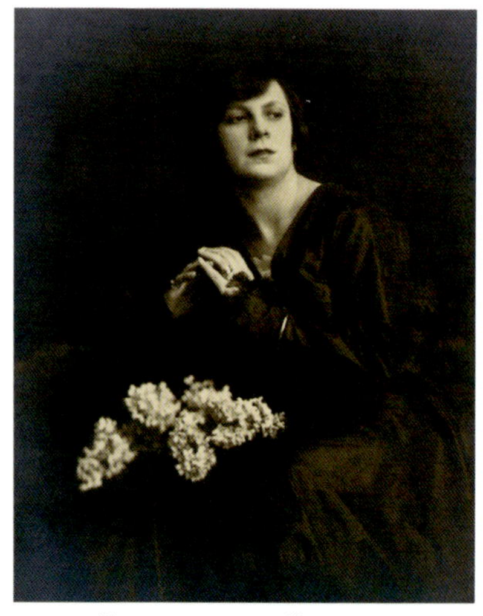

V. J. Bufka (?): Marie Bufková, c. 1914

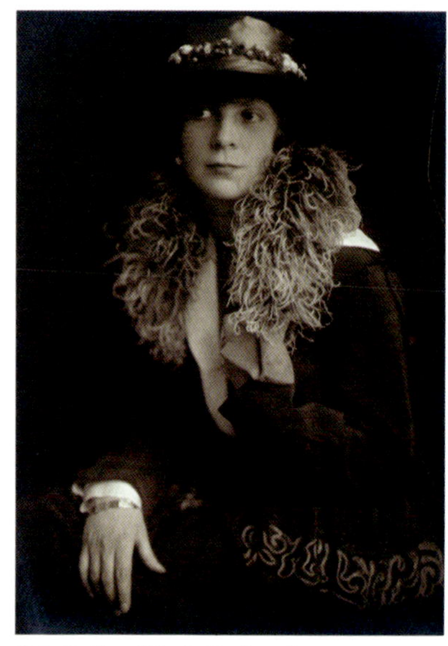

V. J. Bufka: Marie Bufková, c. 1910

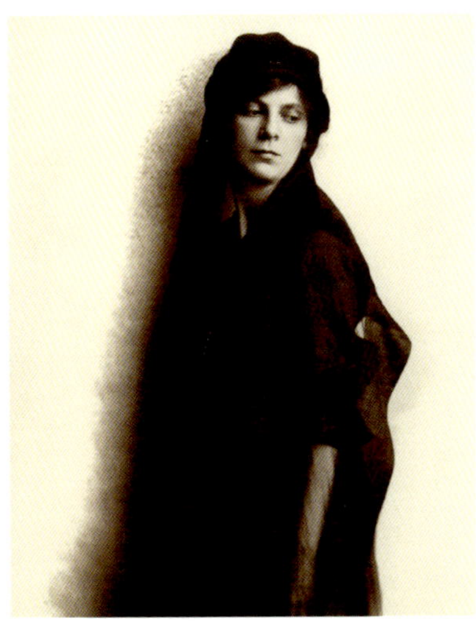

Autoportrét (?) Marie Bufkové, c. 1914

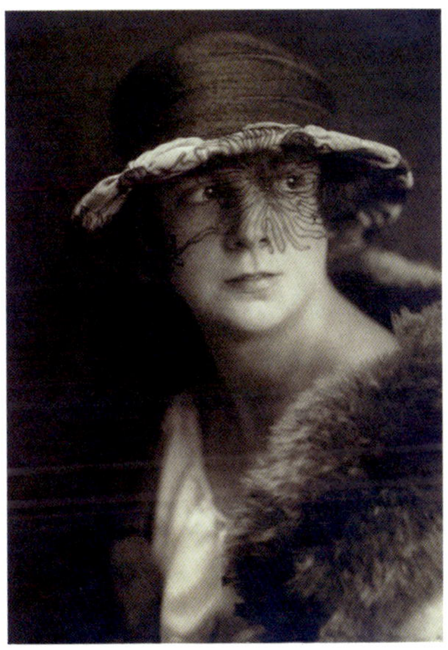

V. J. Bufka: Marie Bufková, c. 1910

Prestiž Vladimíra J. Bufky dál strmě stoupá. Dostává se mu cti napsat úvodník do nového ročníku časopisu *Fotografický věstník* (1911). Zakončuje ho připomínkou rčení Per aspera ad astra! (Přes překážky ke hvězdám!) a sám se jím zřejmě hodlá řídit důsledně. Po návratu z Vídně pořádá od 15. března fotografické kurzy, nabyté vědomosti si tedy nenechává pro sebe.

Následuje jarní *Výstava Českého klubu fotografů amatérů v Praze* v Lucerně, jíž se poprvé od roku 1903 účastní řada dalších klubů, vystaveno je přes tři sta děl. Kromě Františka Drtikola vzbudil největší pozornost referenta právě V. J. Bufka: „Primát výstavy nesporně náleží pp. Bufkovi a Drtikolovi. – Bufkova ‚Urania' nemá na výstavě sobě rovného, pokud se týká delikátnosti. Mlhavá nálada deštivého dne vystižena zde okem uměleckým a provedení je důkazem naprosté suverenity v ovládání tisku platinového. Podobizna H. C. Kosela je nejlepší podobiznou výstavy a nemohl zajisté Koselův žák lepším způsobem odměnit se svému učiteli, než vystavením výtečné podobizny svého mistra. V tónech a světlech prvotřídním výkonem Bufkovým jest gumotisk ‚The Sculpture'; ač místy ruční práce na obraze jest viditelna poněkud více, než bylo by si přáti, působí obraz dojmem velice dobrým. Neméně i ‚Letní večer na Kampě' a ‚Poslední paprsky' svědčí o vybraném uměleckém vkusu Bufkově a technické jeho dokonalosti. Přál bych si ve prospěch našeho amatérstva, aby Bufka stal se učitelem všech, kteří chtí věnovati se fotografii umělecké."[29]

Pravděpodobně v létě odcestoval Bufka do Petrohradu a Varšavy reprodukovat obrazy pro tiskařskou firmu Neubert. Je pravděpodobné, že ho zajímala možnost tiskové reprodukce fotografie, především autochromů. Po barevných pohlednicích Prahy to byla druhá zakázka, o níž víme. Z cest se Bufka vrátil v říjnu, oženil se, otevřel nový ateliér v proslulé Lucerně, který se dle Rudolfa Skopce stal uměleckým střediskem. Spolupracoval s vynálezcem Jaroslavem Husníkem v novém Technickém muzeu v Praze na expozici amatérské fotografie, v níž patrně instaloval i vlastní díla. Jeho život zřejmě dosáhl zenitu. Ateliér v Lucerně následujícího roku z neznámých důvodů opustil a nakonec zakotvil v roce 1913 na výborném místě v centru, v Jindřišské ulici naproti hlavní poště. Dál je o něm málo zpráv, koncem roku 1914 zveřejnil početnou kolekci svých volných i zakázkových prací na výstavě živnostenských fotografů k 75. výročí zveřejnění daguerrotypie v nejčestnějším výstavním prostoru, v Rudolfinu. Většinou to byly podobizny, jen některé z nich označené jmény portrétovaných.[30] Z ostatních fotografií se vztahují k dochovaným pozitivům názvy kombinovaných gumotisků Večerní vlak, Chuchelský hřbitov v den dušiček, možná i Večer na hřbitově košířském a Na řece Vltavě. Připomeňme si, že v zahraničním oddílu výstavy figurovala i díla některých z nejuctívanějších reprezentantů umělecké fotografie, především Hugo Erfurth a Nicola Perscheid. Pokud jde o Bufkovy konkurenty, byli to zejména Drtikol & Škarda, Schlosser & Wenisch, Vaněk & Kanderál. Žádný z nich neměl na růžích ustláno.

Po jeho smrti v roce 1916 ateliér nezanikl, manželka Marie ho vedla až do roku 1928. Dokonce signovala některé pozitivy „V. J. Bufka", ať už proto, že chtěla udržet jméno firmy, nebo proto, že je zhotovila či nechala zhotovit z manželových negativů.[31] Ne vždy je možné tento problém vyřešit.[32] Série (auto)portrétů Marie Bufkové vznikla zčásti podle datovatelných módních prvků až po manželově smrti, zčásti za jeho života (jeden z nich je podepsán „Maňa 1919", jiný „atelier Bufka 1914"). Podobné provedení jako některé autoportréty má i herecká podobizna Anny Sedláčkové publikovaná v *Rozpravách Aventina* roku 1927 a signovaná „M. Bufka".[33] Autorství některých nedatovaných fotografií, například (auto)portrétů V. J. Bufky, je nejisté, na druhé straně lze předpokládat spoluúčast Marie Bufkové na stylizaci svých portrétů fotografovaných manželem.

Dílo Vladimíra J. Bufky se člení do několika okruhů. Nejprve zaujaly snímky, jejichž shrnutím je album třinácti pozitivů *Večerní Praha* (1909). Pět z nich ukazuje zasněženou Prahu se zcela zamrzlou Vltavou (sníh, odrážející světlo, umožňoval i při tehdejší nižší citlivosti negativů fotografovat i v podvečer). Na bílých plochách se v silném kontrastu rýsují siluety objektů a postav, fotografické pozitivy se přibližují grafickým listům. Proti tomu pozitivy jako Praga caput regni jsou celé pokryty jemnými šedými valéry, jež dokázal nejlépe podat platinotisk. Objekty jsou obaleny přísvitem, který stírá jejich hranice, silueta Hradu plynule přechází do zamračené oblohy. Dalšímu snímku dominuje noční osvětlení nábřeží. Světlo, přesněji proměna vizuální reality světlem, je tím, co celé album propojuje. *Večerní Praha* je zřejmě prvním námětově i metodicky sjednoceným souborem v české umělecké fotografii, cyklická tvorba se měla dostat na pořad dne až v moderní fotografii (propagoval ji hlavně jeden z jejích průkopníků László Moholy-Nagy). Ve výtvarném umění 19. století byly však cykly běžné. Vznik souboru mohl být inspirován večerními obrazy Jakuba Schikanedera z devadesátých let 19. století a následujícího desetiletí.[34]

Nové rysy přibírá tematizace světla v Bufkově díle ve Vídni. Bufka zde fotografuje jednak v kontrastním protisvětle, jednak v mlze, snad i za deště. Snímky v protisvětle jsou až dodnes testem schopnosti fotografů zvládat světelné kontrasty. Bufka fotografiemi z podloubí vídeňské Opery a radnice podává jedny z prvních a zároveň vzorových příkladů využití šikmého i čelního protisvětla pro kompozici obrazu s vrženými stíny, jejichž čerň se v struktuře obrazu uplatňuje často výrazněji než stínící objekty, v našem případě šedé stavební prvky. Do fotografií tak vstupuje výrazná grafická (a díky členění architektury často i geometrická) složka. Ve Vídni vyfotografoval Bufka také „The Sculpture", bělostné sousoší u Uměleckohistorického muzea, ozářené sluncem před tmavou fasádou budovy. Vznikl tak mimořádně působivý přídavek k jeho dílům využívajícím světelných kontrastů. Mnohé z těchto pozitivů byly vytvořeny technikami platinotisku a gumotisku, ale jejich tvůrce se v nich nevzdaloval vzhledu ani možnostem čisté fotografie.

Stejně mistrovské jsou záběry Vídně v mlze. Často fotografovanou Uranii zobrazuje Bufka nejen v obvyklém předním pohledu (s úžasnou stafáží), ale také v neobvyklém pohledu od Dunaje. Votivkirche za deště se zrcadlí na zaplavené dlažbě a vypadá, jako by plul po vodní hladině. Vyniká i záběr Karlskirche s fiakrem, blízký opět Schikanederovi a žánrové malbě 19. století. V případě Schikanedera to není jen motivická příbuznost, ale – stejně jako v případě ostatních zamlžených a zešeřelých fotografií – splývavé vykreslení hranic mezi atmosférou a zobrazenými objekty, vypadajícími v černobílém podání jako stíny. Připomíná se tu také Monetův impresionismus a Seuratův pointilismus.

Celý svět si pak můžeme představit jako prostupný, jako hustší či řidší mlhu nebo oblaka, kontrast mezi nebem a zemí je potlačen. Dalším překvapením vídeňského pobytu je portrét Hermanna C. Kosela, vykreslený s podobnou měkkostí jako venkovní snímky v mlze. Další takový Bufkův portrét se nedochoval. Je možné, že v tomto případě tovaryš použil některého z prvních měkce kreslících objektivů z majetku svého mistra, i když zneostření se dalo dosáhnout i jinými způsoby. Ušlechtilá reprodukce, kterou můžeme považovat za originál, ukazuje tvář tetelící se světlem, jako by byla pozorována přes horký vzduch. Skupina prací, využívajících světelných kontrastů a neostrého vykreslení vizuality, se hlásí k impresionismu. V tomto smyslu navrhoval Bufka termín „stylová fotografie" namísto „umělecká fotografie". Neomezoval se však jen na jeden styl.

Z hlediska fotografického kontextu je Bufkovo dílo spjaté s řešením světelných problémů příznačné pro počáteční období práce s příručními kamerami. Nová technika a nové možnosti se staly výzvou k tematizaci samotného média fotografie, ke zkoumání jeho možností ve srovnání s manuálními zobrazovacími technikami malby, kresby a grafiky. Světlo, tento nástroj fotografa, se zákonitě muselo stát i předmětem jeho zájmu, ale fotografů, kteří zkoumali hraniční možnosti fotografování, byla jen hrstka. Iniciační úlohu měl svými snímky za noci a nepohody Alfred Stieglitz. V Evropě se většina fotografů dala cestou zpracování negativů pomocí gumotisků a dalších procesů umožňujících ovlivnit pozitivní proces. Bufka, inspirovaný snad drážďanskou výstavou v roce 1909, je v tomto směru ojedinělou postavou. Jeho dílo vychází z vidění, z originálních vizuálních postřehů. K nejlepším ukázkám v tomto smyslu patří miniaturní zobrazení všední (pražské?) ulice s lesknoucí se kaluží. Nebýt dobové stafáže, mohli bychom tento snímek přičlenit ke Skupině 42, jejímž hlavním námětem se za druhé světové války stala pražská periferie.

Nejslavnější Bufkovy fotografie jsou však zhotoveny technikou gumotisku. Časovou následností si nemůžeme být jisti, řada z nich nenese žádný letopočet a vročení negativu známe jen v několika nepříliš důležitých případech. Pozitivy jsou obvykle datovány rokem jejich zhotovení, tak jak postupně vznikaly. Nejstarší barevný gumotisk nese vročení 1908 a zobrazuje pravděpodobně západ slunce, tedy hlavní námět všech náladových fotografií. Do běžného repertoáru secesního krajinářství patří také snímky s topoly a zvlášť zdařilými břízami, zatímco nebarevné záběry zasněžených lesů u Říčan (1911) a diagonálně komponované nokturno (Po západu slunce, 1908)[35] mohou připomenout například rané práce Jaromíra Funkeho asi z roku 1920. Ostatně pokud jde o tematizaci média fotografie, Funke je bezděčným Bufkovým pokračovatelem.

Vedle prací, jimiž se Bufka zařazoval mezi virtuózní interprety povinného repertoáru secesní fotografie, vytvářel i námětově a stylově originální dodatky k tehdejší obrazové fantazii. Nejpřekvapivějším z nich je hlava Marie Bufkové v čelence Siouxů (gumotisk je bohužel bez názvu). O portrét zde patrně nejde, hlava a čelenka by správně měla patřit muži (ozdoby žen byly jiné). Profil hlavy s čelenkou musel být koncipován jako symbol ušlechtilosti, čestnosti, statečnosti, nepoddajnosti, hrdosti, vzdoru, tedy hodnot, s nimiž si až dodnes původní obyvatele Ameriky spojujeme. Právě pro tyto hodnoty indiáni překvapivě figurovali jako vzor nepoddajného vlastenectví i v českém národním obrození, v cyklu Mikoláše Alše Živly (1881). Pro V. J. Bufku však byl spojnicí k indiánům (byť jihoamerickým) spíše cestovatel Alberto Vojtěch Frič, jejž portrétoval. Frič také přivezl do Prahy Čerwuiše, indiána z kmene Čamakoko (kvůli stanovení diagnózy a následnému vyléčení celého kmene), který pobýval v Praze v letech 1908–1909. Bufkův gumotisk je koncipován v temné tonalitě (low-key), z níž se vynořuje ušlechtilý profil hlavy, na jejíž střed a odvrácenou tvář dopadá světlo (tzv. rembrandtovský profil). Ruka u brady a sklopená víčka naznačují kontemplaci, světlo z neznámého zdroje má snad symbolický význam úsvitu či odkazu k budoucnosti.

Večerní vlak odjíždějící pod obrovským příkrovem kouře s rozsvícenými červenými koncovými svítilnami v jinak nebarevném podání je v Bufkově díle dalším ze vzorových příkladů ztvárnění námětu, který byl později tak oblíben. Bufka ovšem nebyl prvním „železničním fotografem", jeho předchůdcem byl i v tomto případě Alfred Stieglitz, jenž s charakteristickou výřečností pojmenoval svůj proslulý, rovněž temný snímek kolejiště s kolmo kouřící lokomotivou Ruka člověka (Hand of Man, 1902). Jsou to radikálně odlišná díla. Stieglitzův záběr lze chápat jako symbol industriální civilizace (přitom mračna kouře dnes vnímáme s opačnými pocity než před sto lety), Bufkův vlak (nepochybně expres) se řítí do dálek (přesto, že v okamžiku expozice asi stál) a je jejich romantickým symbolem. Pozemská diagonála kolejnic a nebeská diagonála kouře se sbíhají kdesi před viditelným koncem vlaku, možná v nekonečnu. Stroj je rychlost, jako ve futurismu.

Bufka zobrazil i nákladní loď s kouřící Chuchlí v pozadí, to byl jeho obraz příměstského průmyslu. Jeho parník plující po řece nemá daleko k parníkům Schikanederovým. Zájem o techniku, vědu, exaktnost zjevnou ve všech jeho textech, se však u něho spojoval se smyslem pro iracionalitu a pro hřbitovní tematiku. Noční snímky z chuchelského a smíchovského hřbitova (nyní části Prahy) patří k charakteristickým dílům dekadentního umění, kdežto záběr z Košíř je impresionistickým dílem. Gumotisková provedení těchto děl sice autorovi umožnila i manuální zásahy, přesto se zde fotografie nezapře a může být vnímána i jako pozoruhodný pendant k rukodělným výtvarným dílům s podobnými náměty.

Ojedinělé zátiší s vázou a porcelánovou figurkou (gumotisk) je celé provedeno v modrém tónu a svědčí o tom, že si v tomto žánru autor ponechával větší volnost. Má blízko k Artělu a především k rodícímu se slohu art deco. K nejvíc abstrahovaným dílům patří krajina, provedená v sépiovém tónu. Vizualita zde má podobu dekorativních grafických siluet, podobně jako na gumotisku Na starém a báječném hřbitově smíchovském, 1914.

Nevíme, co všechno z díla Vladimíra Jindřicha Bufky postrádáme, ale vezmeme-li v úvahu krátkou dobu, po kterou vznikalo, chybějí pravděpodobně zejména autochromy a samozřejmě většina zakázkových portrétů, stranou zůstaly také snímky publikované v ilustrovaných časopisech. Bufka byl i vynikajícím publicistou a autorem fotografických příruček. Jeho život zůstává napůl skryt. Byl snad skutečným géniem v době, kdy se za génia považoval téměř každý umělec. Kulturní vazby jeho fotografického díla jsou daleko početnější a hlubší, než lze vyčíst z této publikace. Byl typem tvůrce, který byl schopen samostatně reflektovat a realizovat jako jeden z prvních nebo vůbec první nové možnosti svého média a zároveň je vztahovat ke kulturním tématům své doby. Byl průkopníkem čisté fotografie v rámci fotografického purismu i skvělým stylistou za jeho hranicemi. Vycházel z vidění, z vizuálních postřehů, a snad právě proto se často pohyboval na hranicích viditelnosti, kdy nedostatek světla potlačuje uchopitelnost tvarů a akcentuje podíl světla na vzhledu reality i význam vidění. V tomto směru jsou jeho fotografie blízké pozdní tvorbě Josefa Sudka.[36] Bufka nebyl typem umělce, jemuž jde jen o sebevyjádření. Spíše se zdá, že svoji dobu chápal jako pluralitu možností, včetně stylové plurality, která již tehdy byla markantní. Impresionismus, postimpresionismus, secese, symbolismus, kubismus, futurismus koexistovaly zčásti vedle sebe a Bufkův postoj k této pluralitě byl téměř postmoderní. Lze si představit, že jeho díla vznikala na základě strategií, vyplývajících z impozantních vědomostí a z pochopení možností a úkolů doby.

Poznámky

1 Scheufler, Pavel: Historické fotografické techniky, Praha a Plzeň, Ipos Artama a Společnost IF Plzeň 1993.

2 Mühldorf, Josef & Vrbová, Pavla: *Od sportu fotografického k umělecké fotografii, Historie prvního klubu fotografů amatérů v Čechách a Svazu československých klubů fotografů amatérů, 1889–1945*, Praha, Národní informační a poradenské středisko pro kulturu 2010.

3 Jiránek, Otakar: *Život a dílo prof. Rudolf Skopce*, diplomová práce, oddělení fotografie, Praha, FAMU 1980; Dufek, Antonín: Rudolf Skopec in Relation to Helmut Gernsheim, in: Anna Auer and Alistair Crawford (ed.): *Helmut Gernsheim Reconsidered. Symposium 2003 Mannheim*, Passau 2004, s. 53–56; Dufek, Antonín: Rudolf Skopec, předseda poradního sboru fotografické sbírky Moravské galerie v Brně, 62. *Bulletin Moravské galerie v Brně / 2006*, s. 29–32.

4 Ústní sdělení Rudolfa Skopce autorovi.

5 -ec. [Skopec, Rudolf]: V. J. Bufka. *Československá fotografie* 12, 1961, č.4, s. 58–59, 7 reprodukcí. Na výstavě *Dějiny fotografie II* prezentoval Skopec tři přílohy *Fotografického obzoru*. Pro dvě reprodukce v jeho knize *Dějiny fotografie v obrazech od nejstarších dob k dnešku*, Praha 1963, byly předlohou pravděpodobně originály.

6 „Trvání české fotografické moderny můžeme zhruba vymezit od roku 1908 do roku 1926.“ Kroutvor, Josef: *Česká fotografická moderna*, Praha 1989, nestránkováno.

7 Kroutvor, Josef: Die tschechische Moderne, in: *Photographie der Moderne in Prag 1900–1925*, katalog výstavy, ed. Monika Faber, Wien 1991, s. 6–13.

8 Kroutvor, Josef: *Česká fotografická moderna*, Praha 1989, nestránkováno.

9 Faber, Monika: Portraits zwischen Versunkenheit und Pose, in: *Photographie der Moderne in Prag 1900–1925*, katalog výstavy, ed. Monika Faber, Wien 1991, s. 103.

10 *České centrum fotografie, Praha 1999–2000*, katalog Jan Mlčoch a Pavel Scheufler.

11 Hrubeš, Martin: *Vladimír Jindřich Bufka*, bakalářská teoretická práce, FAMU 1994; Hrubeš, Martin: *Vladimír Jindřich Bufka*, magisterská teoretická práce, FAMU 1998.

12 Anděl, Jaroslav & Tucker, Anne (ed.): *Czech Modernism 1900 – 1945*, Boston, Toronto and London, Bulfinch Press 1989, Houston, Museum of Fine Arts 8. 10. 1989 – 7. 1. 1990, s. 123–147. Reprízy výstavy: Akron Art Museum, Akron; Brooklyn Museum, International Center of Photography, Anthology Film Archives, New York 2. 3. – 13. 5. 1990.

13 Clegg, Elizabeth: *Art, Design and Architecture in Central Europe 1890–1920*, New Haven and London, Yale University Press 2006. Do knihy autorka začlenila jen několik málo fotografů, z českých zemí ještě Františka Drtikola.

14 *La photographie pictorialiste en Europe 1888–1918*, Rennes, Musée des Beaux-arts de Rennes 2005; *Impressionist Camera. Pictorial Photography in Europe, 1888–1918*, Sant Louis, Sant Louis Art Museum.

15 Bufková-Wanklová, Karla: Vzpomínky, in: Berthold Kladivo (ed.): *Zlatá rodina*, Blansko, Masarykova měšťanská škola 1936, s. 41–42. Za upozornění a zapůjčení děkuji Petře Trnkové.

16 Kotěšovec, Miroslav: *Karel Kruis. Fotografie z let 1882–1917*, Praha, Libri 2009.

17 Číp, Jiří & Jung, Rudolf & Scheufler, Pavel: *Karel Šmirous – výběr barevných fotografií z rastrových diapozitivů z let 1908–1955 / Selection of color photographs from the screened positives from 1908–1955*, Praha, Národní technické muzeum 1993.

18 *Paměti Josefa Váchala, dřevorytce* (1935), Praha, Prostor 1995.

19   Portrét je reprodukován in: Šejn, Miloš: *Josef Váchal. Dílo*, Roudnice nad Labem, Galerie výtvarného umění 1984. Podle Šejna se oba umělci seznámili roku 1906.

20   Brož, Jaroslav & Frýda, Myrtil: *Historie československého filmu v obrazech*, Praha, Orbis 1959. Údaje shromáždil Martin Hrubeš ve své magisterské práci.

21   V. V. Štech: Estetika fotografie, *Fotografický obzor* 30, 1922 (seriál, upravená přednáška z roku 1914).

22   V. J. Bufka: Fotografie za noci, *Fotografický obzor* 17, 1909, s. 133–137.

23   Praga caput regni je název básně Petra Bezruče ze *Slezských písní*, vydávaných od roku 1903. V. J. Bufka se snad volbou tohoto názvu hlásí k vlastenectví (nepřímo i k sociálnímu cítění). Název byl ovšem rozšířen zejména ve středověku.

24   Dvořák, Karel: Jinde a u nás. 5. výstavní list drážďanský, *Fotografický obzor* 17, 1909, č. 12, s. 182–183.

25   Viz např. Jeníček, Jiří: *Fotografie jako zření světa a života*, Praha 1947, s. 21. Gustav Mautner byl jedním z nejvýznamnějších členů německého klubu fotoamatérů v Praze (Club deutscher Amateurphotographen in Prag). Jeho Praha je z roku 1908.

26   *O fotografii v barvách pomocí desky autochromové*, Praha, E. Weinfurter 1910.

27   Pohlednice vydalo pražské umělecké nakladatelství Minerva roku 1910.

28   -ec. [Skopec, Rudolf]: Mistři světové fotografie. Vladimír Jindřich Bufka, *Československá fotografie* 2, 1961, č.4, s. 58.

29   V[ladimír]. Fanderlík: Jarní výstava klubová, *Fotografický obzor* 19, 1911, č. 5, s. 104.

30   František Kobliha, redaktor Rydlo [snad Jaroslav Rydlo, doložen 1908 jako redaktor ve Dvoře Králové nad Labem], Renata Tyršová, prof. Ostrčil [pravděpodobně hudební skladatel a dirigent Otakar Ostrčil, 1879–1935], dr. Hartmann [originál v Národním technickém muzeu z roku 1912 sig. Atelier Bufka, s podpisem P.(?) Hartmann] a tři portréty Schwarzenbergů („J. J. kníže Karel ze Schwarzenbergů, Portrét J. J. knížete Karla ze Schwarzenbergů se synáčkem, Portrét J. J. kněžny Eleonory ze Schwarzenbergů se synáčkem". Dva poslední jsou ve sbírce Moravské galerie v Brně společně se třemi dalšími Bufkovými portréty Schwarzenbergů.

31   Dokládá to olejotisk bez názvu (břízy na kraji lesa) signovaný „V. J. Bufka 1921", který se dochoval také jako gumotisk signovaný „V. J. Bufka 1912".

32   Kontra, Gabriela: *Fotografky v českých zemích 1839–1918*, diplomová teoretická práce FAMU, Praha 2005.

33   *Rozpravy Aventina*, 1927–28, s. 33. Právě příbuznost tohoto signovaného portrétu s některými z podobizen Marie Bufkové opravňuje k domněnce, že to mohou být autoportréty. Sám podpis „Maňa 1919" by k připsání autorství neopravňoval, byl spíše dedikací.

34   Petr Wittlich ve svém lektorském posudku upozornil na další souvislosti Bufkova díla: „Zejména srovnání Bufkových snímků Prahy s pražskými náměty Antonína Slavíčka by mohlo přinést zajímavé shody a rozdíly. Právě tady je asi skryto jádro problematiky umělecké hodnoty secesní piktoriální fotografie tohoto námětového zaměření."

35   Fotografie (platinotisk) mohla být vystavena roku 1911 pod názvem Poslední paprsky na Výstavě Českého klubu fotografů amatérů v Praze, č. k. 29.

36   Bufkově Večerní Praze není vzdálen také Sudkův první soubor: *Praha. 10 náladových fotografií*, Praha, Ústřední státní ústav grafický, bez data (1922–1924). Album je v majetku UPM Praha.

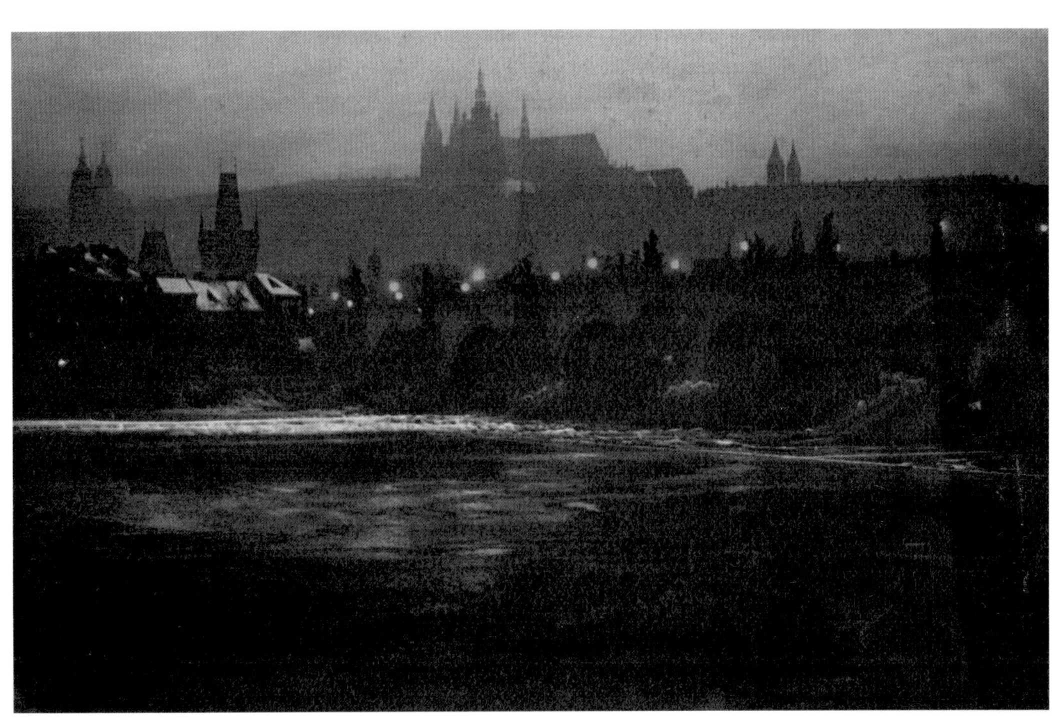

1 **Prague / Praha** 1914

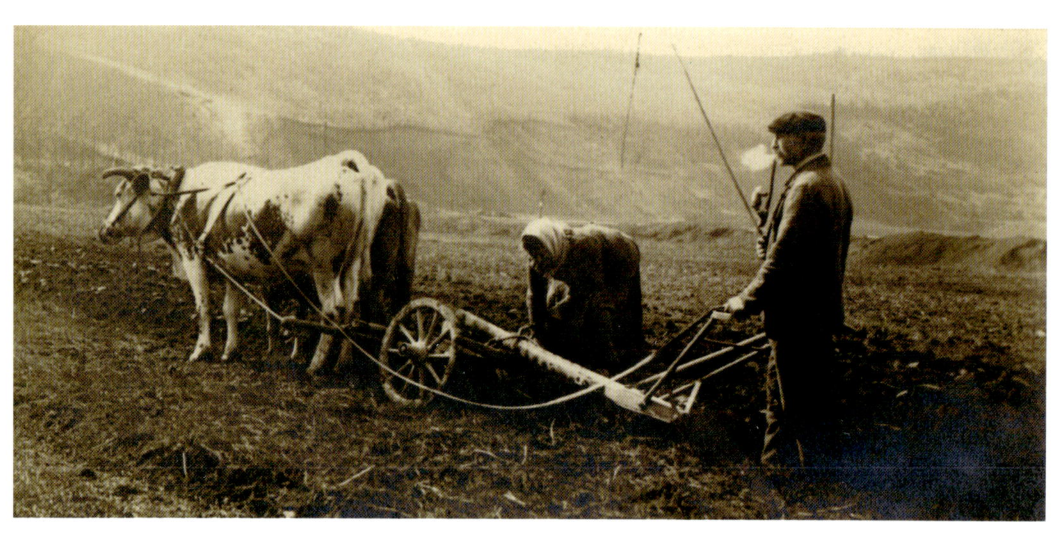

2 **From the Kladno Region / Z Kladenska** 1908

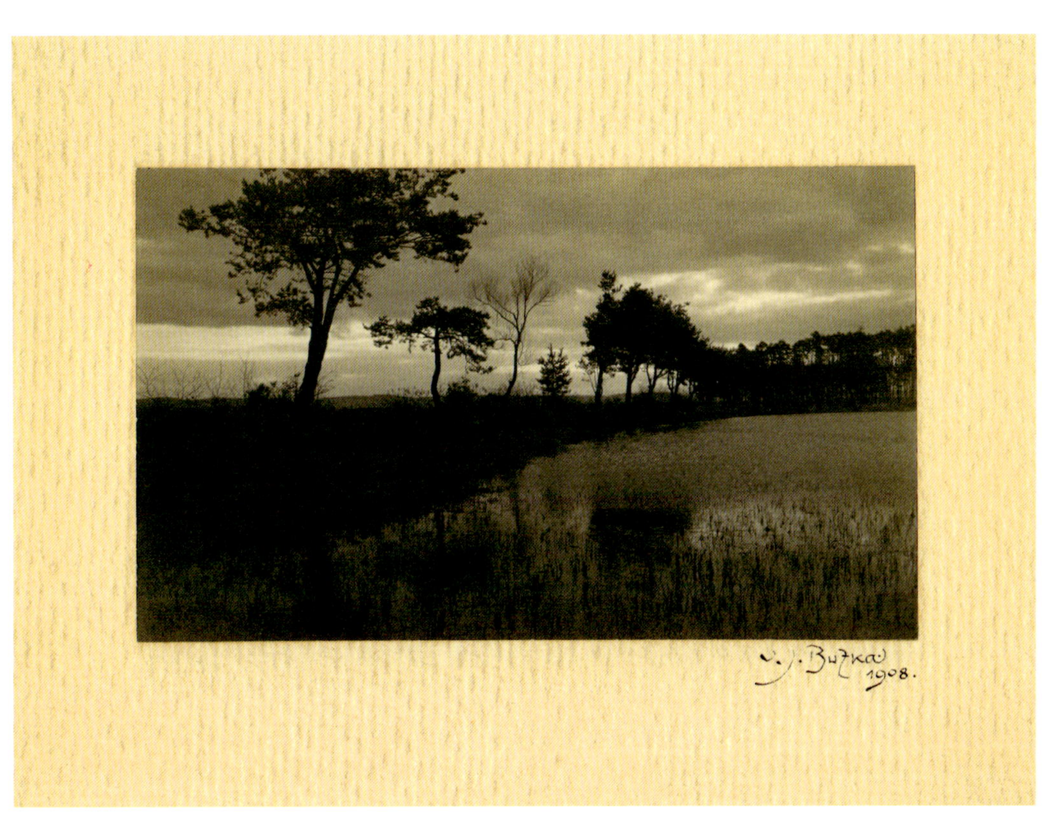

3 **After Sunset / Po západu slunce** 1908

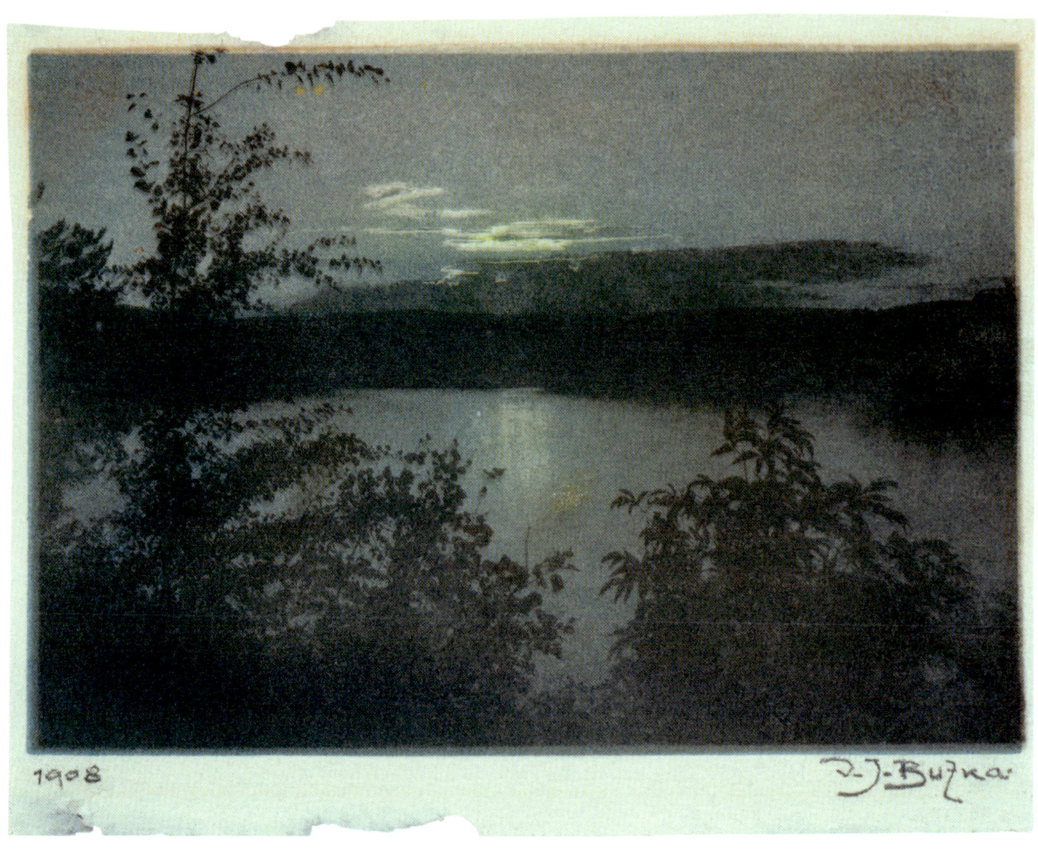

4 **Nocturne / Nokturno** 1908

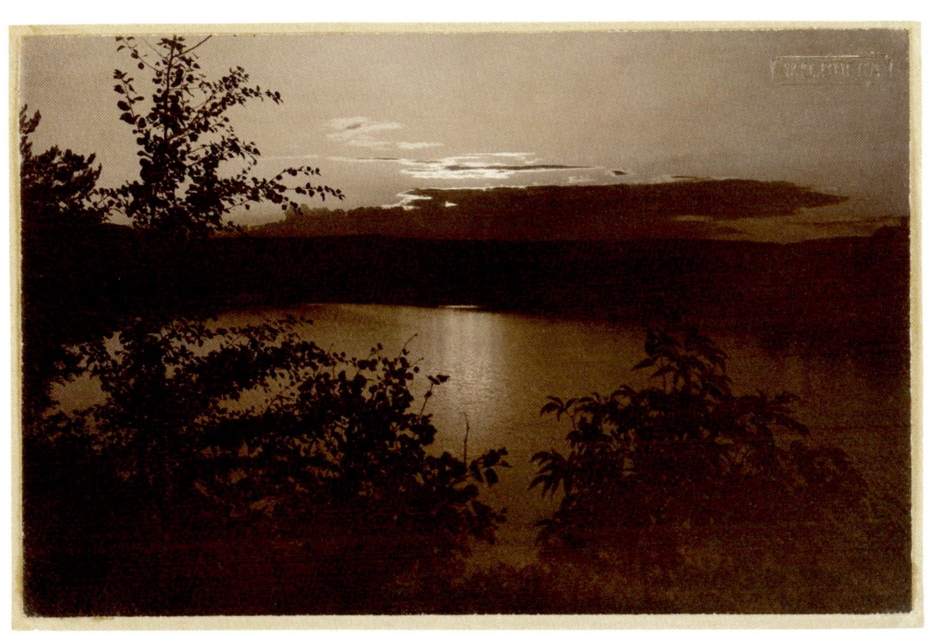

5 **Sunset on a Lake / Západ slunce nad jezerem** c. 1908

6 **The Francis Embankment / Františkovo nábřeží** 1909

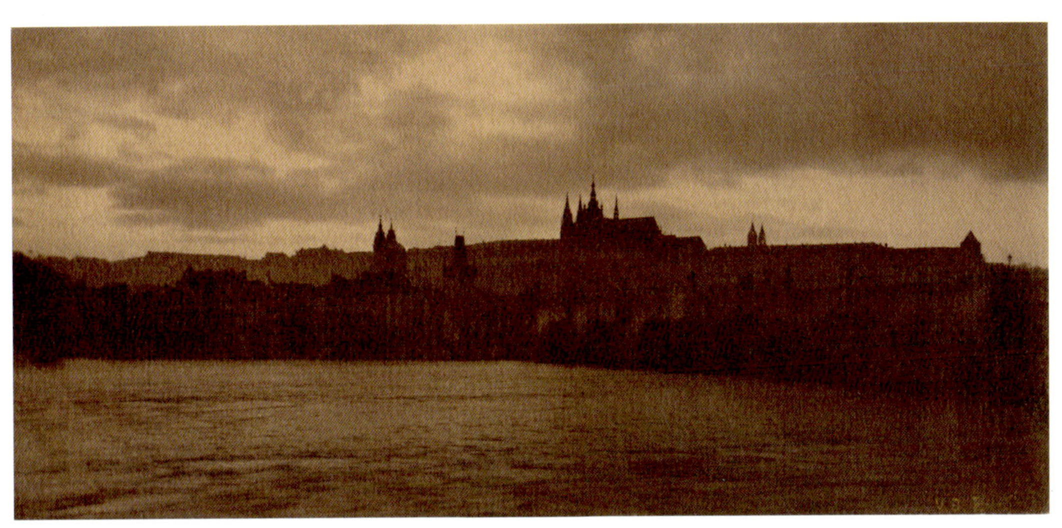

7 **Praga Caput Regni** 1909

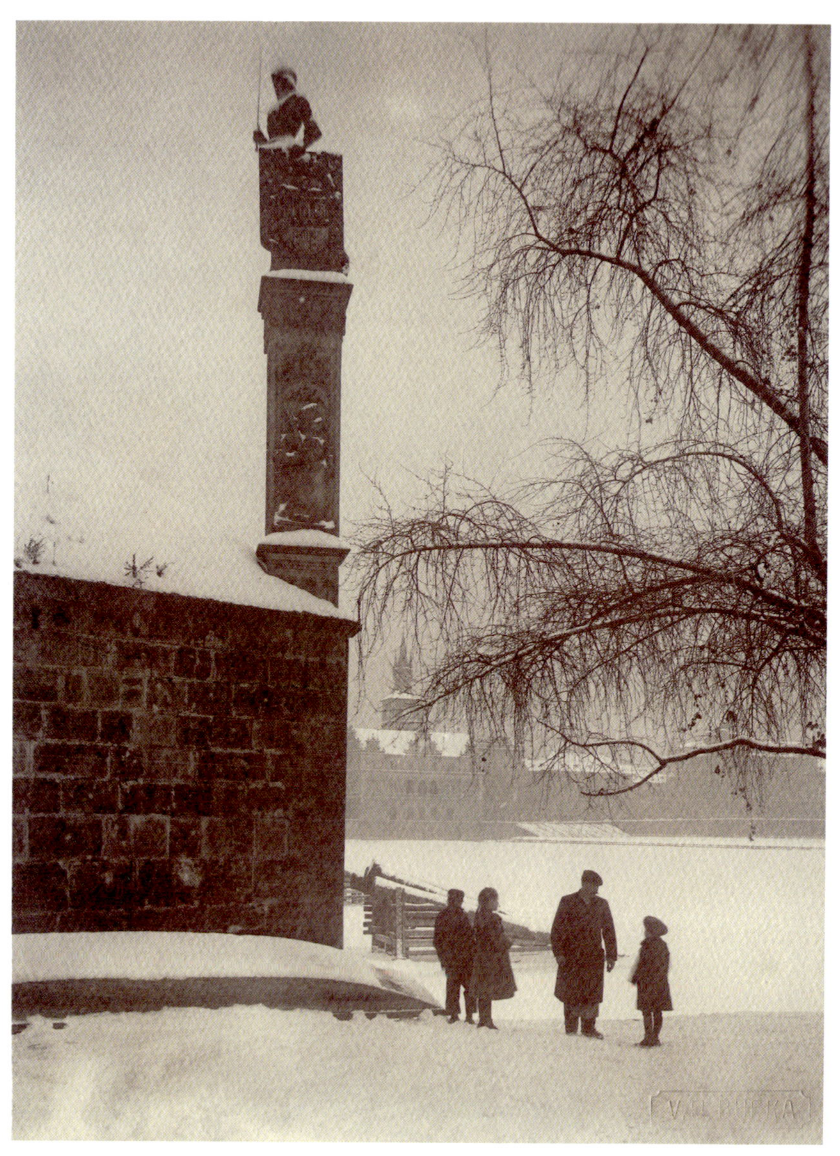

8 **Brunswick / Bruncvík** 1909

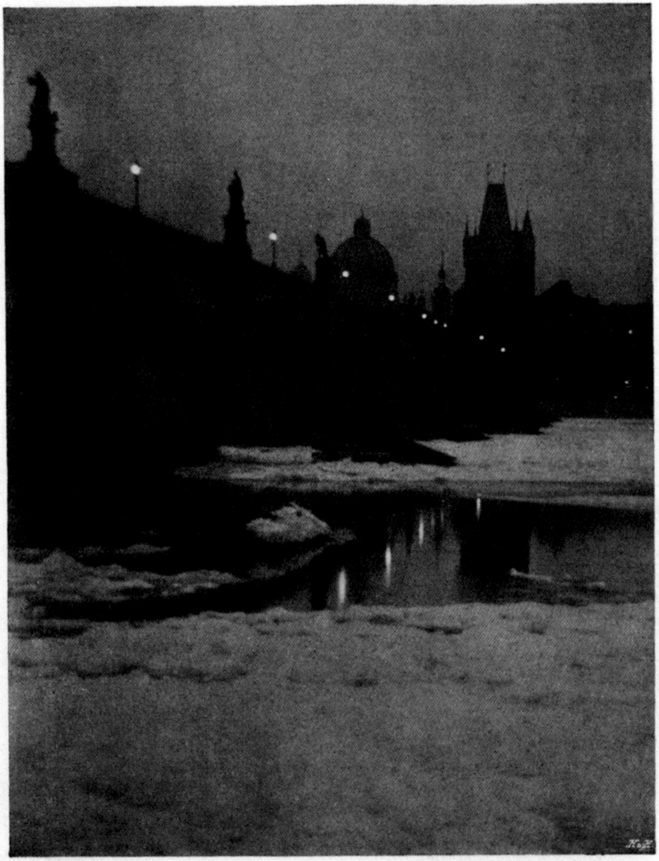

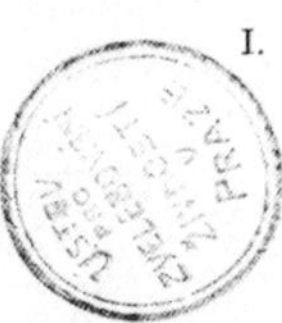

9 A Winter's Evening / Zimní večer c. 1909

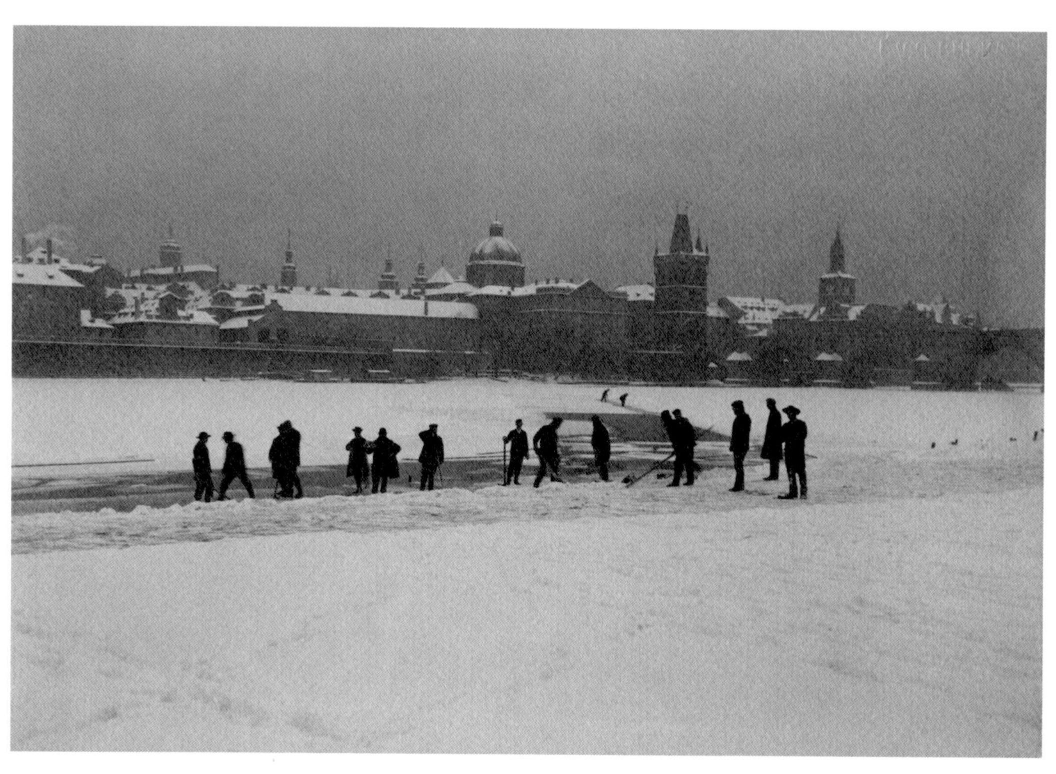

10 **Snow and Ice, Prague / Sníh a led v Praze** 1909

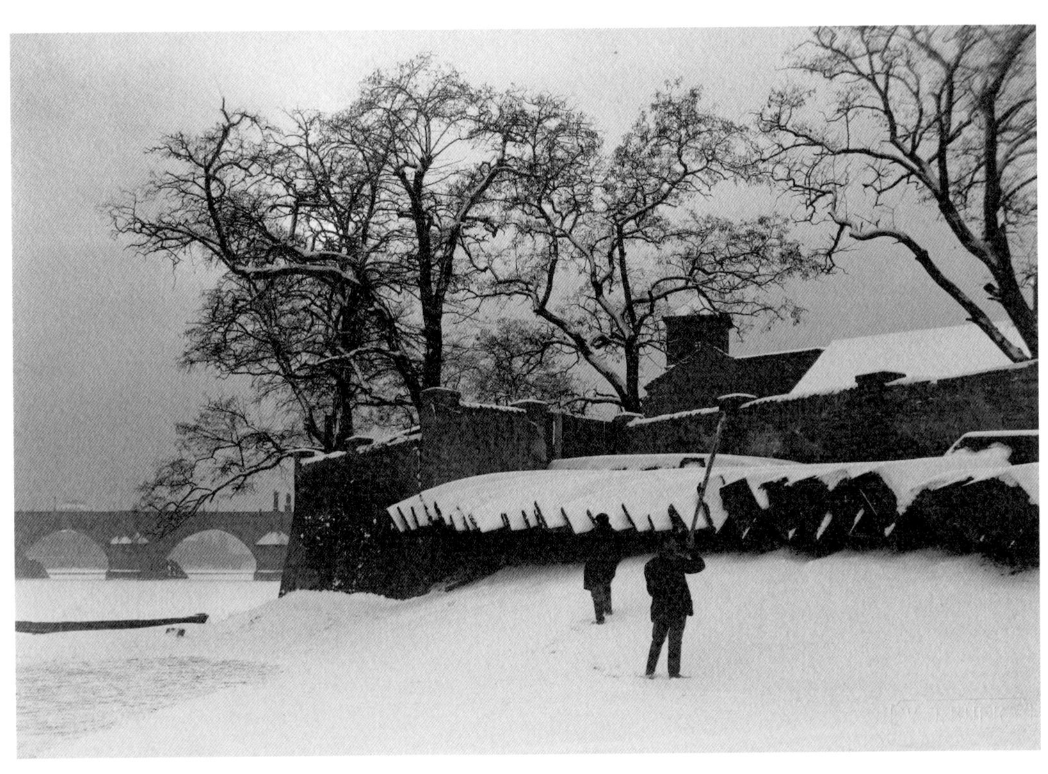

11 **At Kampa / Na Kampě** 1909

12 **Monument to Francis I, on the Smetana Embankment / Pomník Františka I. na Smetanově nábřeží** c. 1909

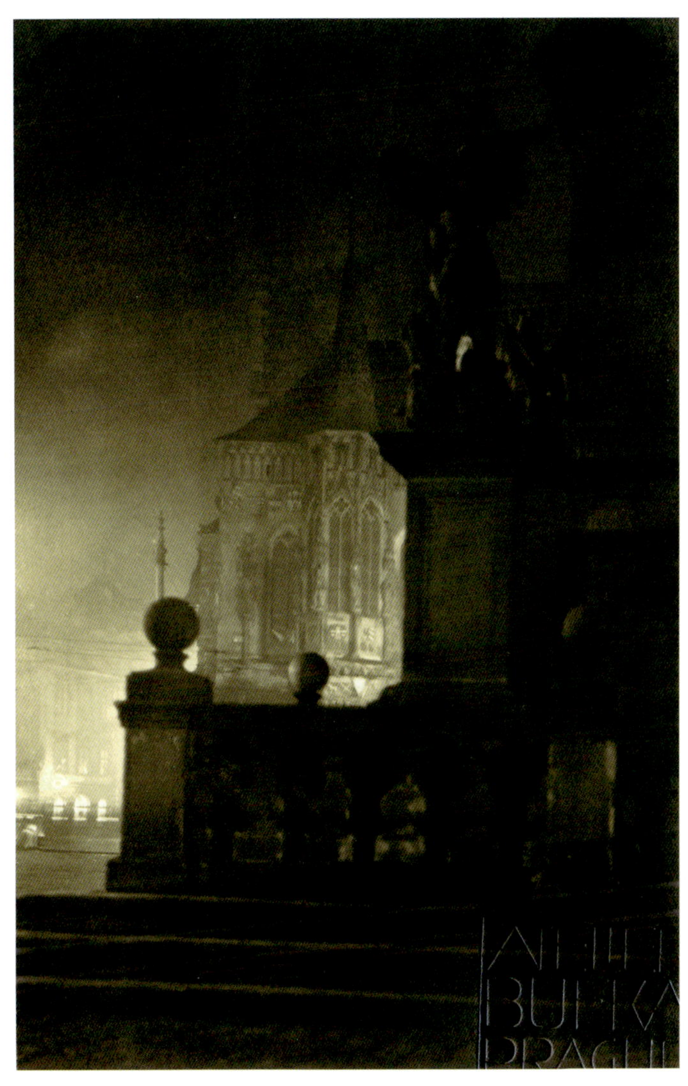

13 **Town Hall, Old Town** / *Staroměstské náměstí* c. 1909

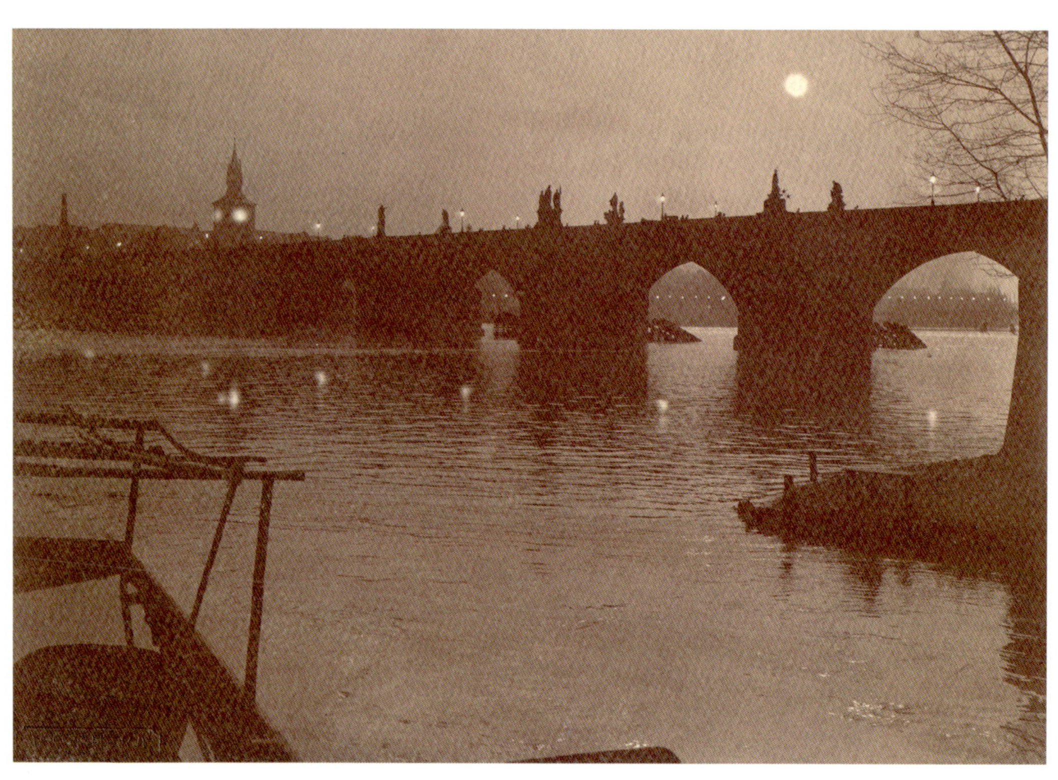

14 **Charles Bridge / Karlův most** 1909

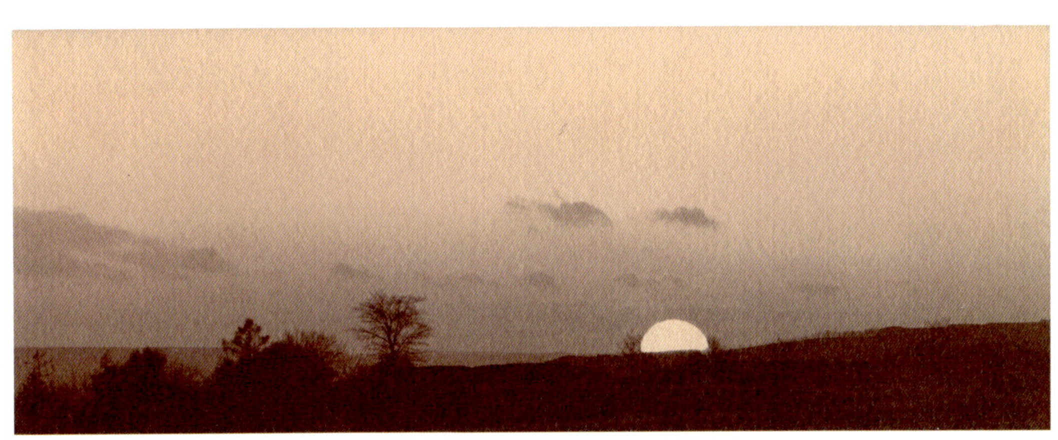

15 **Sunset on Petřín Hill / Západ slunce na Petříně** 1909

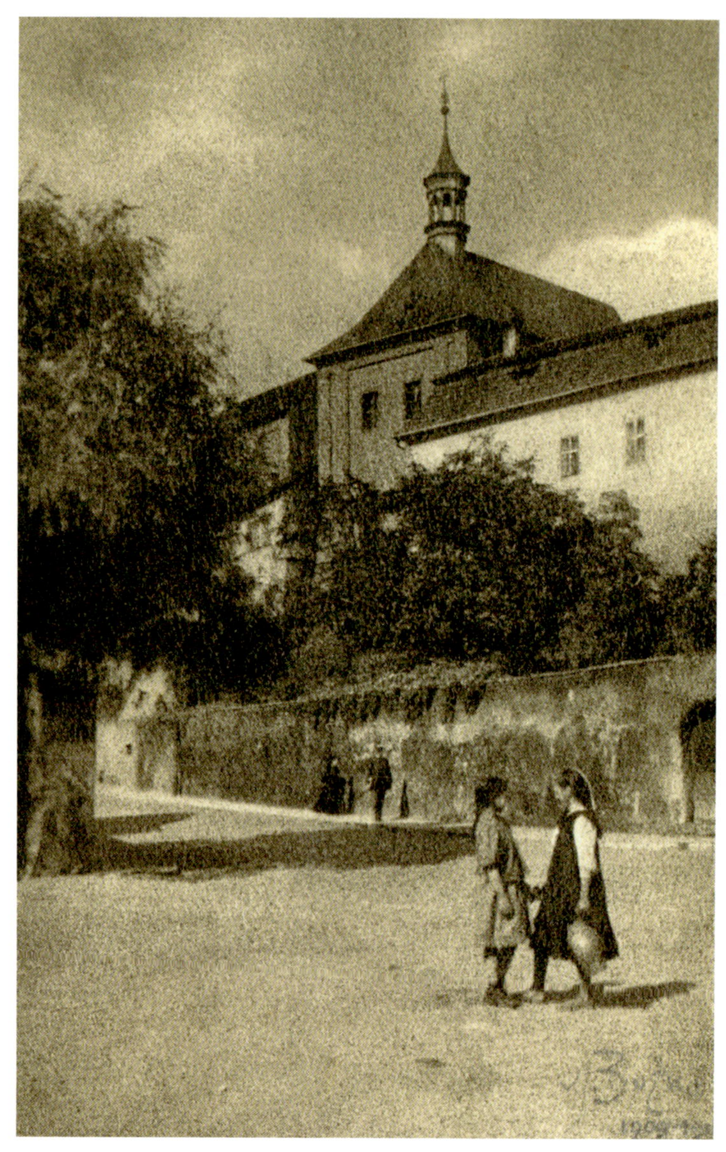

16 **Below the Emmaus Abbey / Pod Emauzy** 1909–14

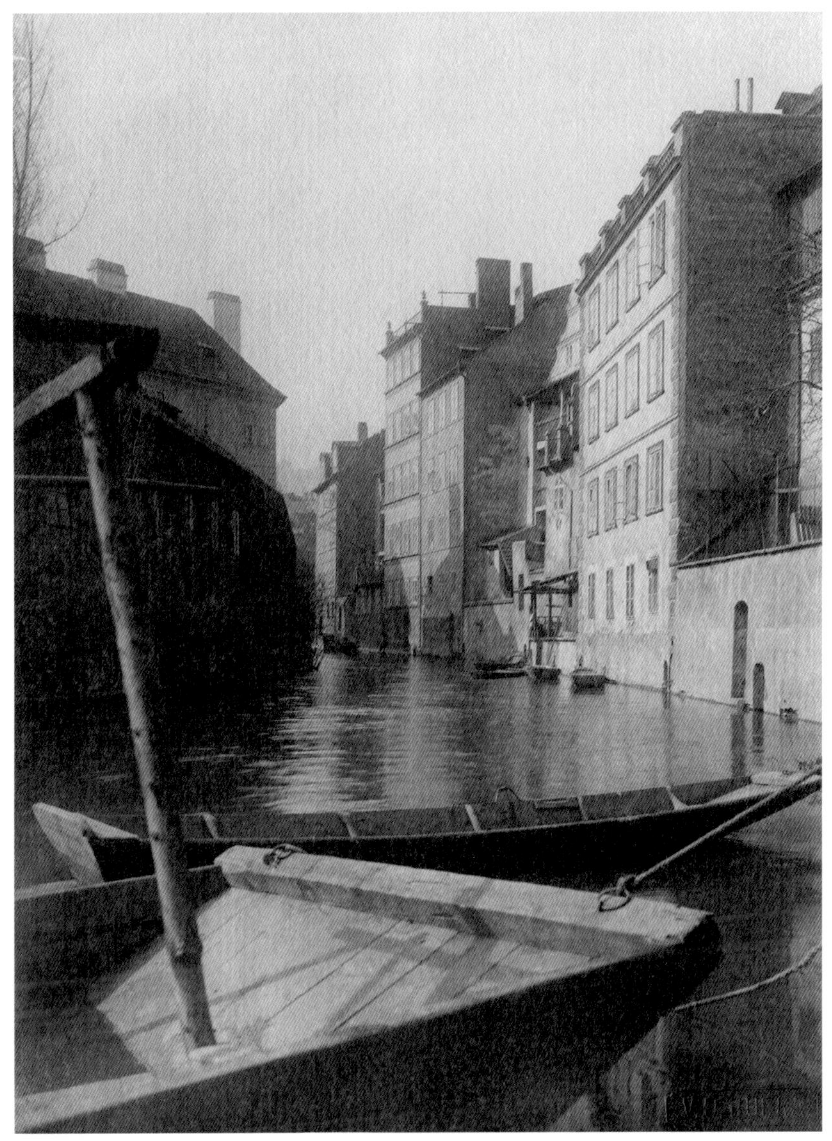

17 **Little Venice, Prague / Pražské Benátky** 1909

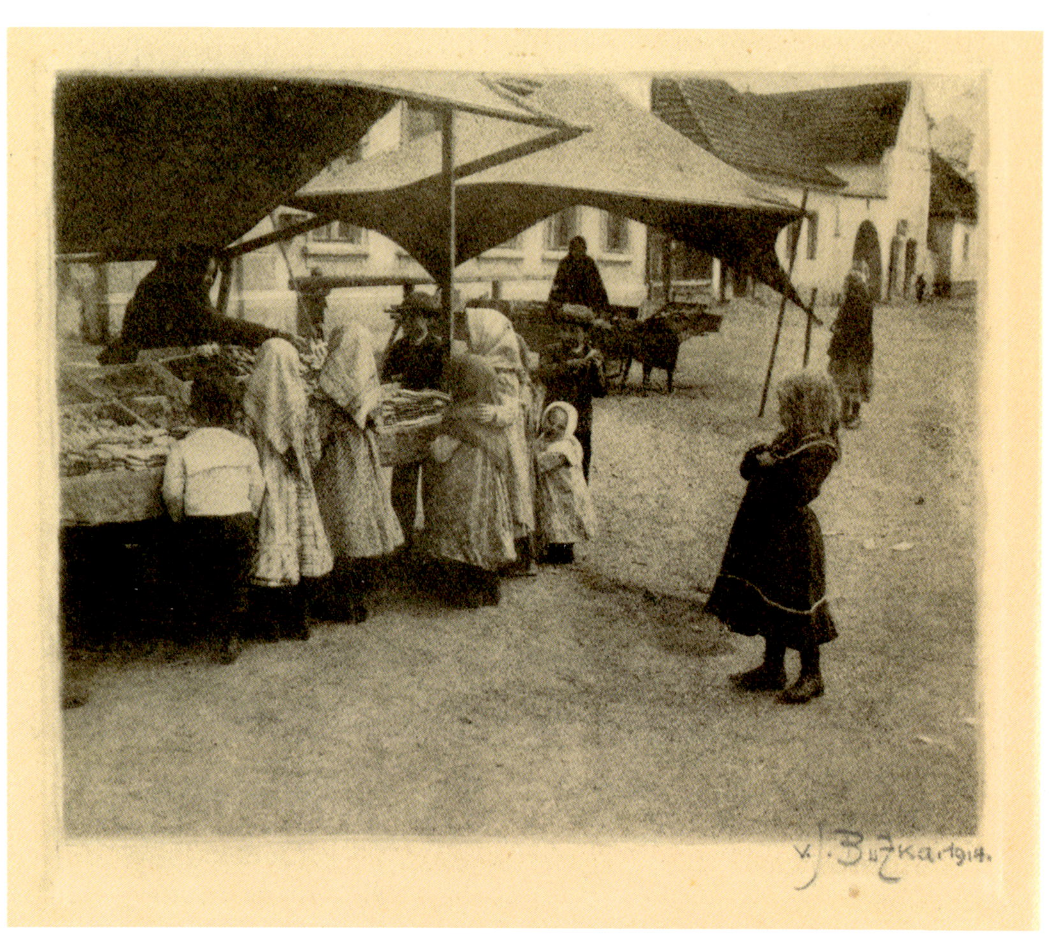

18 Market / Trh 1914

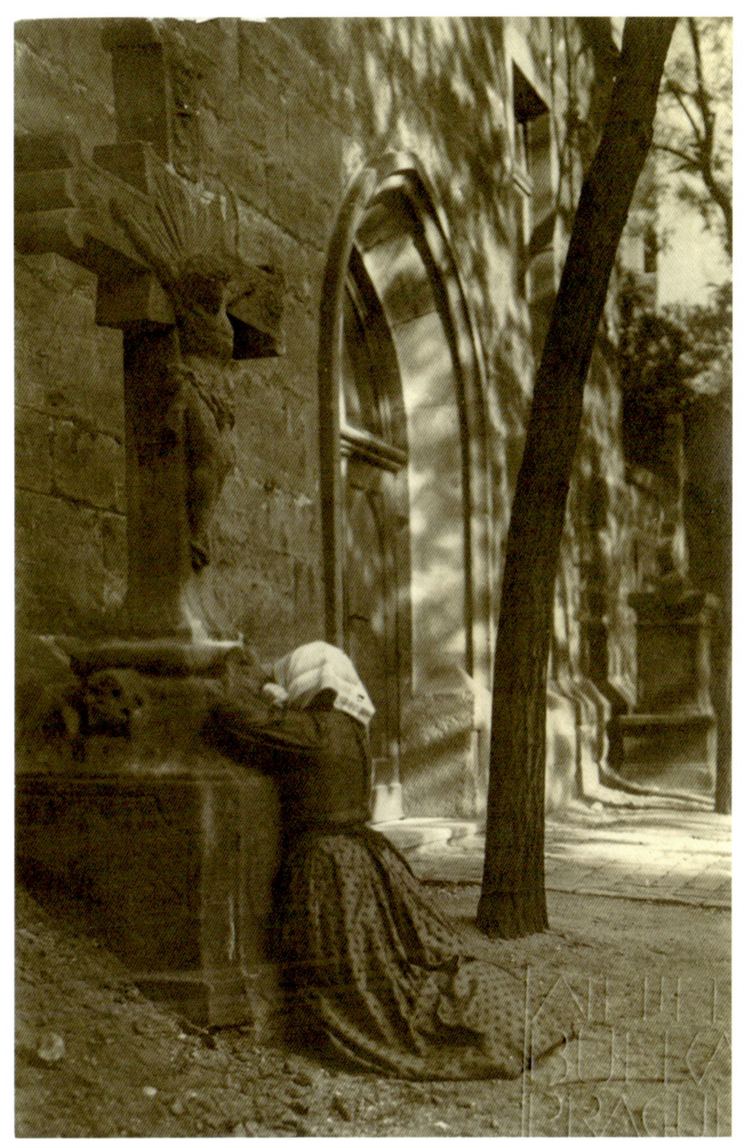

19 **Prayer / Modlitba** c. 1911

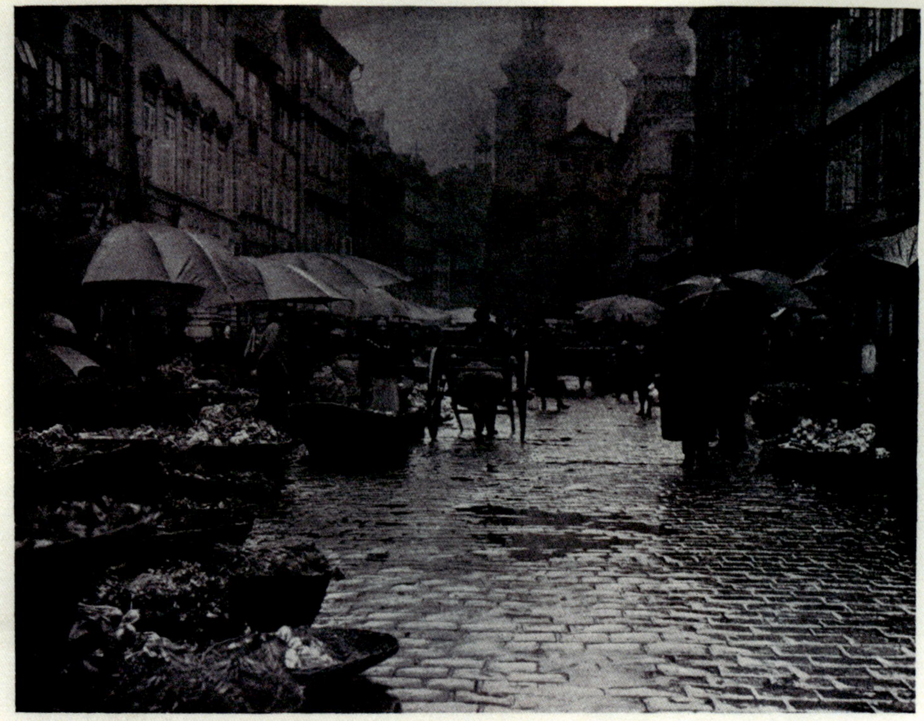

20 **The Vegetable Market in the Rain / Zelený trh v dešti** 1912

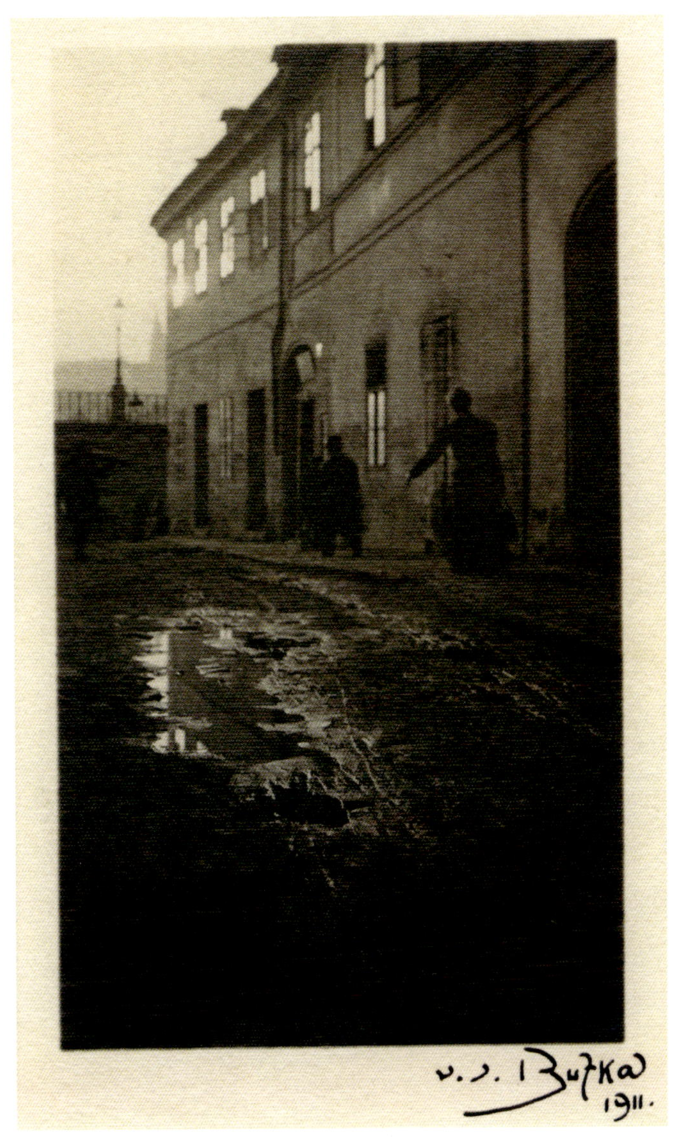

21 **Untitled / *Bez názvu*** c. 1911

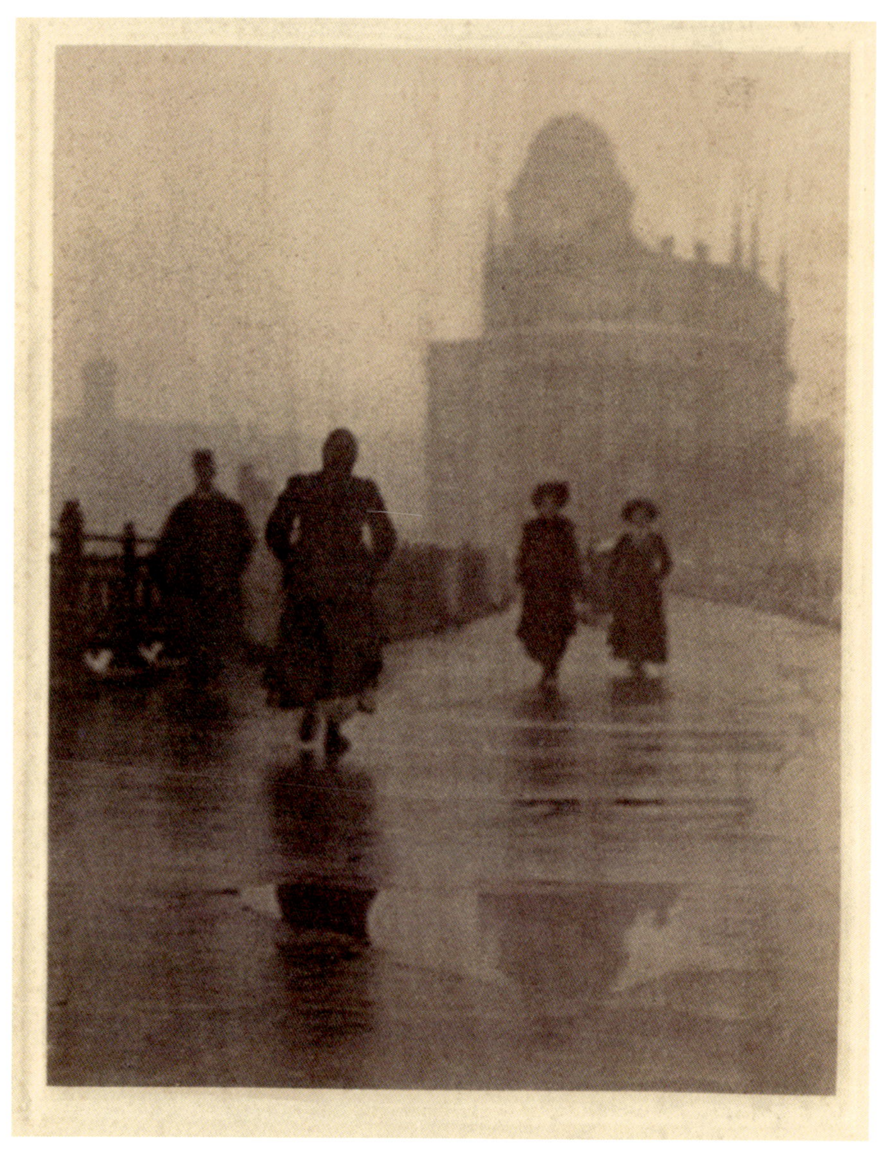

22 **The Urania, Vienna / Urania, Vídeň** 1910–11

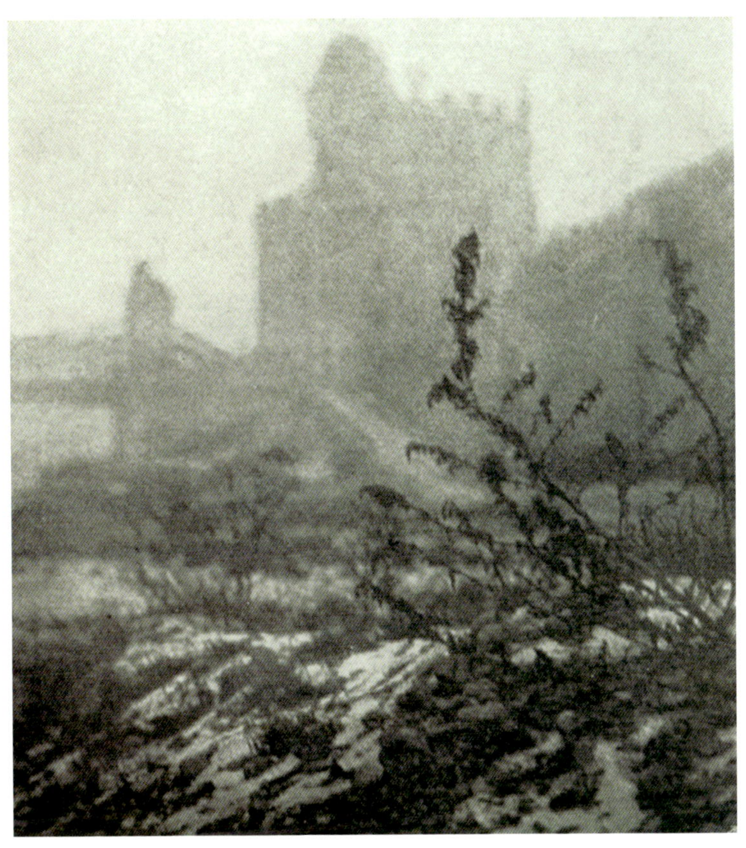

23 **The Urania, from the River, Vienna / Urania od řeky, Vídeň** 1910–11

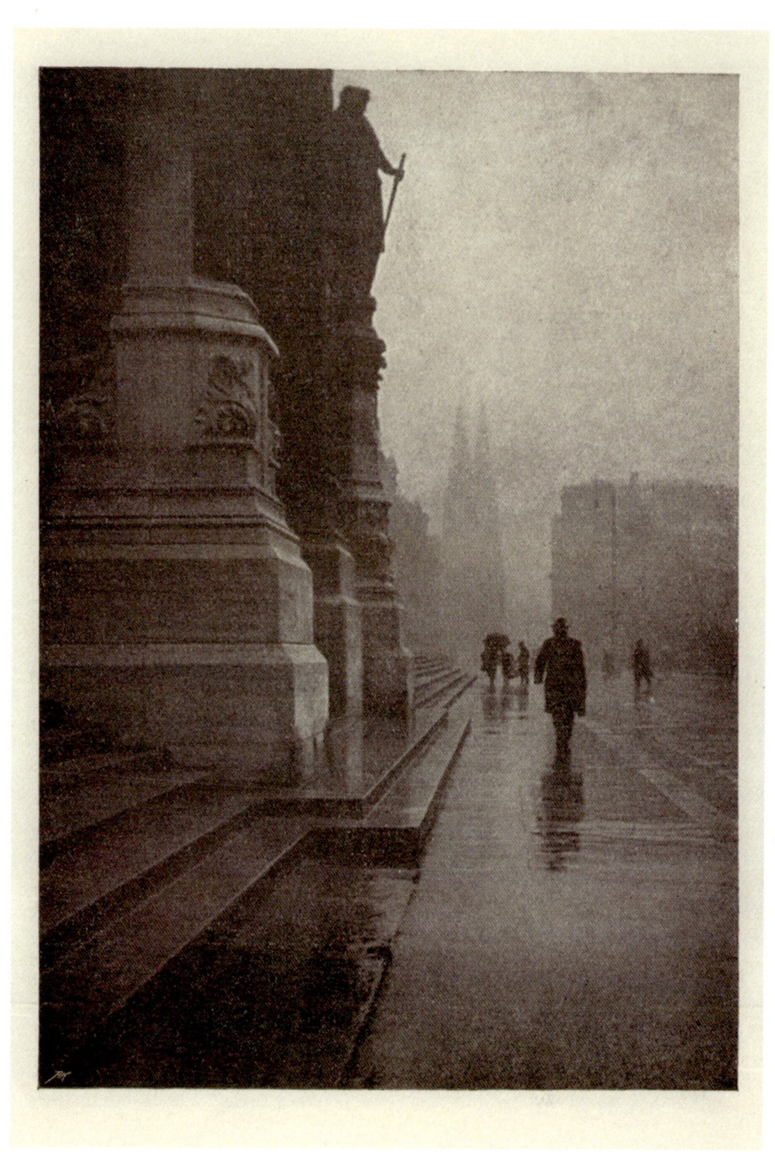

24 **The Town Hall and The Votive Church, Vienna / Radnice a Votivkirche, Vídeň** 1910—11

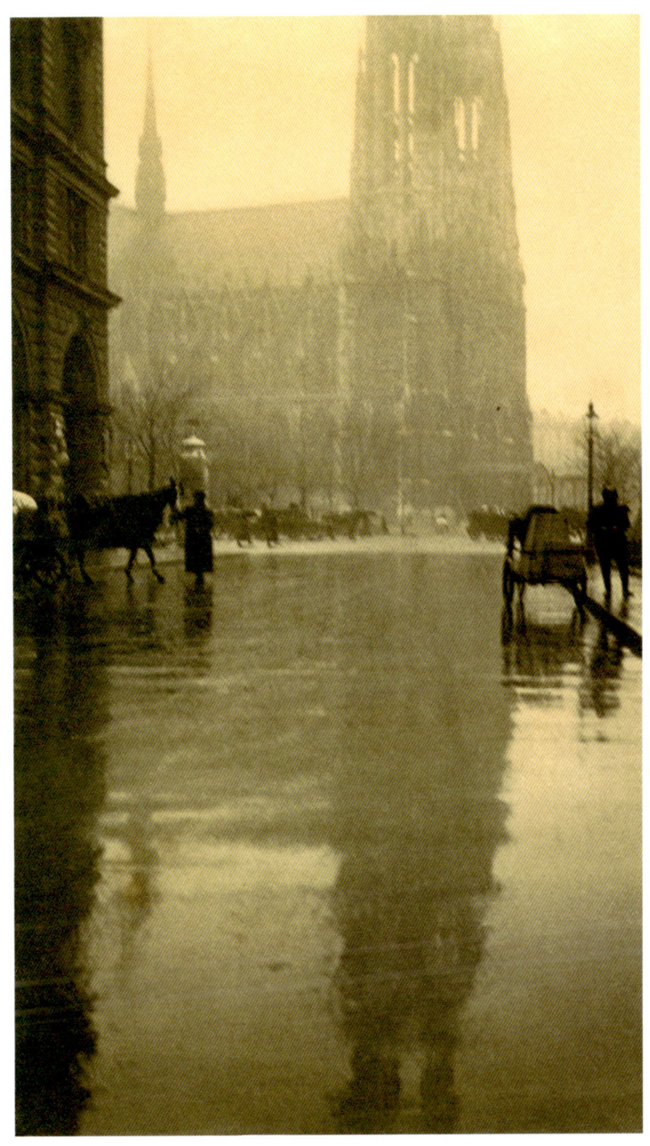

25 The Votive Church, Vienna / U Votivkirche, Vídeň 1910

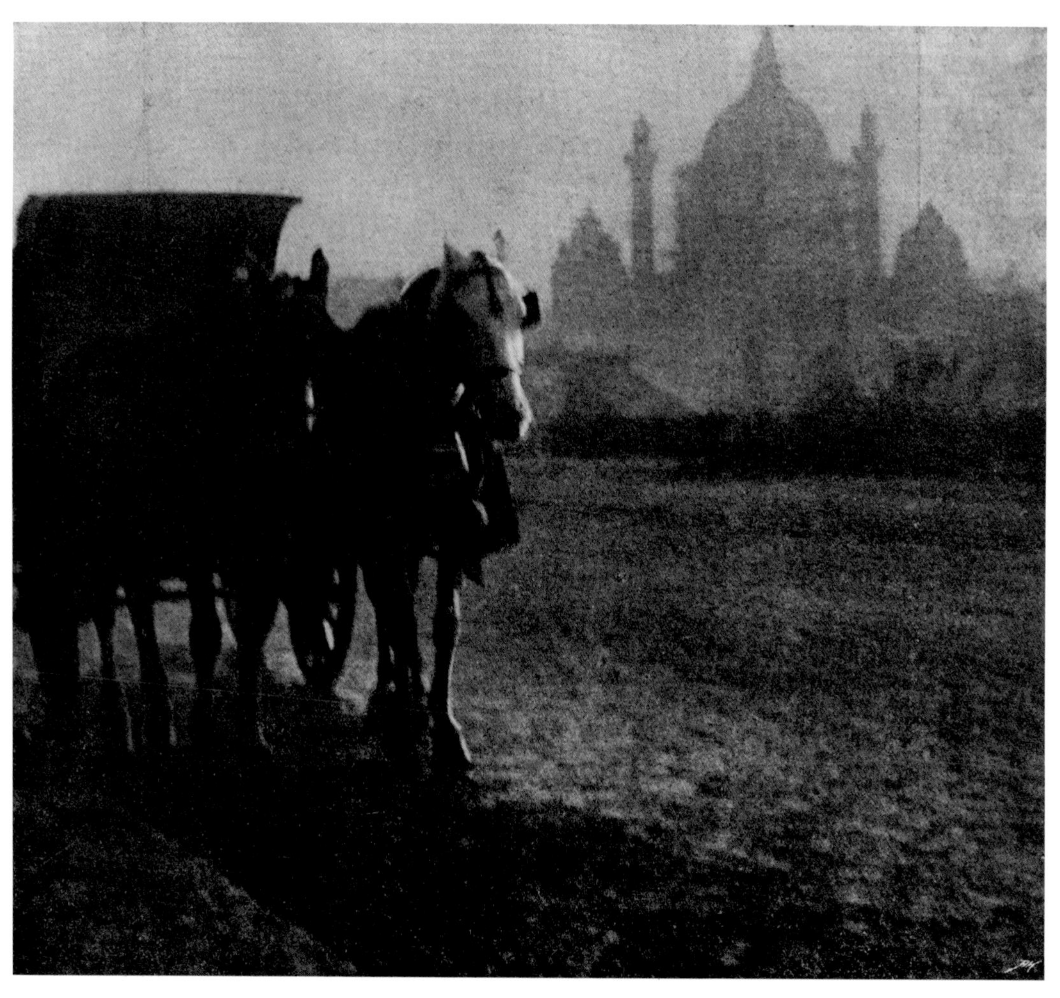

26 **A Landau at St. Charles's Church, Vienna / Fiakr u Karlskirche, Vídeň** 1910–11

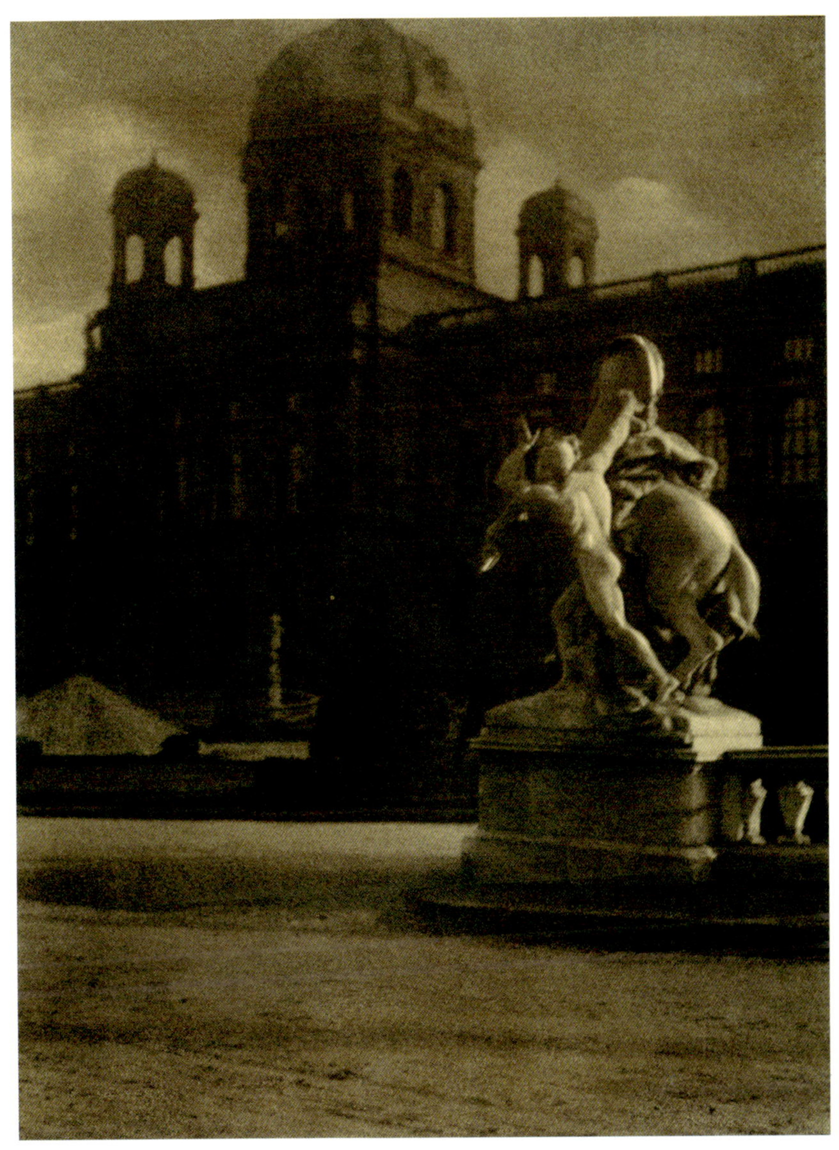

27 **The Sculpture, Kunsthistorisches Museum, Vienna / Vídeň** 1910

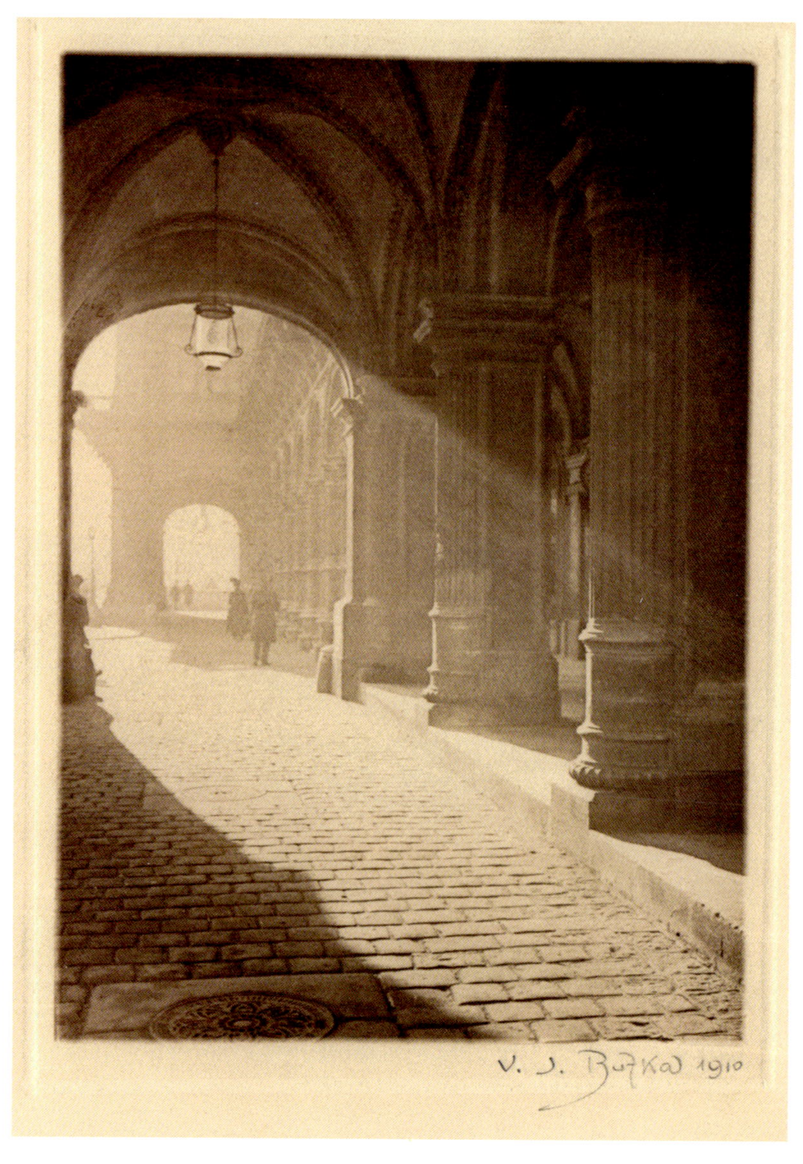

28 **The Opera, Vienna / Opera, Vídeň** 1910

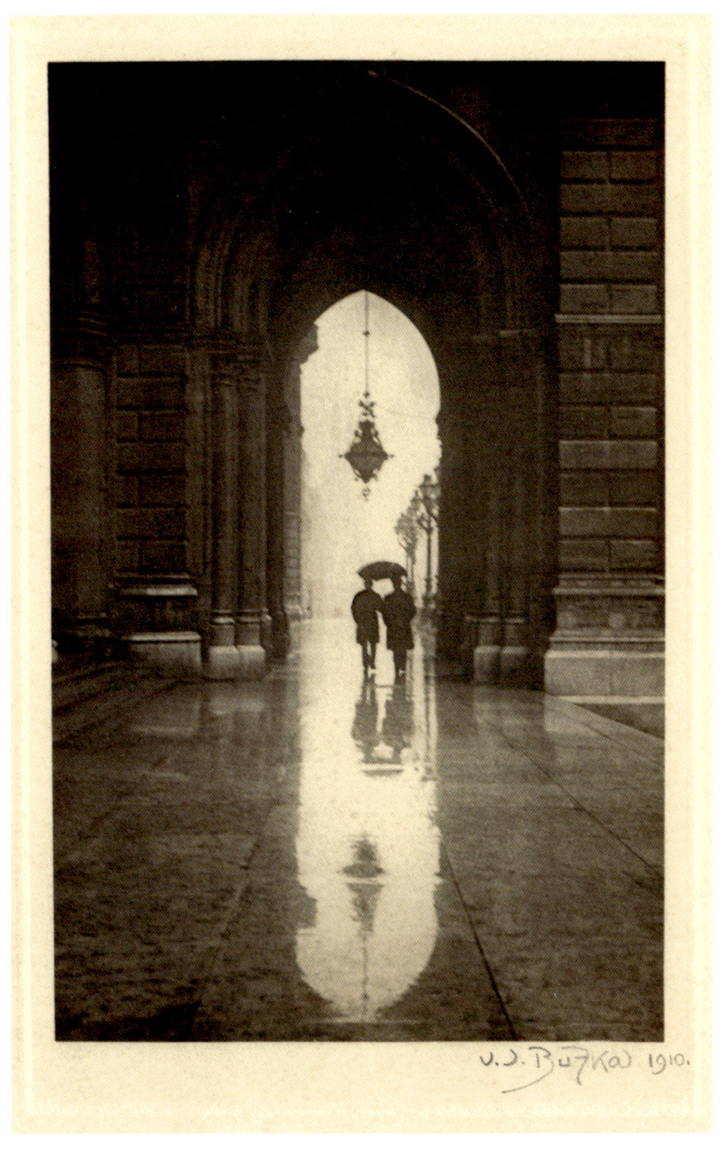

29 **The Town Hall, Vienna / Radnice, Vídeň** 1910

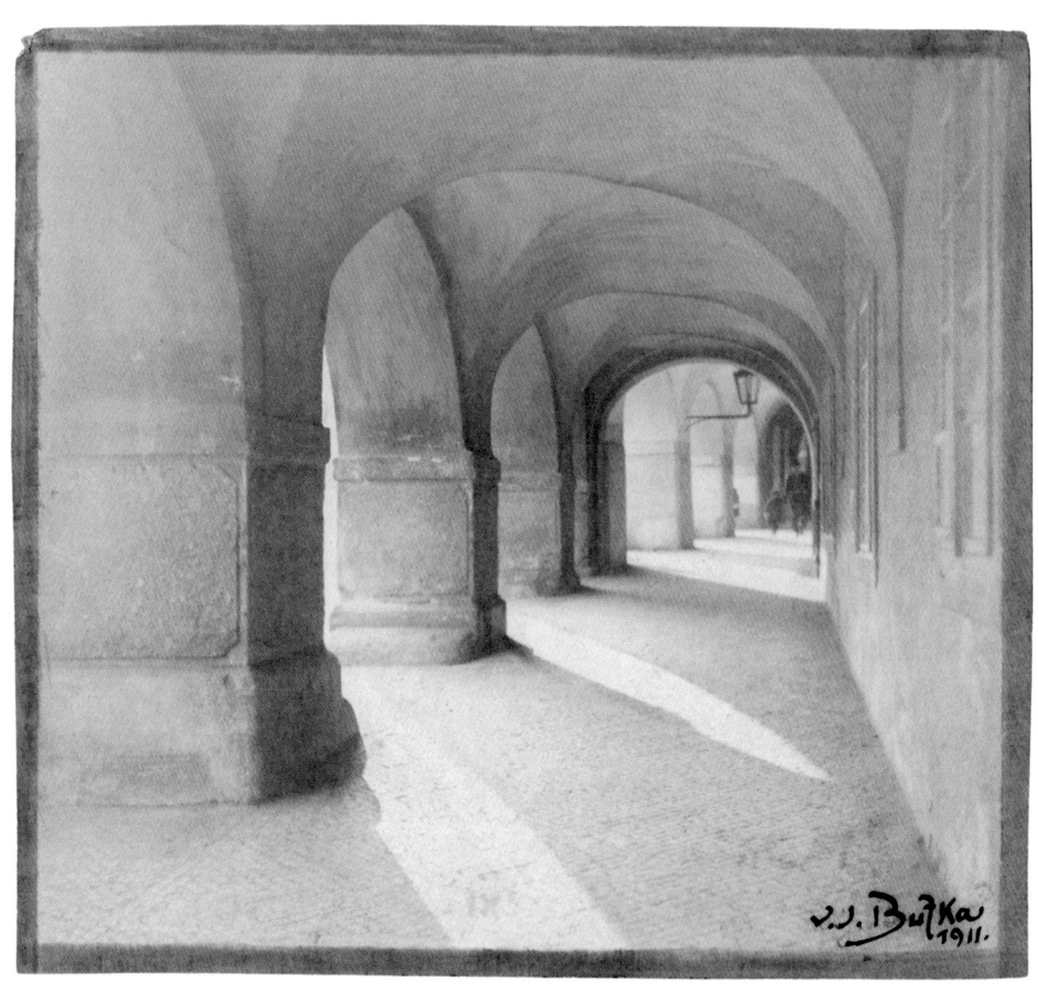

30 **From Prague / Z Prahy** 1911

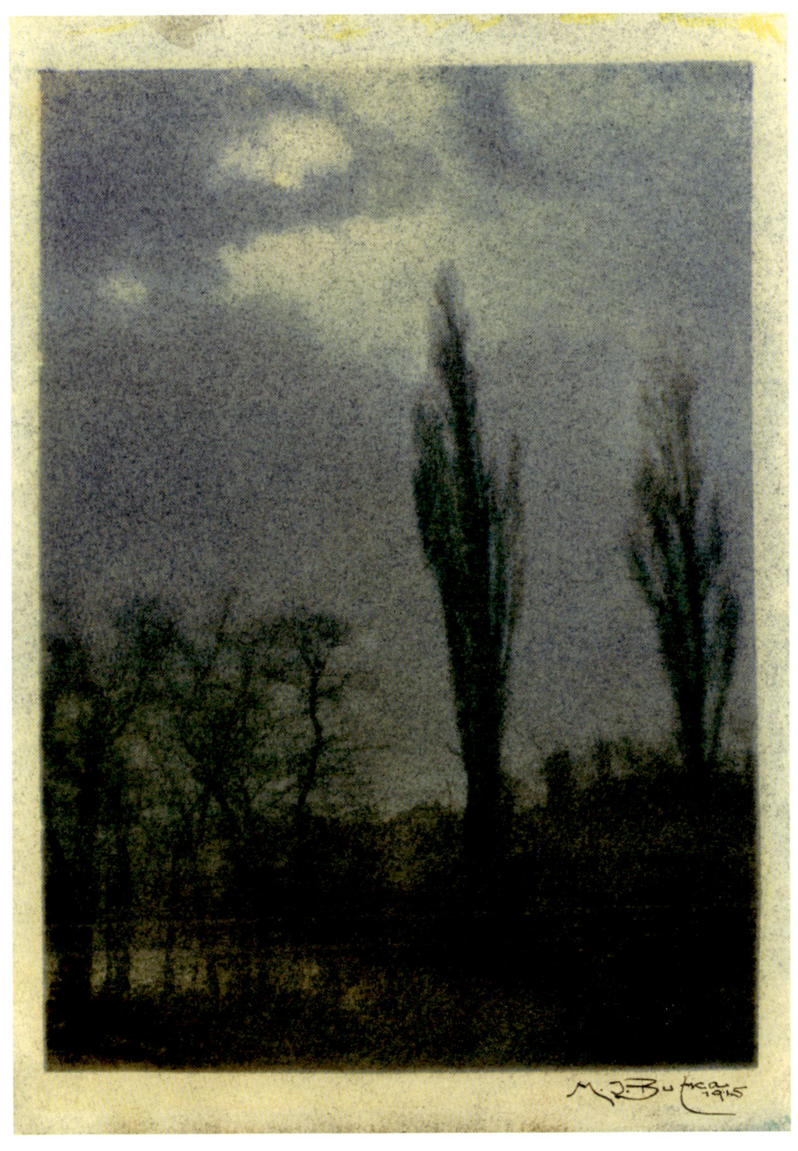

31 **Poplars by the Light of the Full Moon, Vršovice / Topoly při úplňku ve Vršovicích** 1915

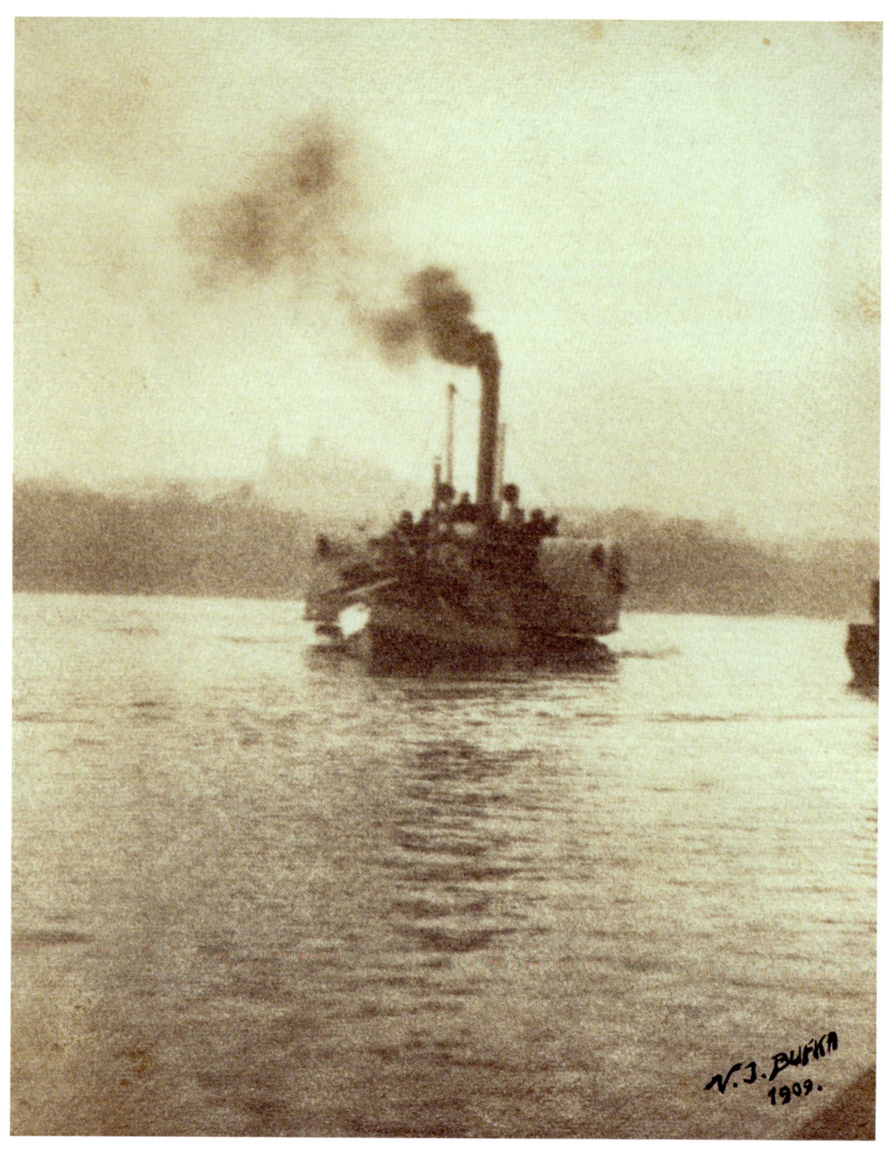

32 **Steamboat / Parník** 1909

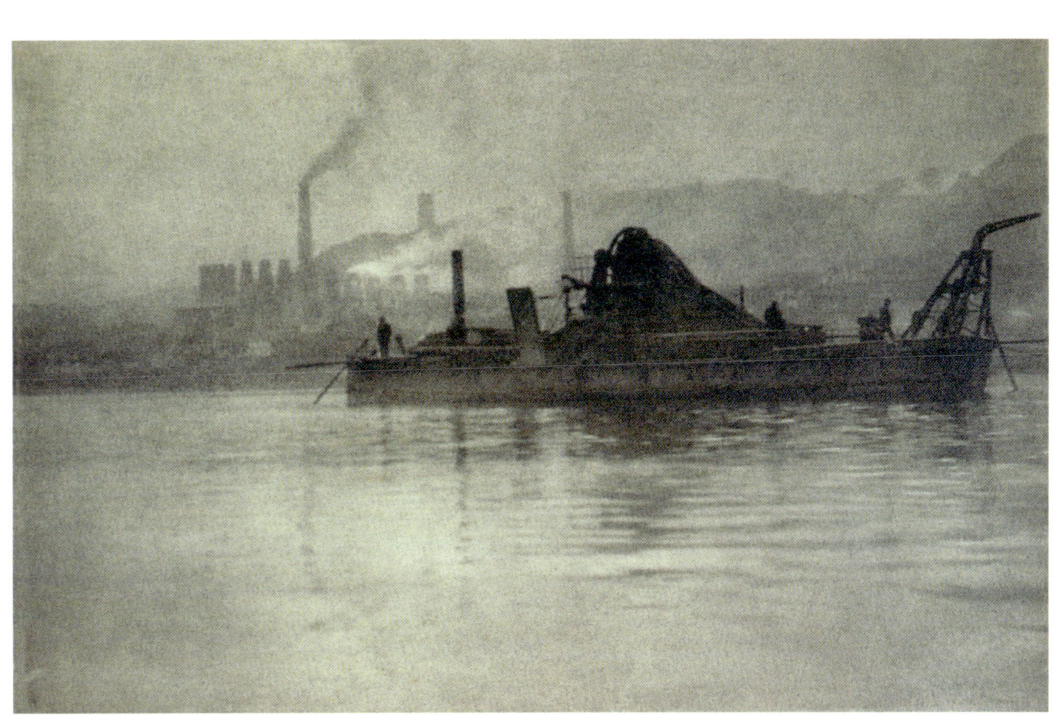

33 **Near Chuchle / U Chuchle** 1913

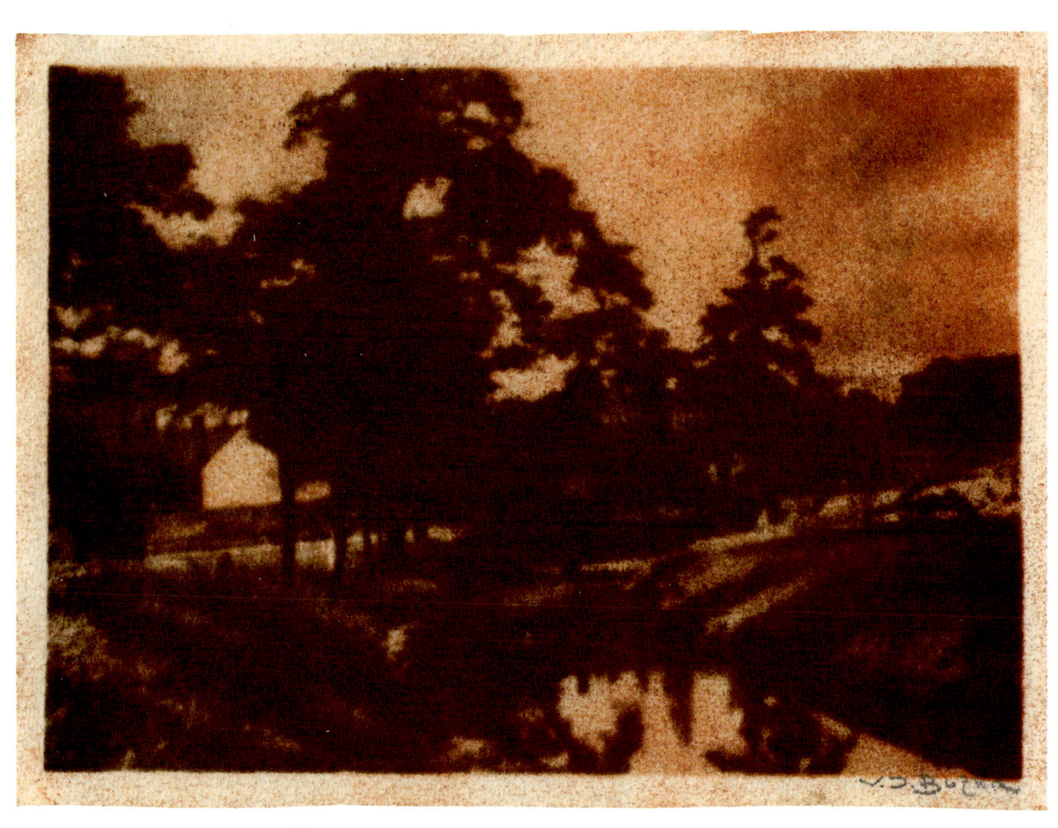

34 **Landscape / Krajina** c. 1914

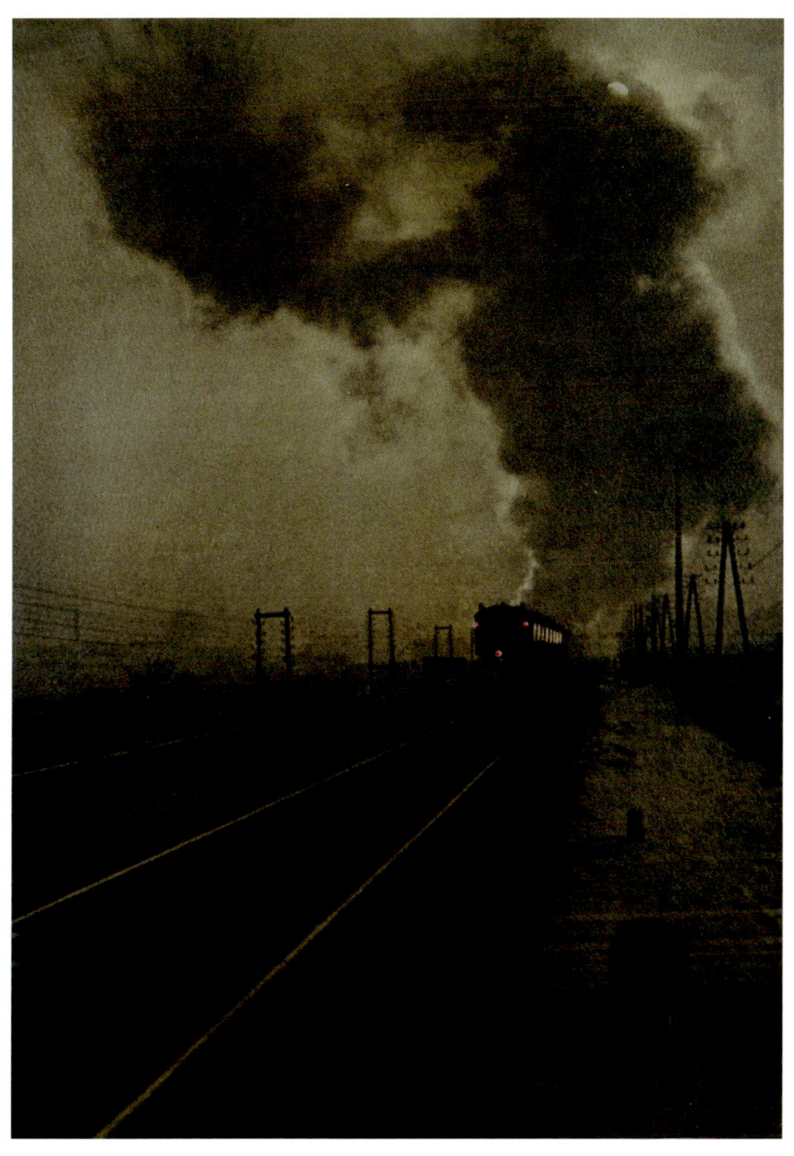

35 **Evening Train / Večerní vlak** 1911

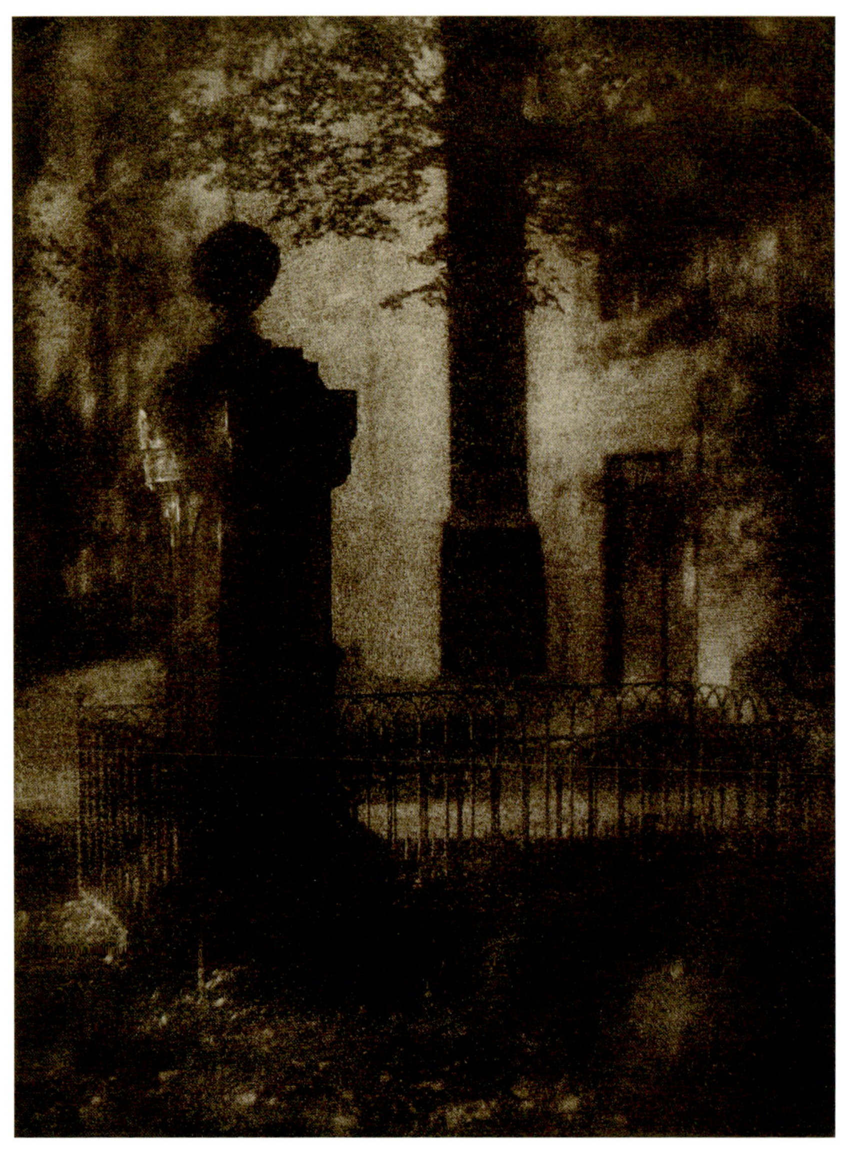

36 **At the Wonderful Old Smíchov Cemetery / Na starém a báječném hřbitově smíchovském** 1914

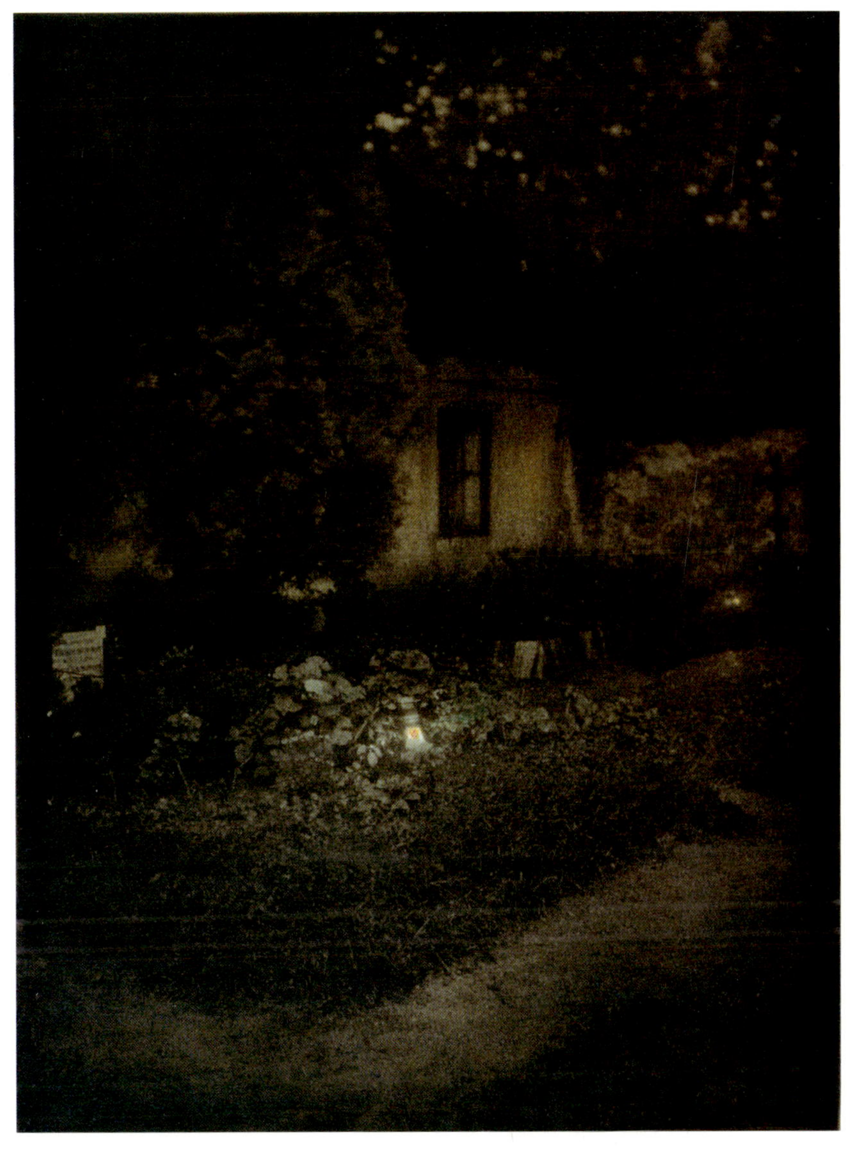

37 **At Chuchle Cemetery / Na chuchelském hřbitově** 1912

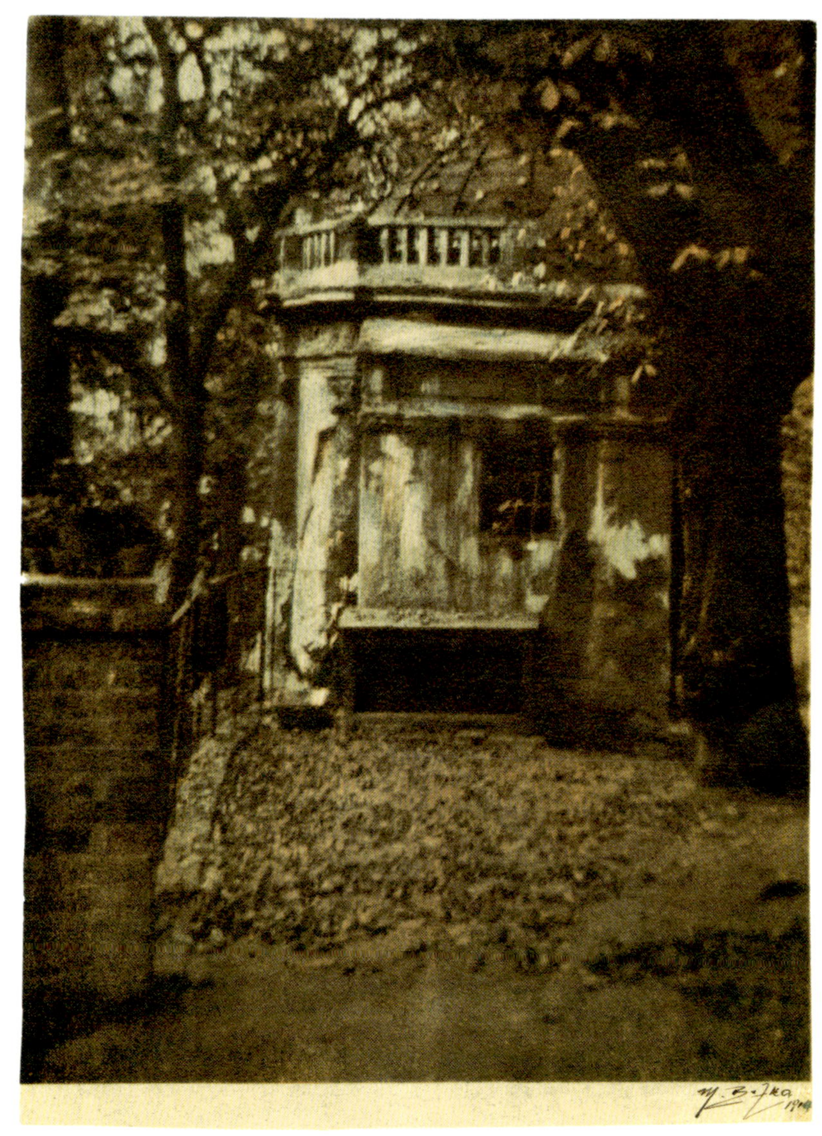

38 From a Košíře Garden / Z košířské zahrady c. 1914

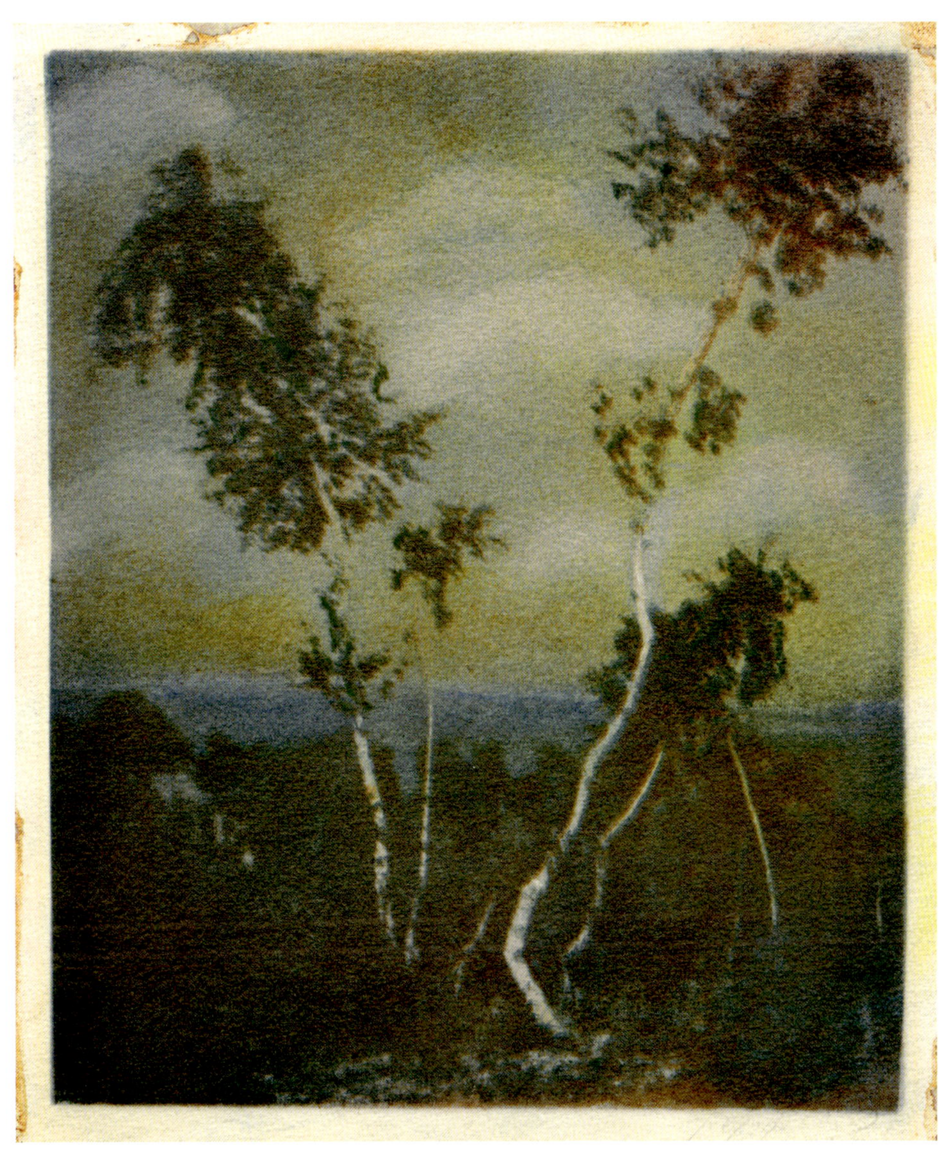

39 **Birches / Břízy** 1913

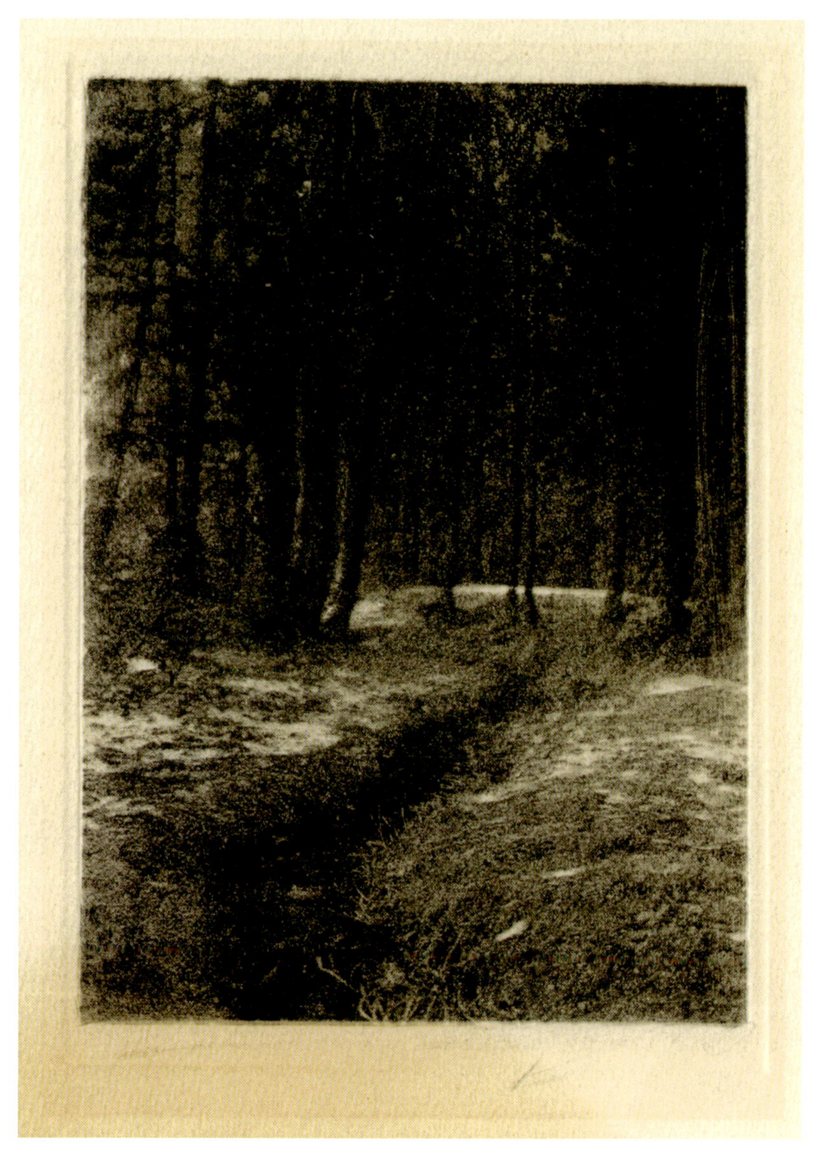

40 **A Wood near Říčany / Les u Říčan** 1911–13

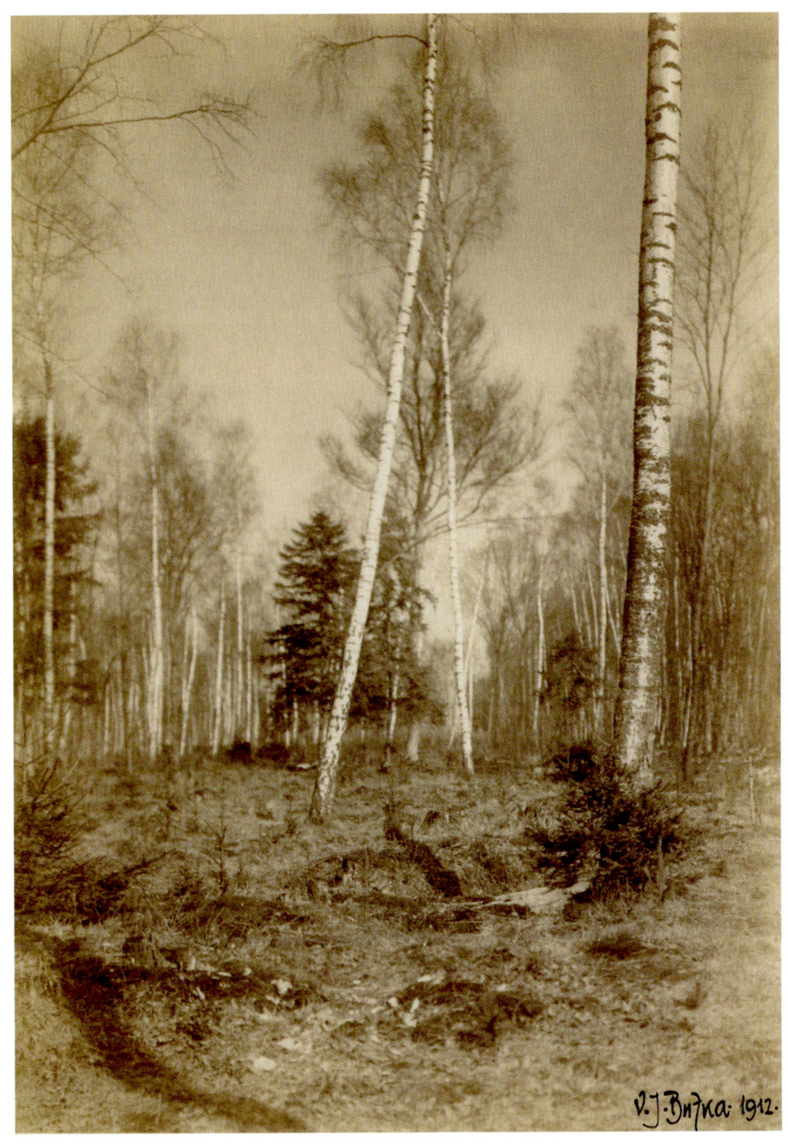

41 **Birches at the Edge of a Wood / Břízy na kraji lesa** 1912

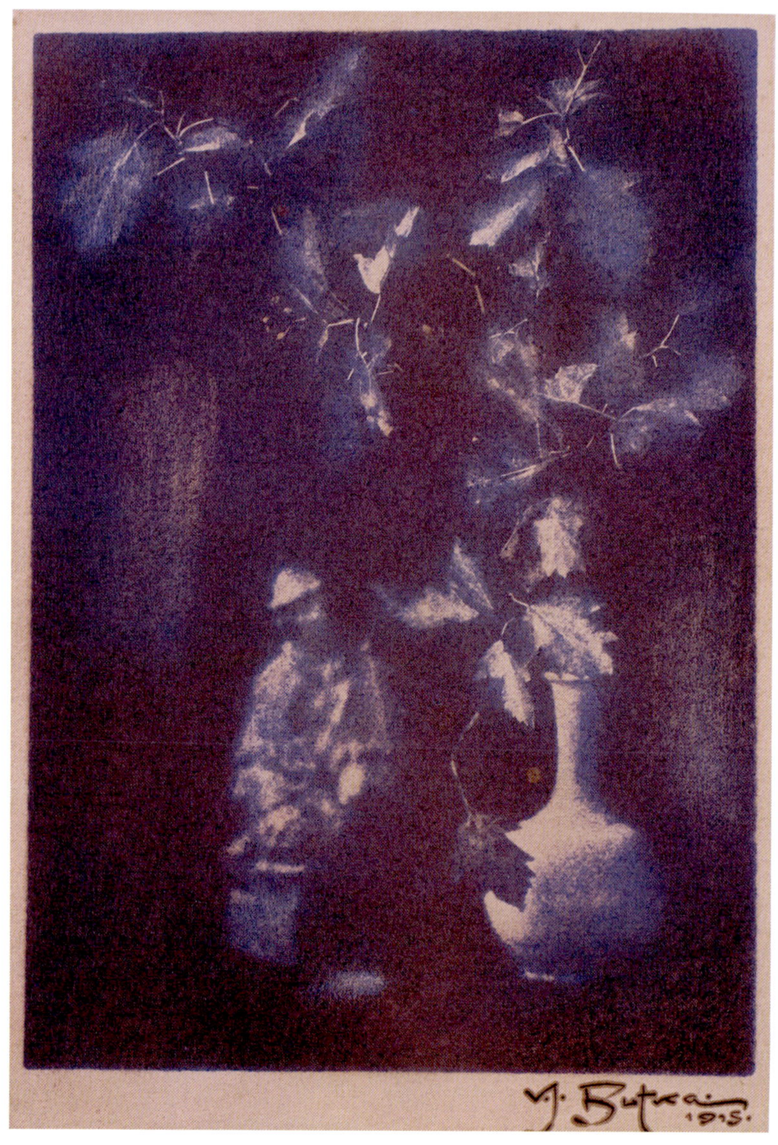

42 **Blue Still Life / Modré zátiší** 1915

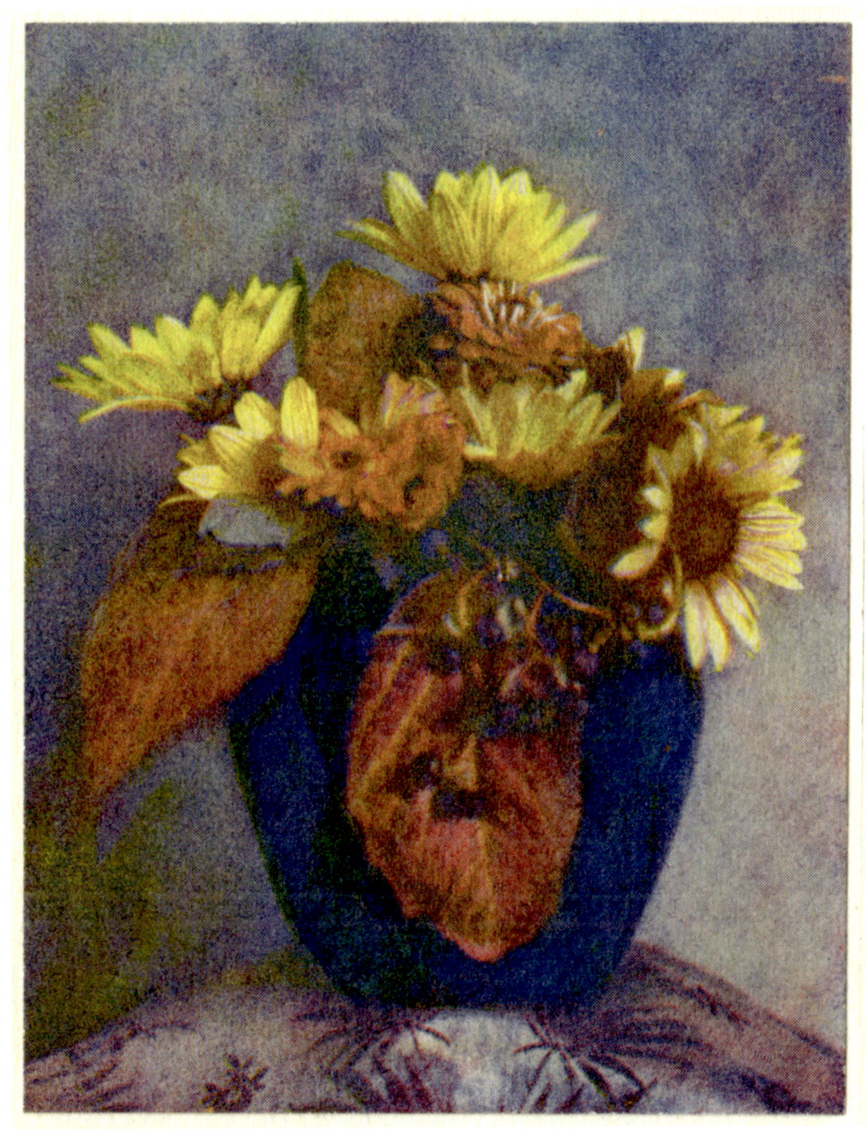

43 **Sunflowers in a Blue Vase / Slunečnice v modré váze** c. 1914

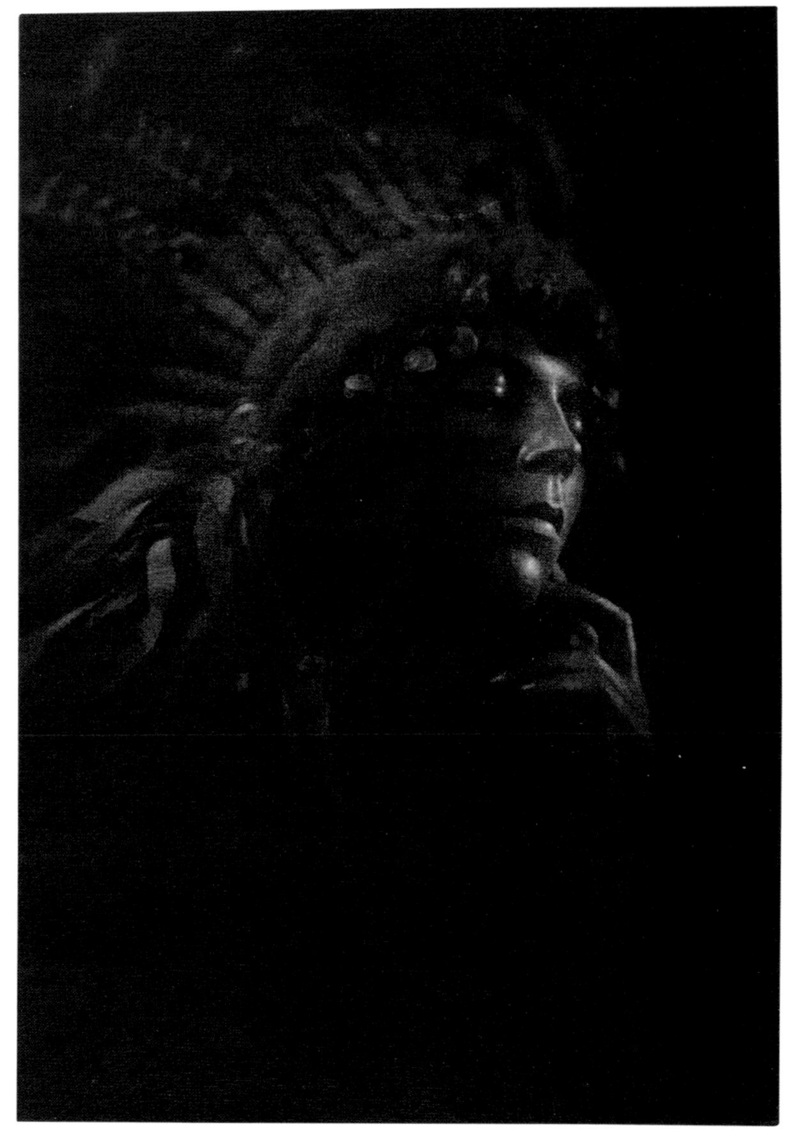

44 **Marie Bufková in a Headdress / Marie Bufková v čelence** c. 1912

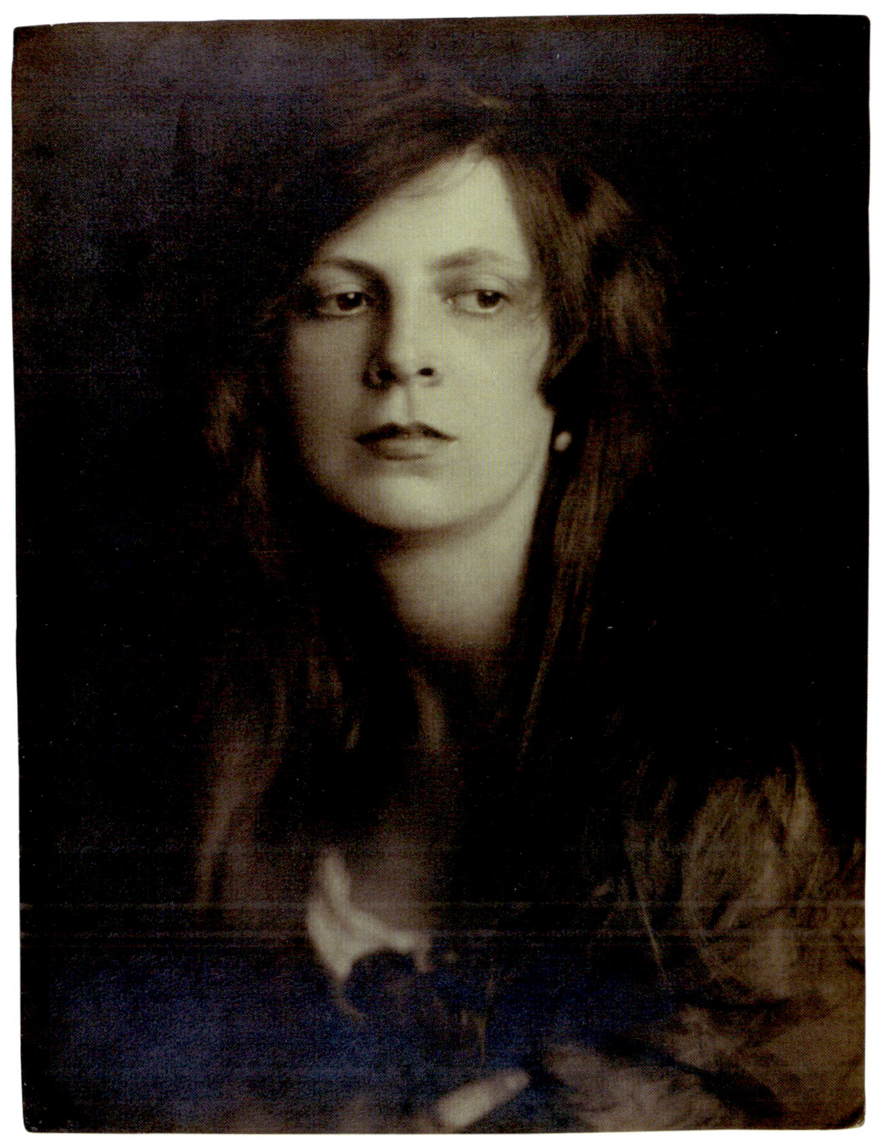

45 **Marie Bufková** c. 1912

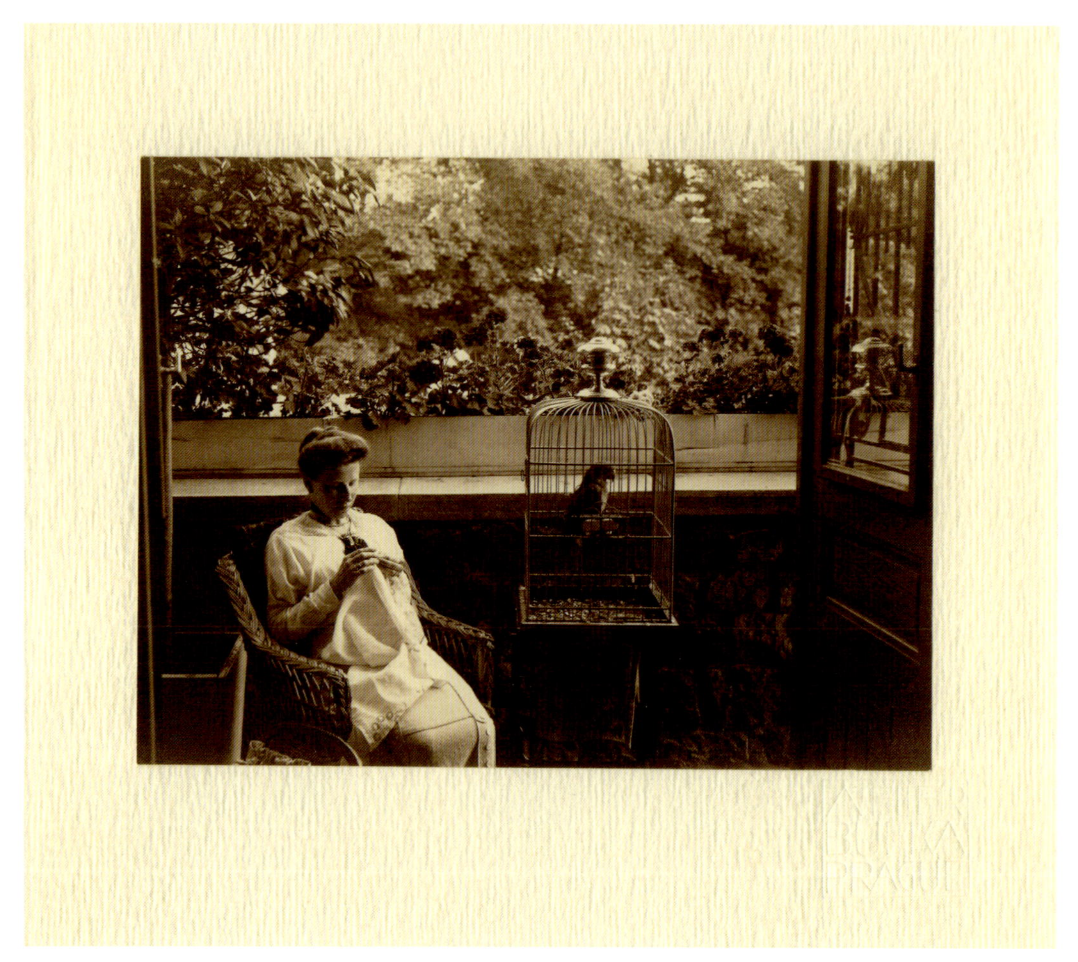

46 **Lucie Bakešová, Brno** c. 1912–15

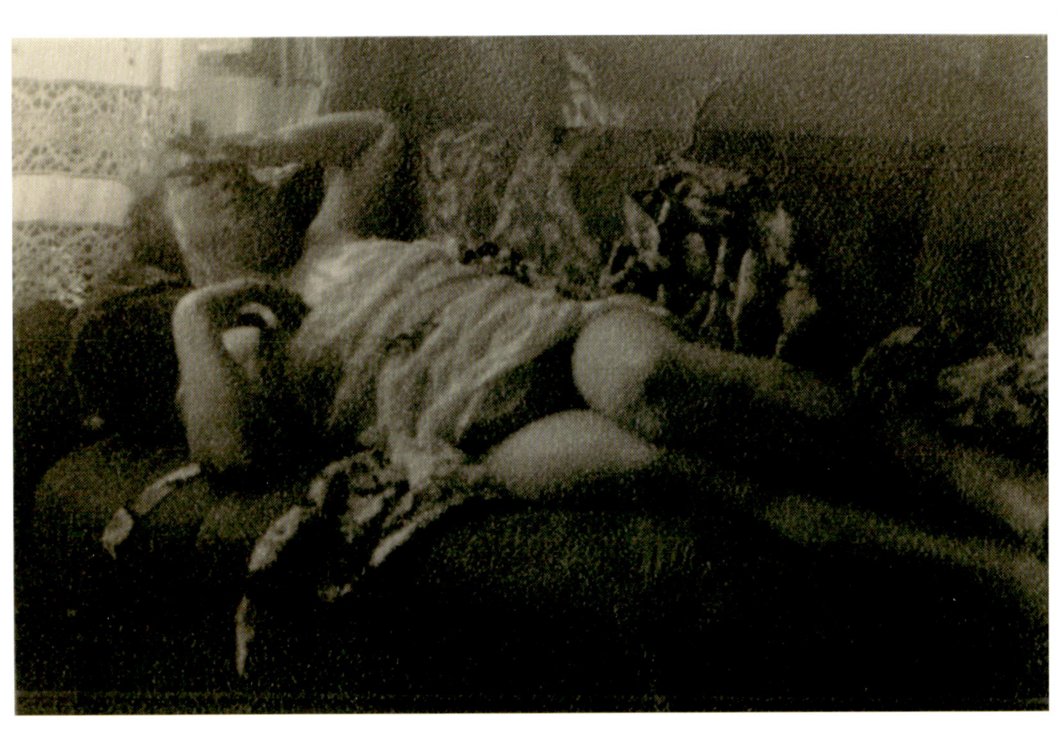

47 **A Woman on a Sofa / Žena na pohovce** c. 1912

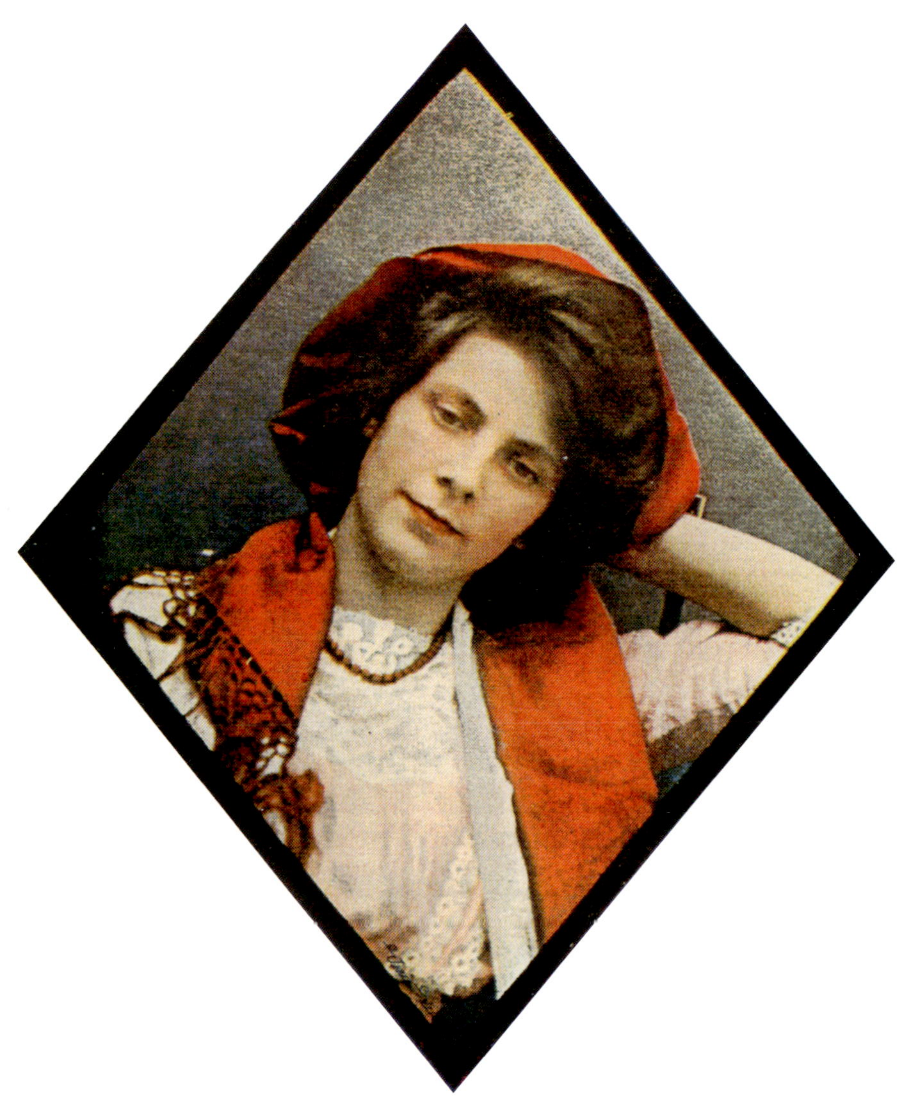

48 **Marie Bufková** 1909–10

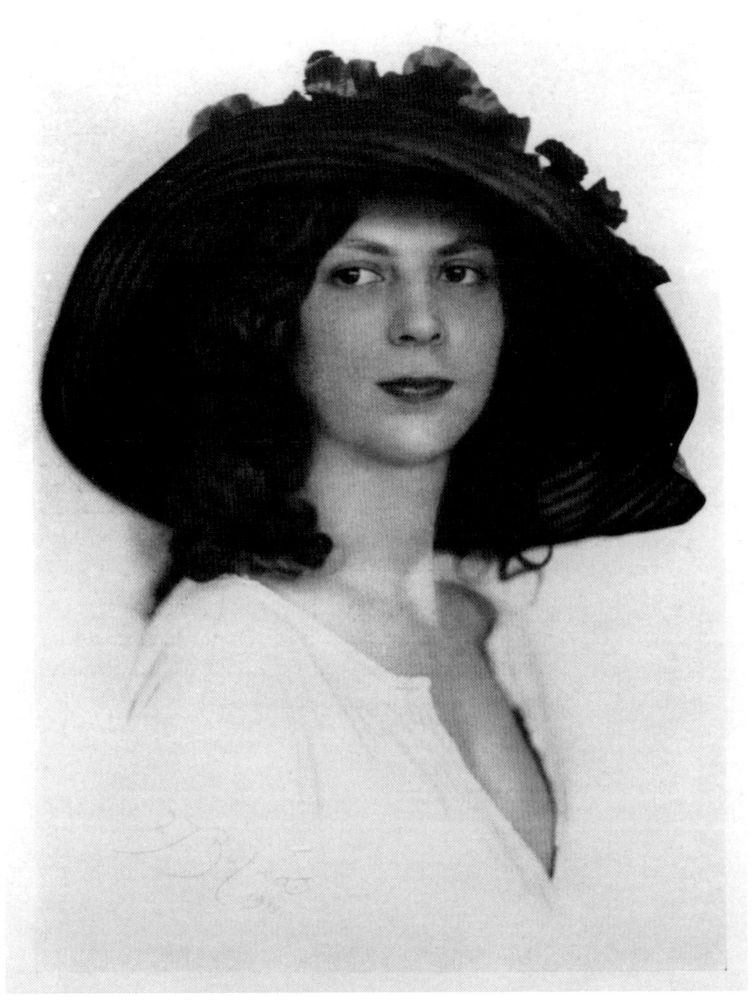

49 The Artist's Wife / Choť umělcova 1909–10

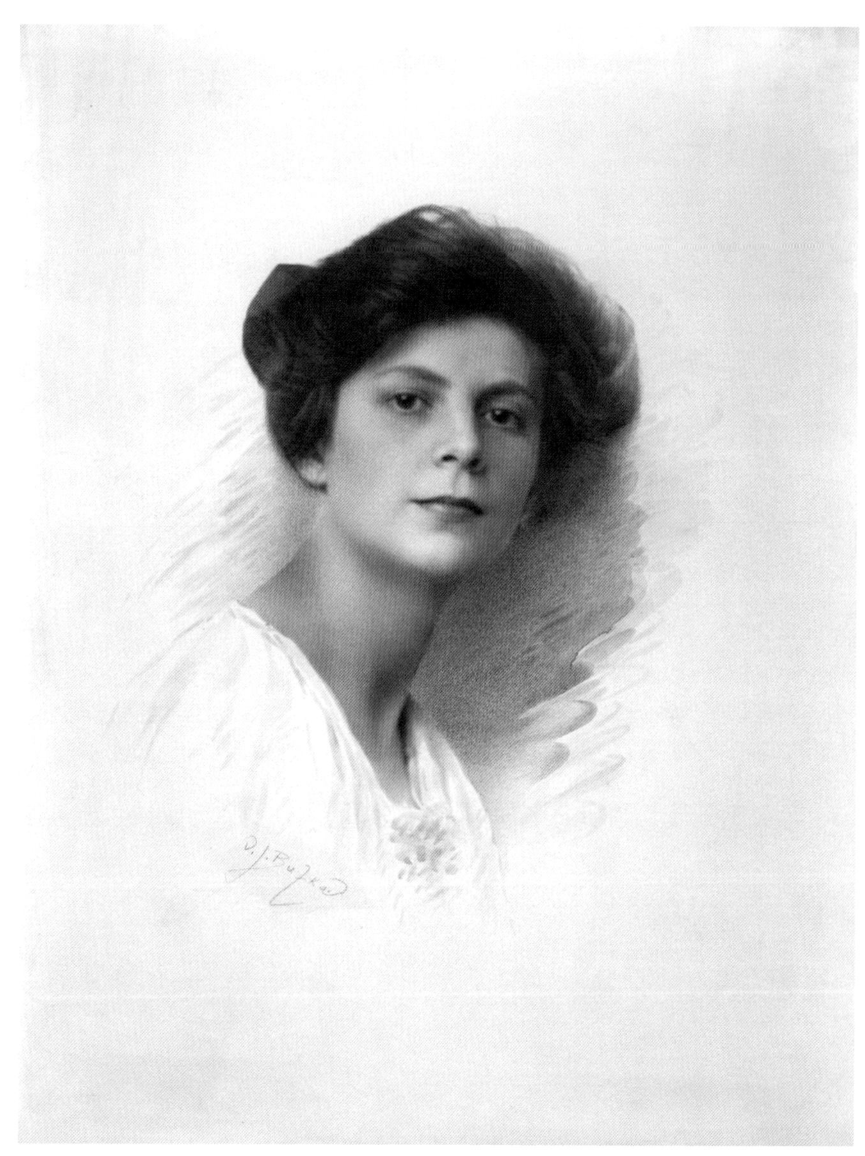

50 Marie Bufková 1914

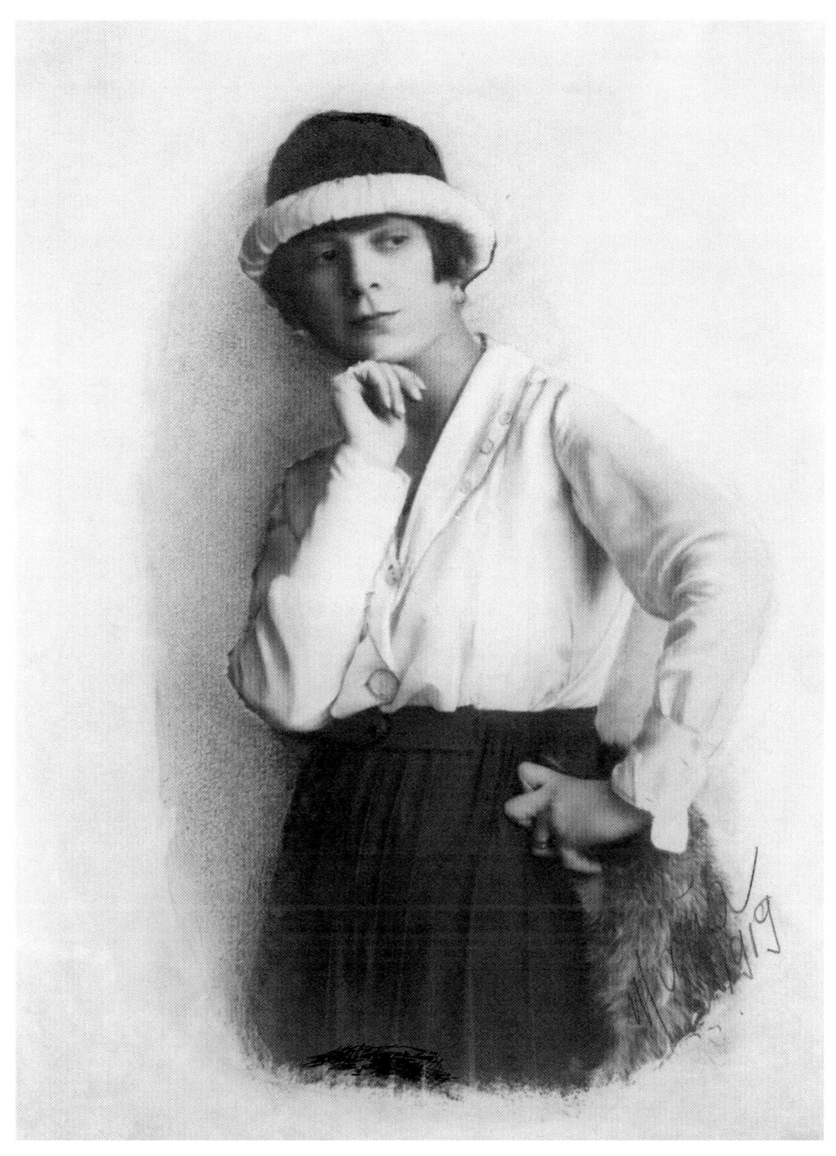

51 Self-portrait, Marie Bufková / Marie Bufková: Autoportrét c. 1919

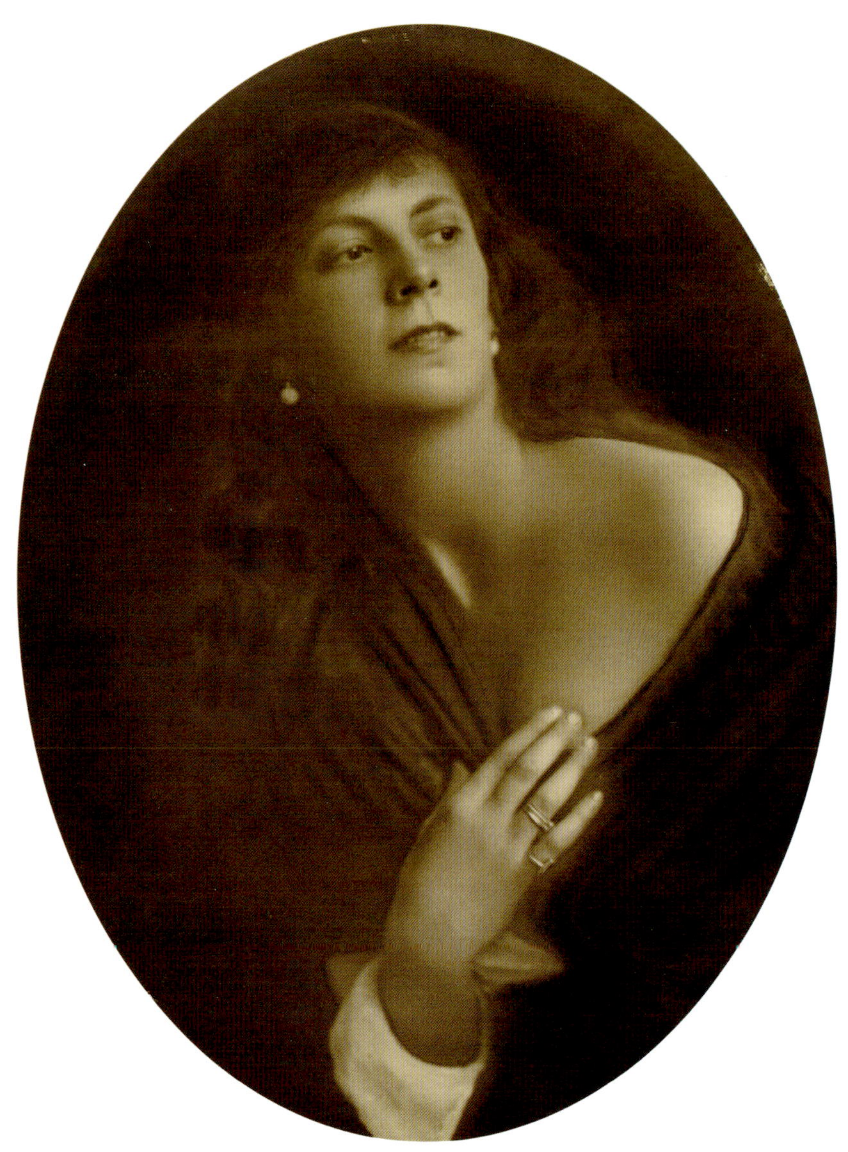

52 **V. J. Bufka?: Marie Bufková** c. 1912

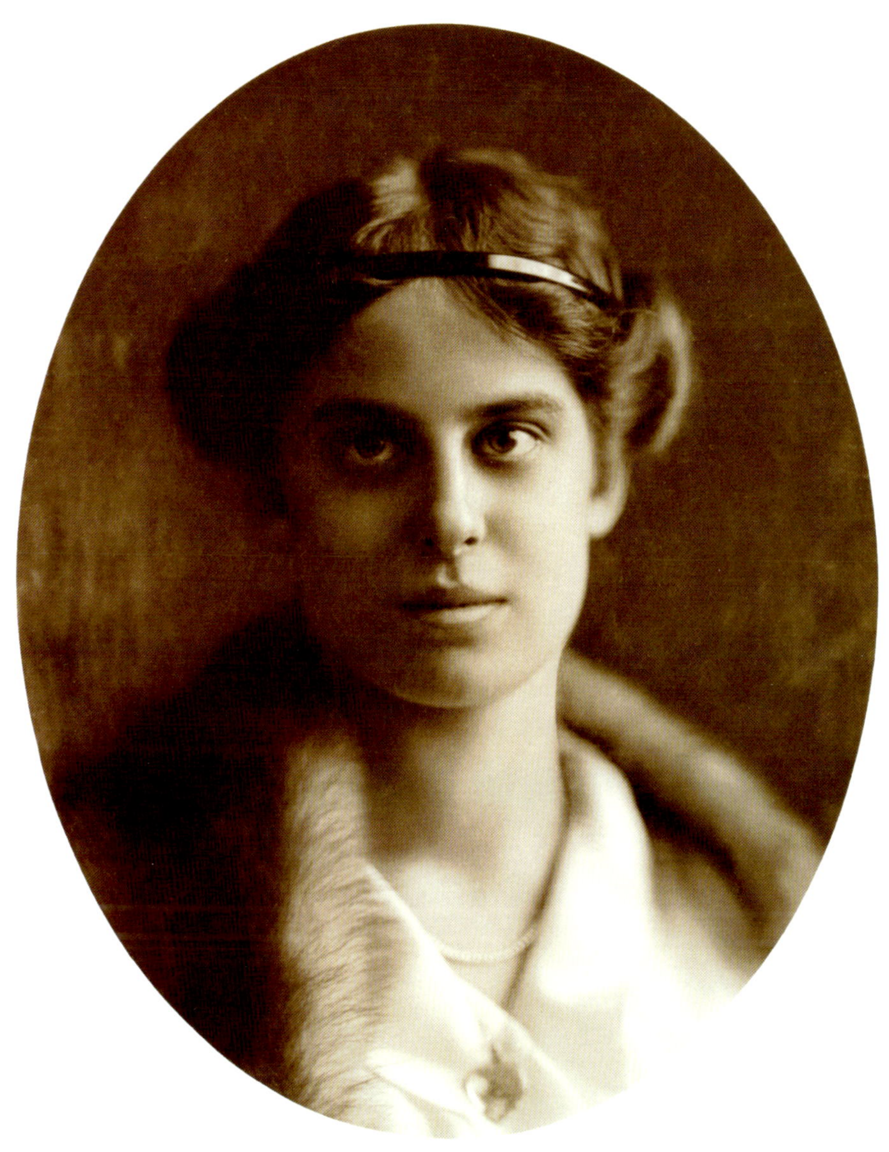

53 **Eleonora Schwarzenberg / Eleonora Schwarzenbergová** c. 1914

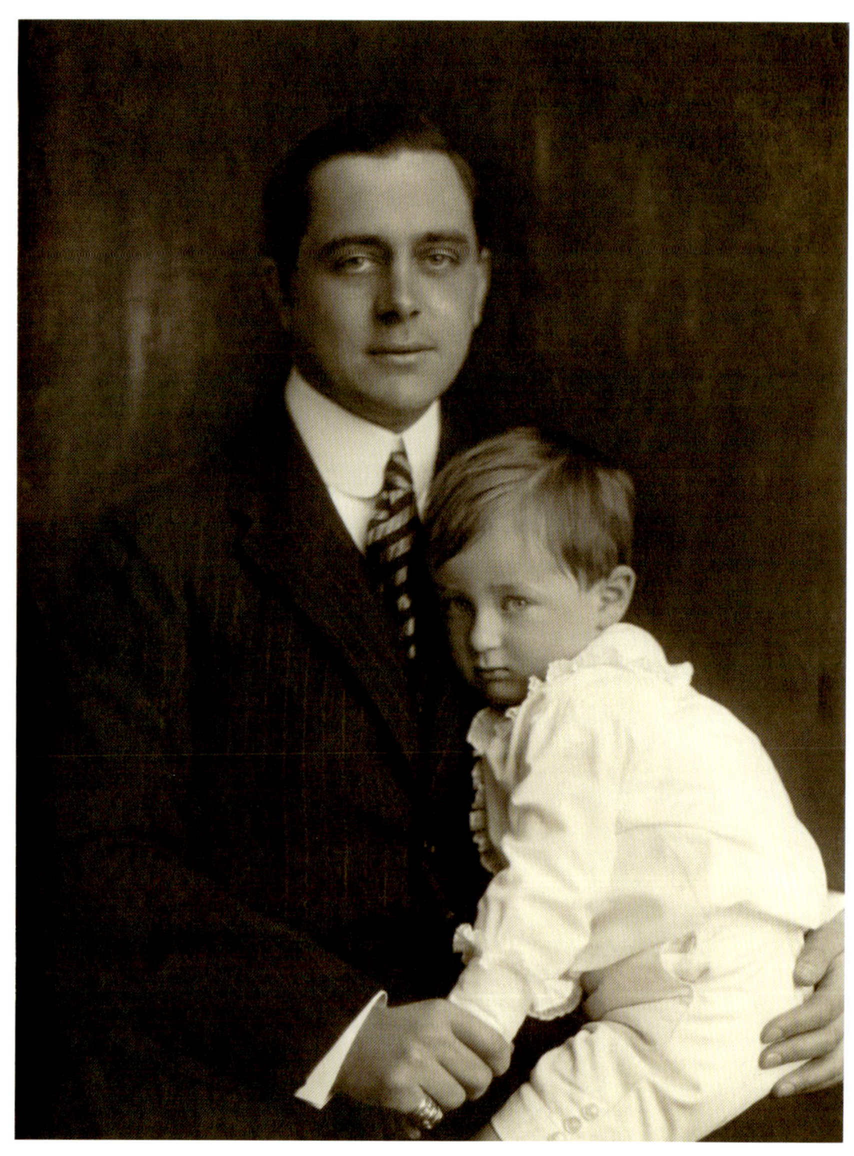

54 **Karl Schwarzenberg (V) with his son, Karl (VI) / Karel V. Schwarzenberg se synem Karlem VI.** 1914

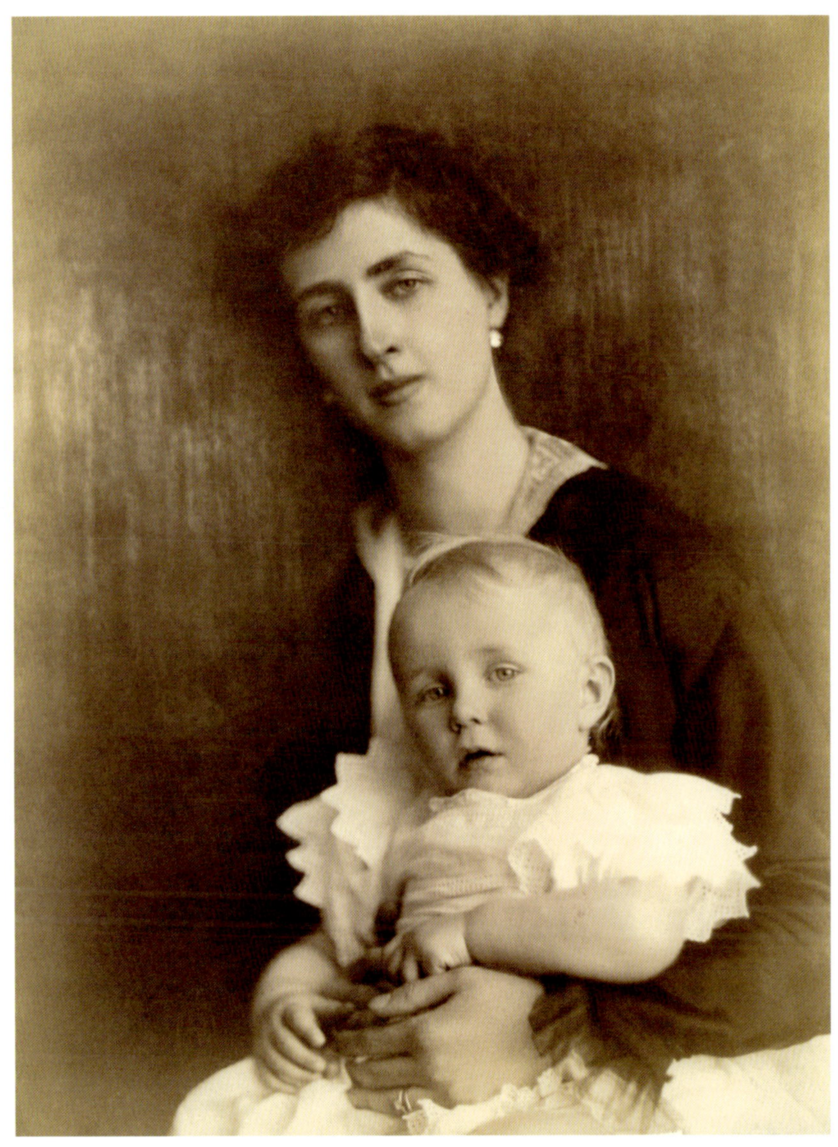

55 **Eleonora Schwarzenberg with her son Franz / Eleonora Schwarzenbergová se synem Františkem** 1914

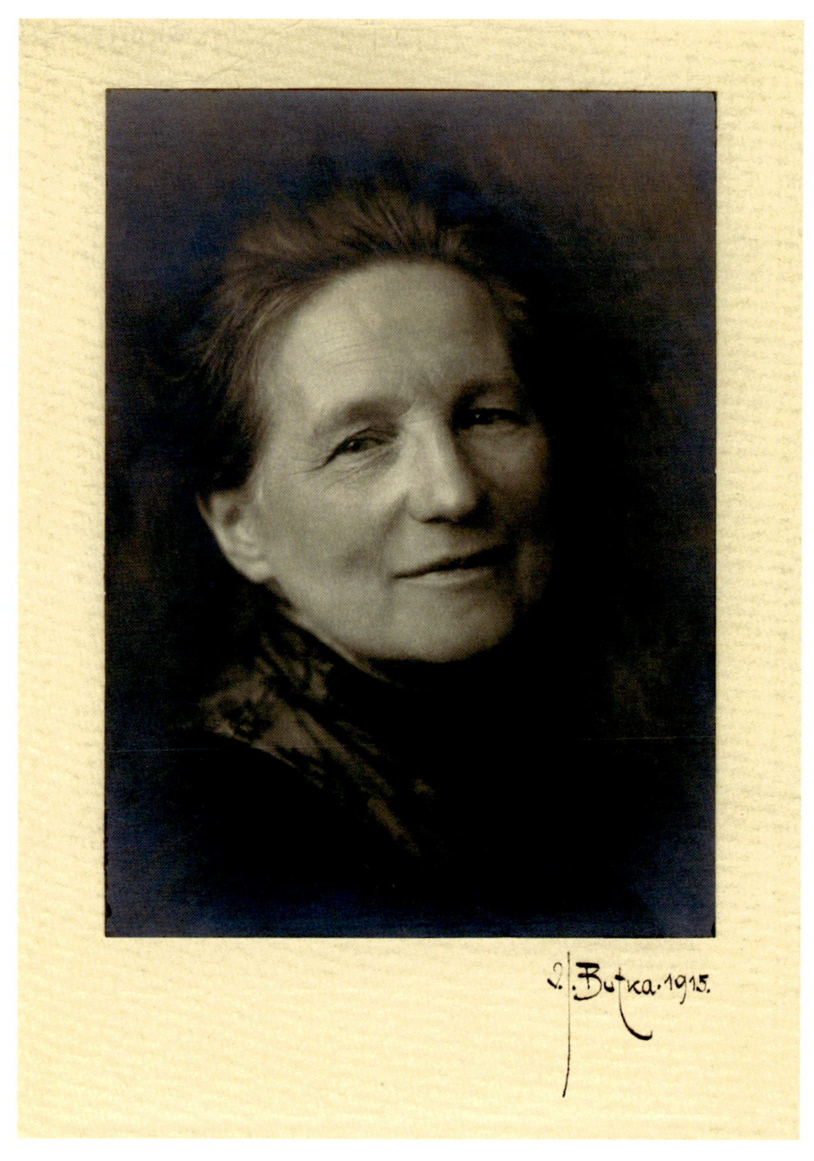

56 **Lucie Bakešová** 1915

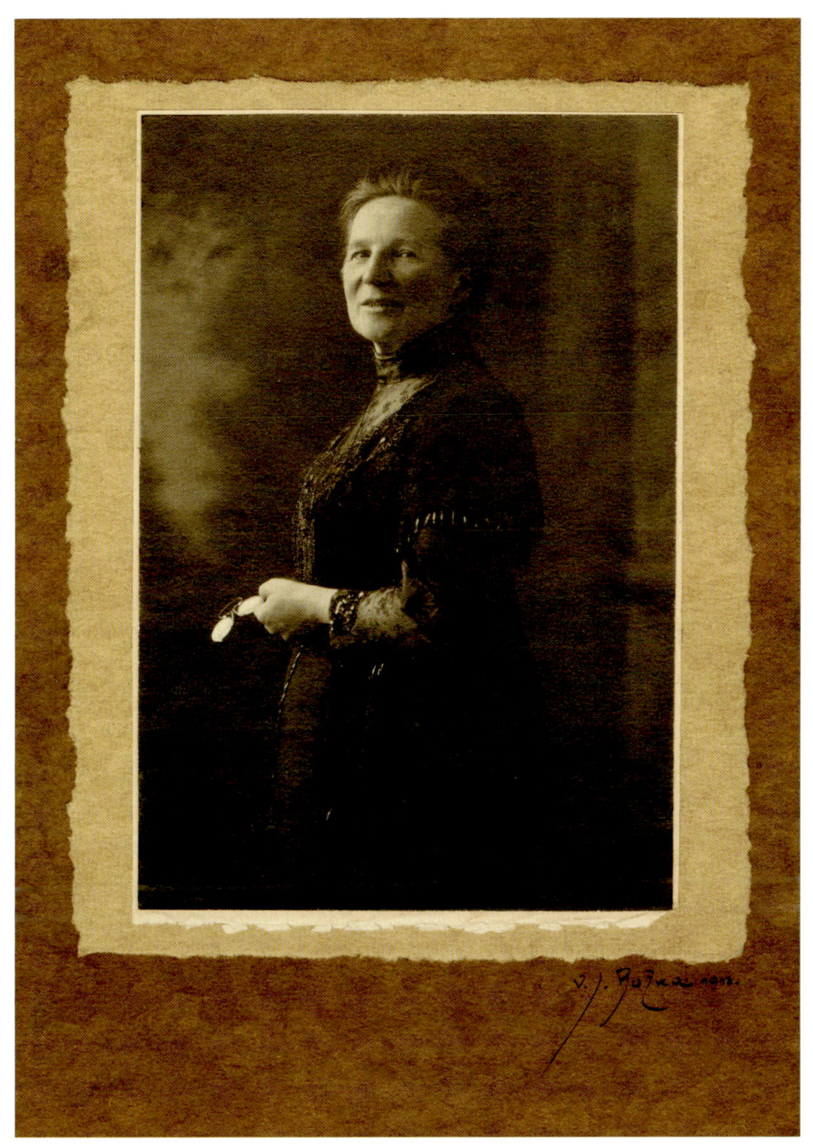

57 **Lucie Bakešová** 1913

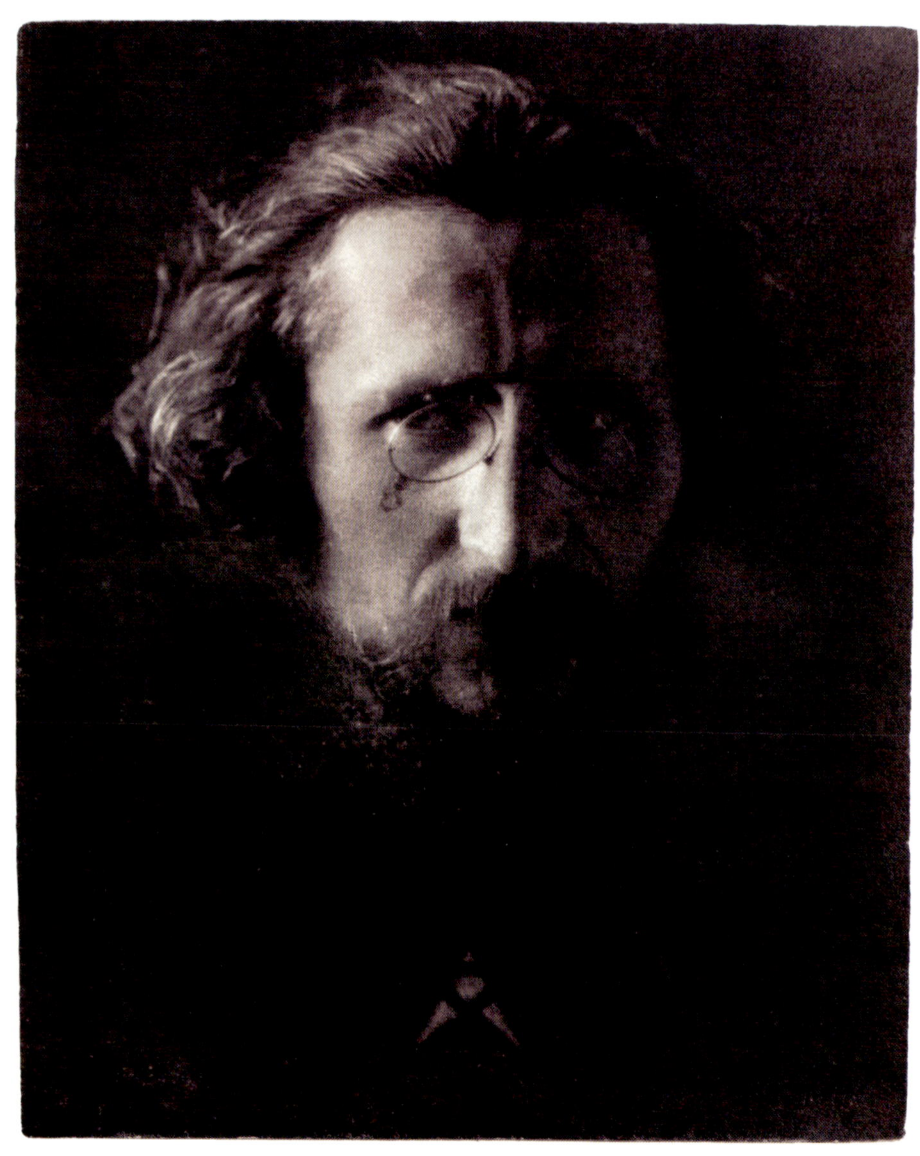

58 **Josef Váchal** 1911

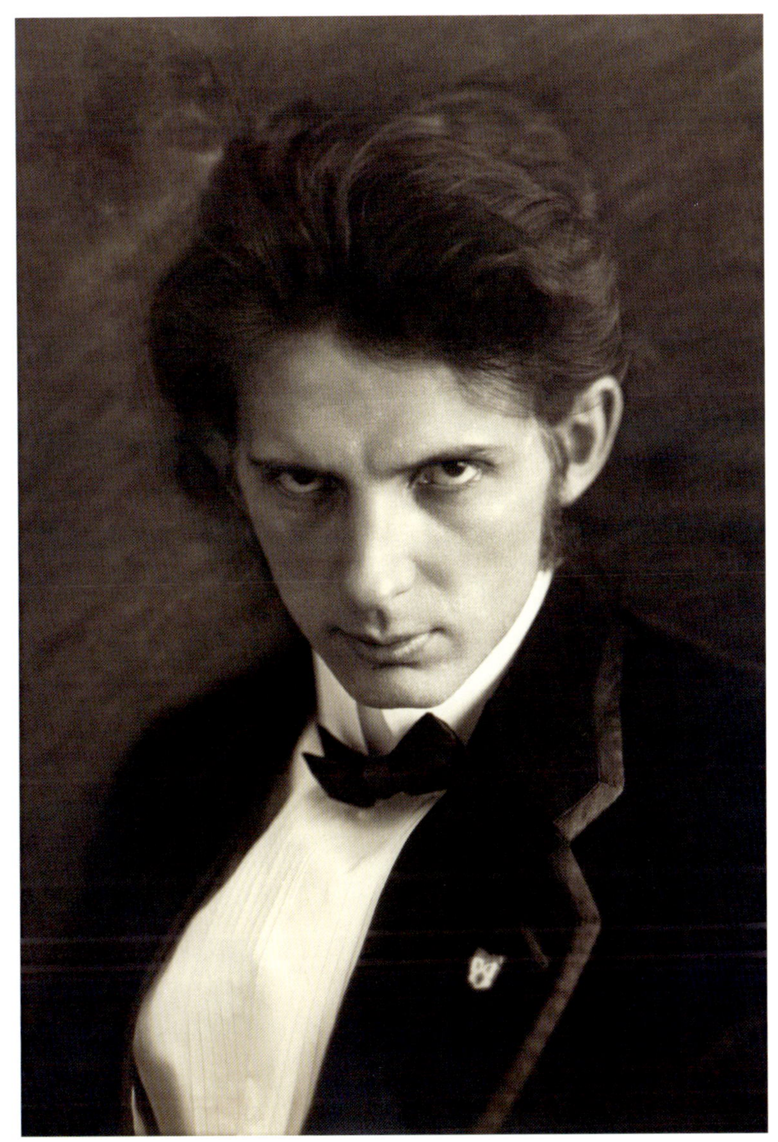

59 **Alberto Vojtěch Frič** c. 1909

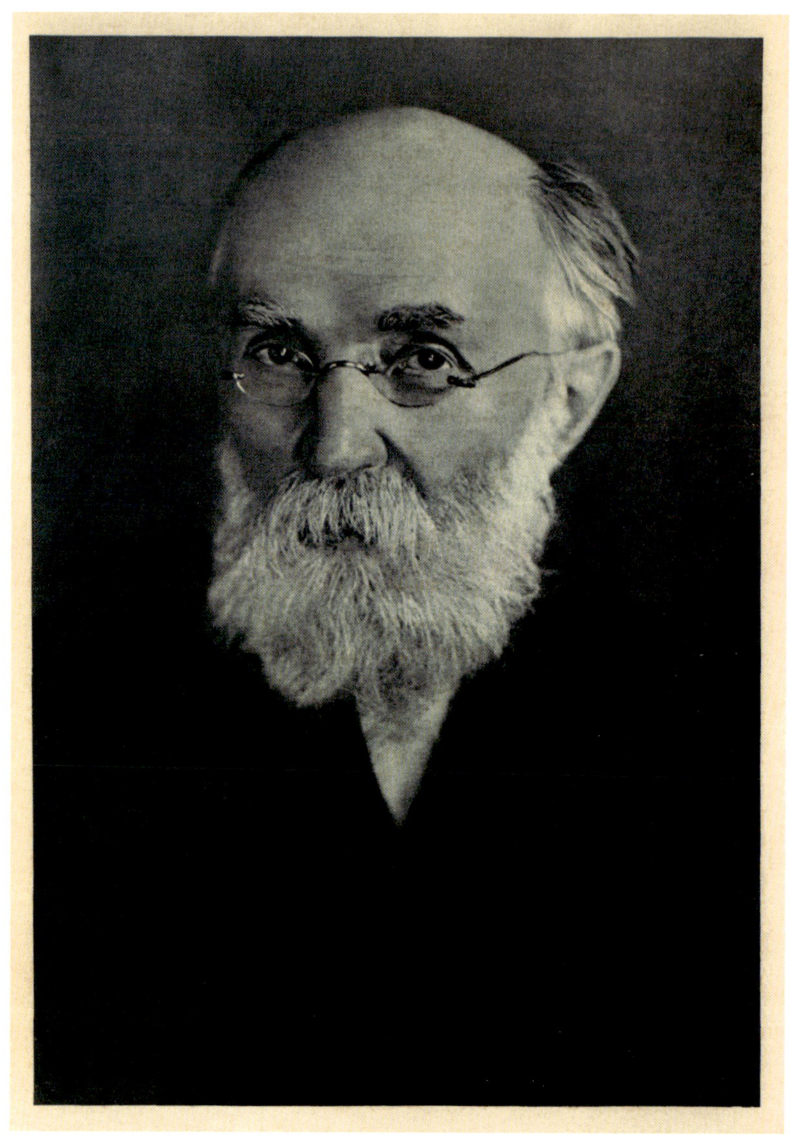

60 **Jakub Husník** 1911–12

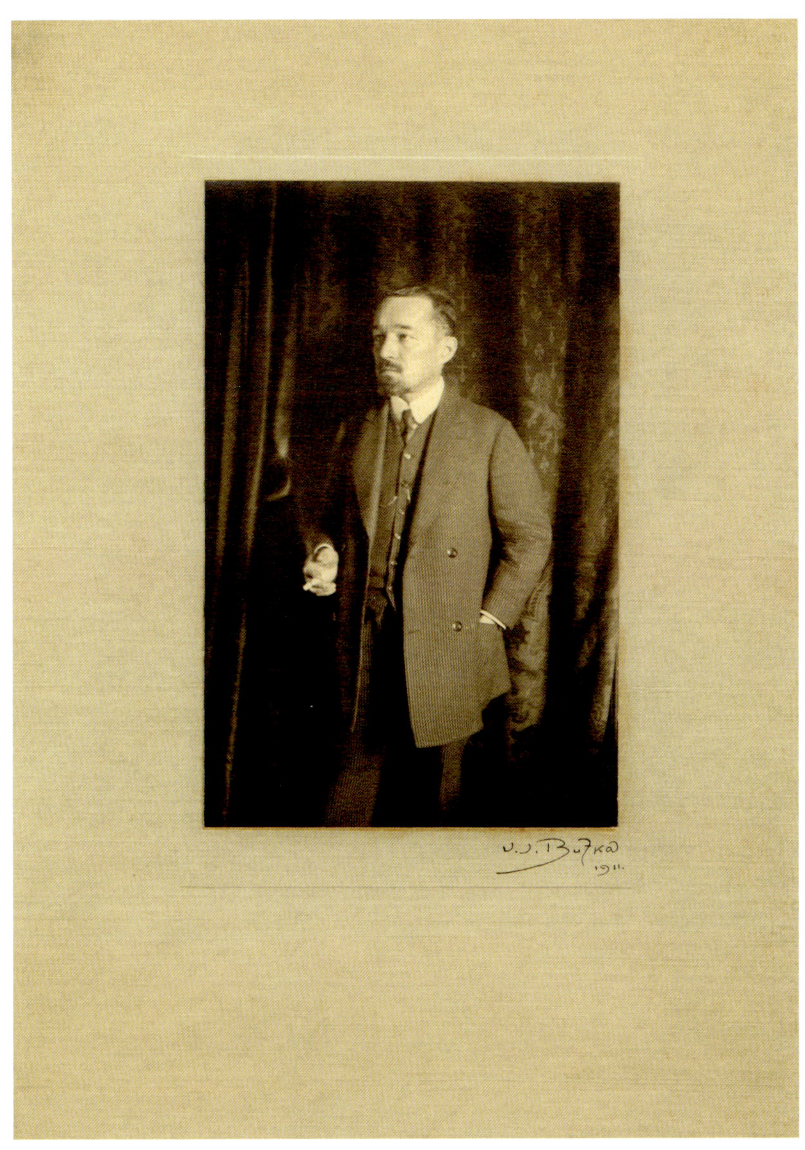

61 **Jaroslav Husník** 1911

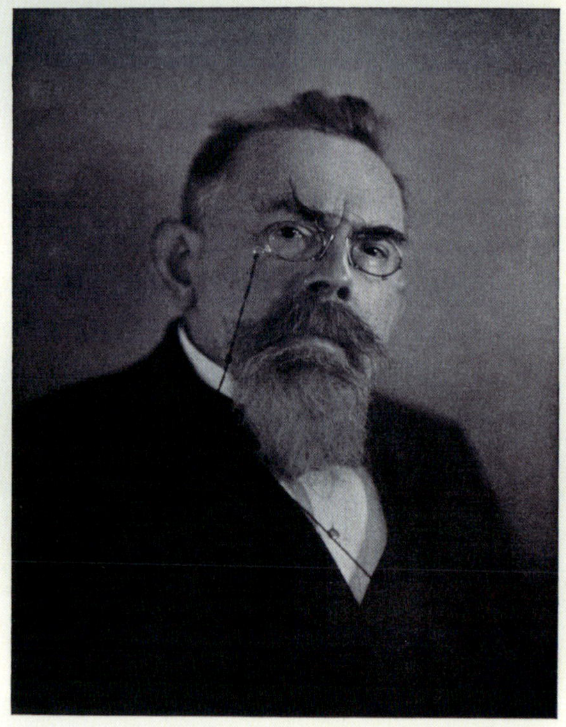

62 Portrait of František Herites, Writer / Portrét spisovatele Františka Heritese
c. 1911

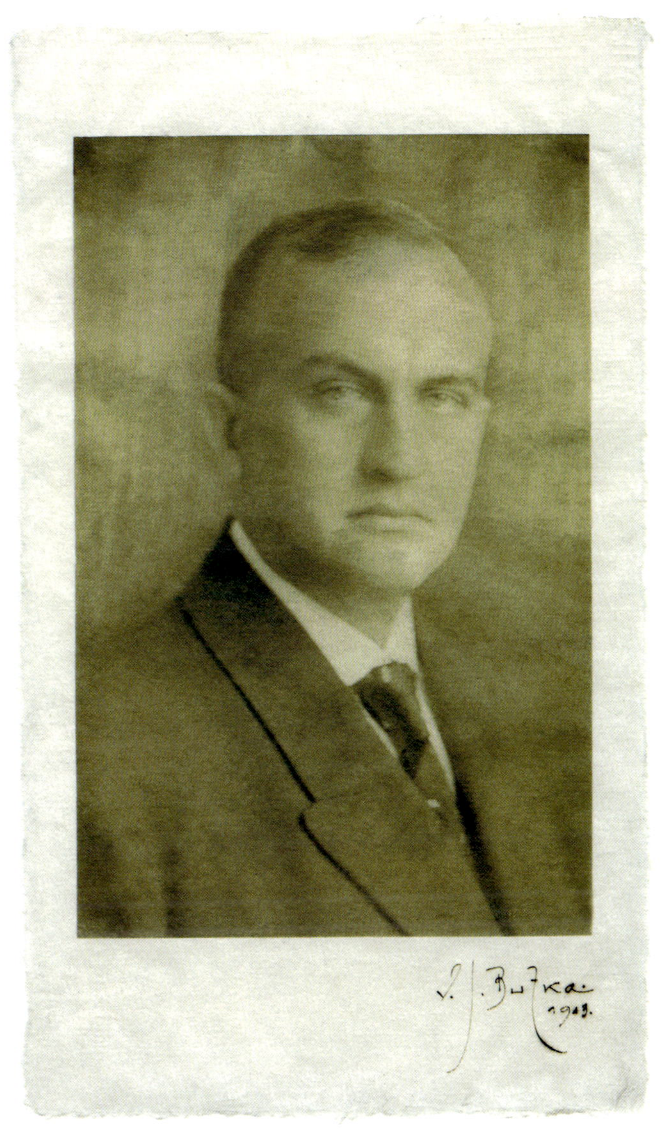

63 **Jan Kotěra** c. 1912

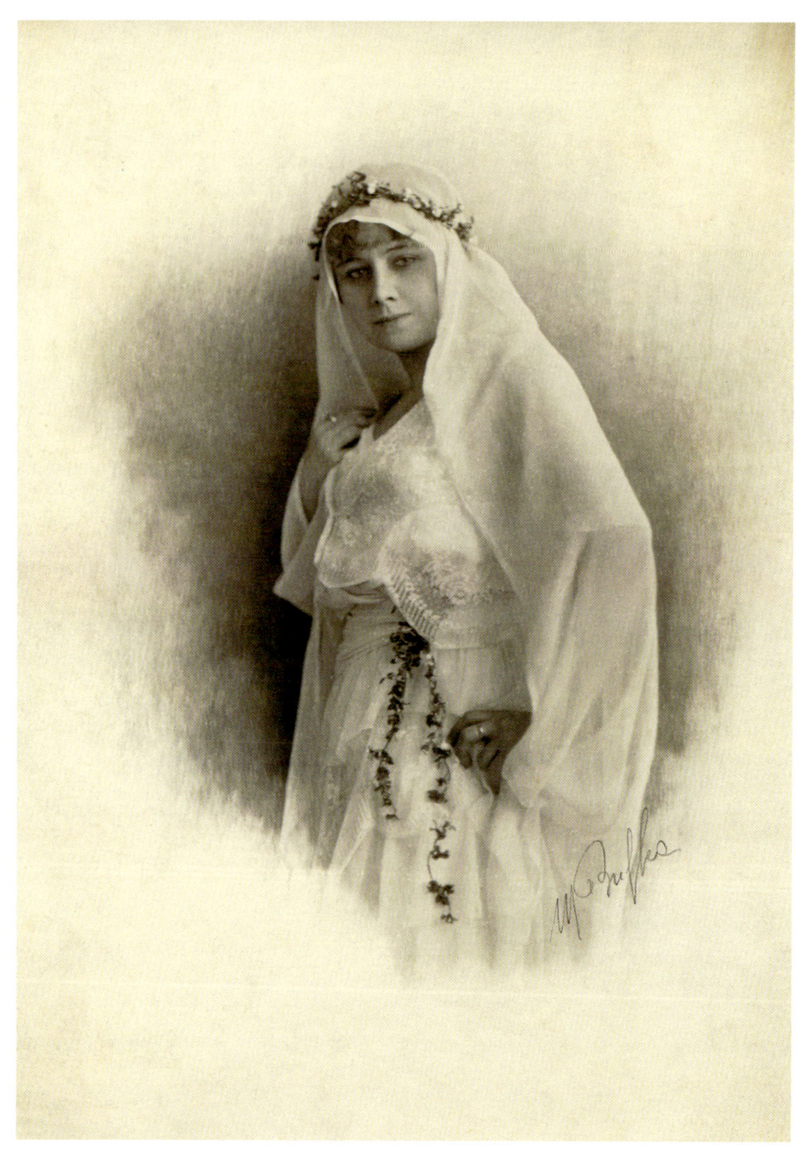

**64 Anna Sedláčková (signed: Marie Bufková) / Marie Bufková:
Anna Sedláčková** c. 1927

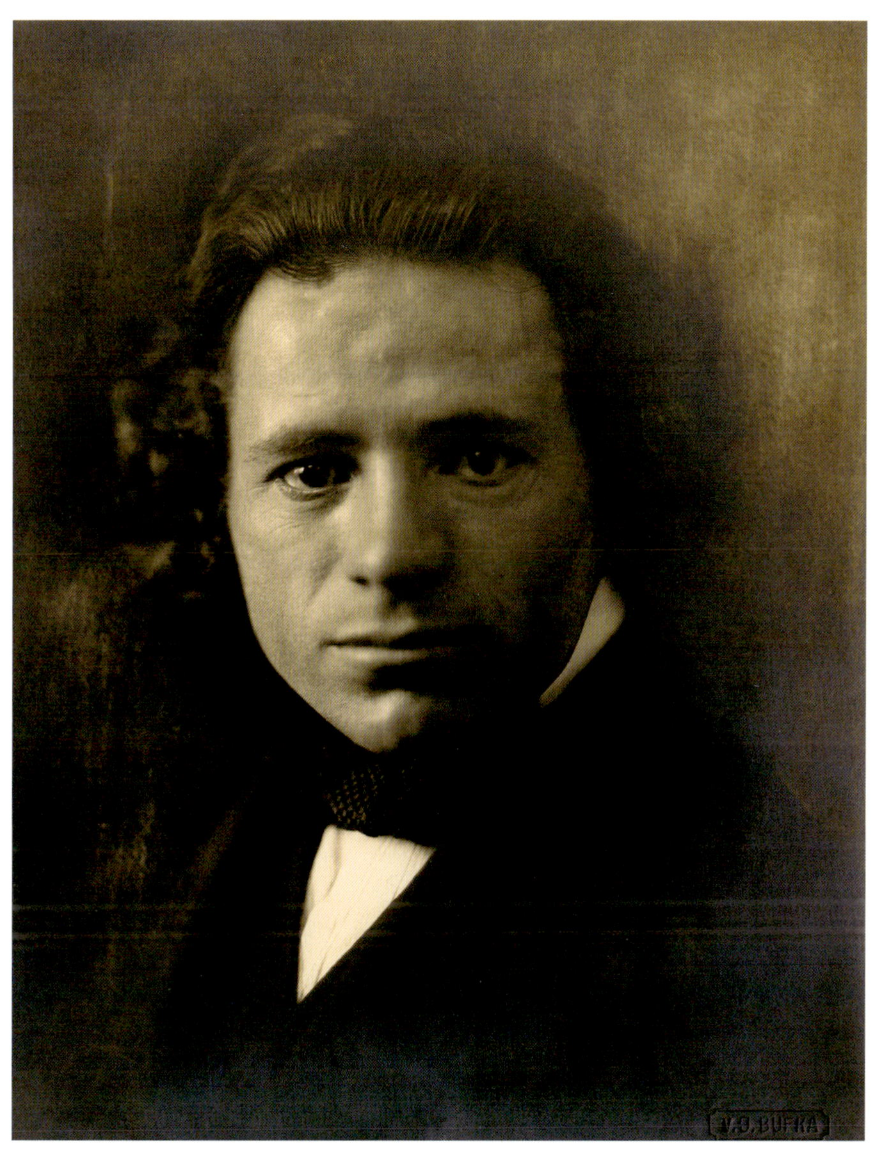

65 **Jan Kubelík** c. 1911–13

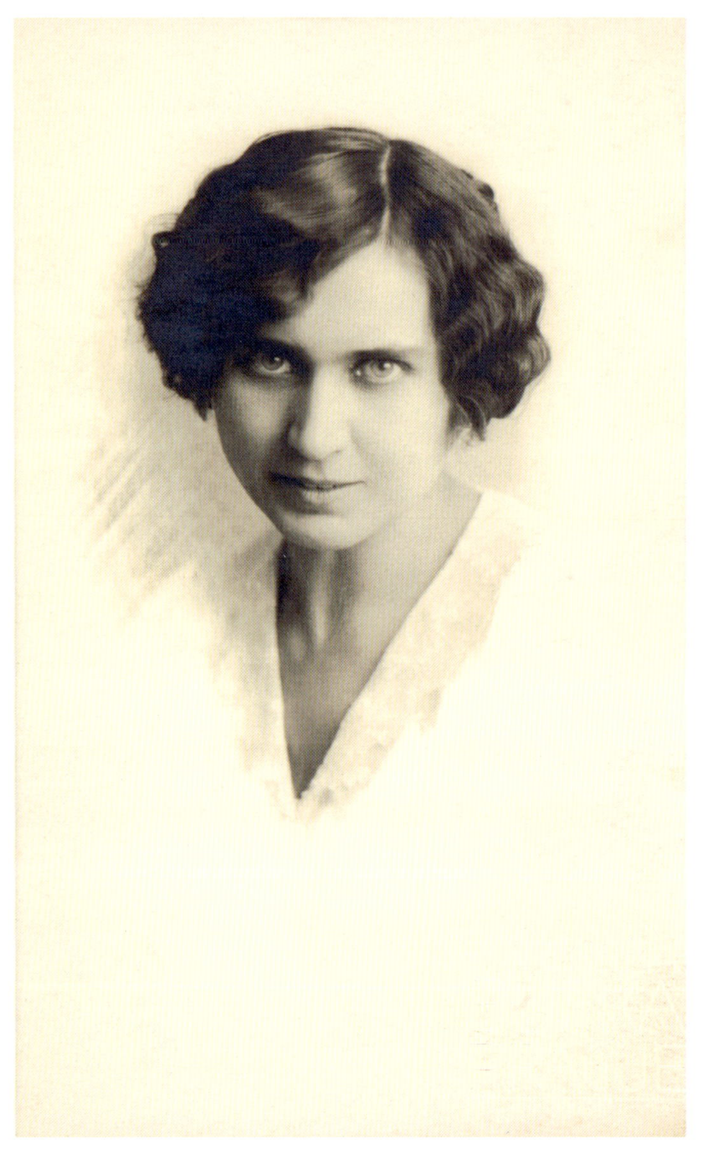

66 **Leopolda Dostalová (signed: Marie Bufková) / Marie Bufková: Leopolda Dostalová** c. 1920

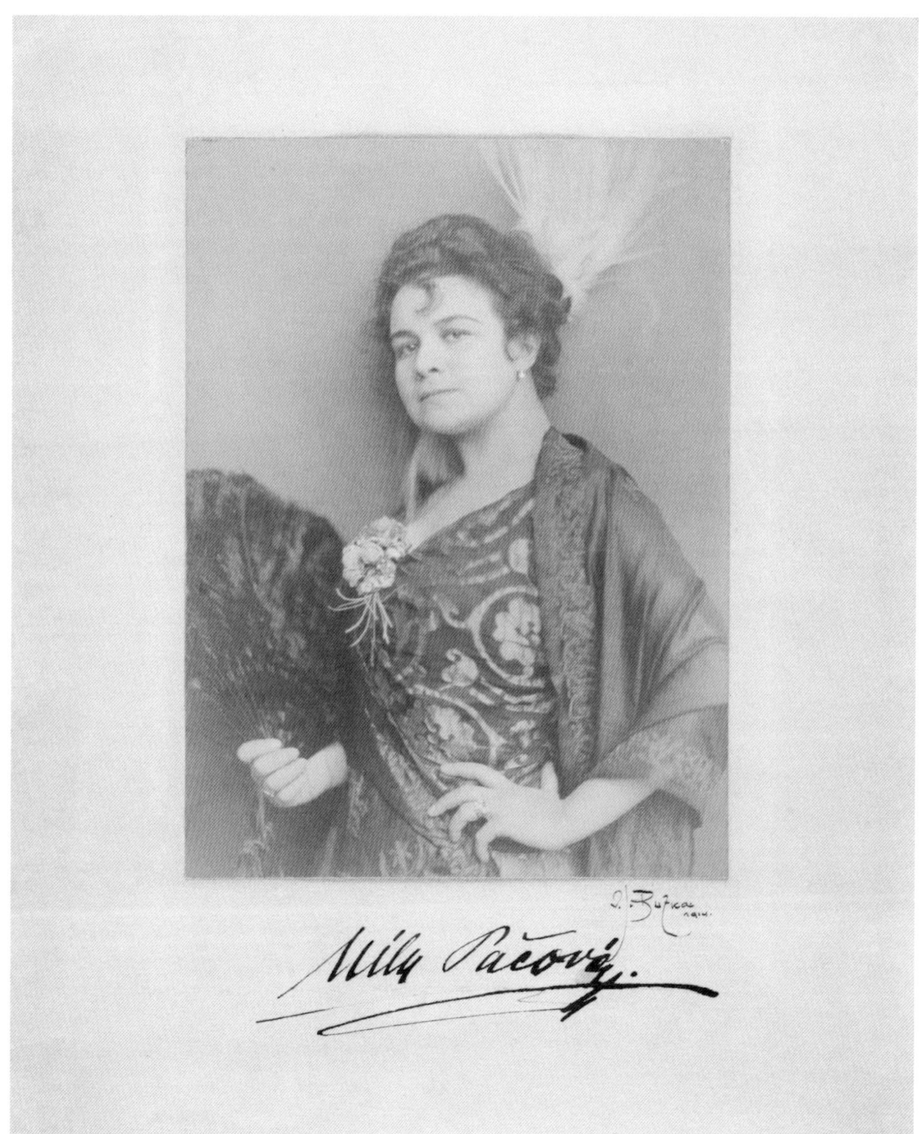

67 **Míla Pačová** 1914

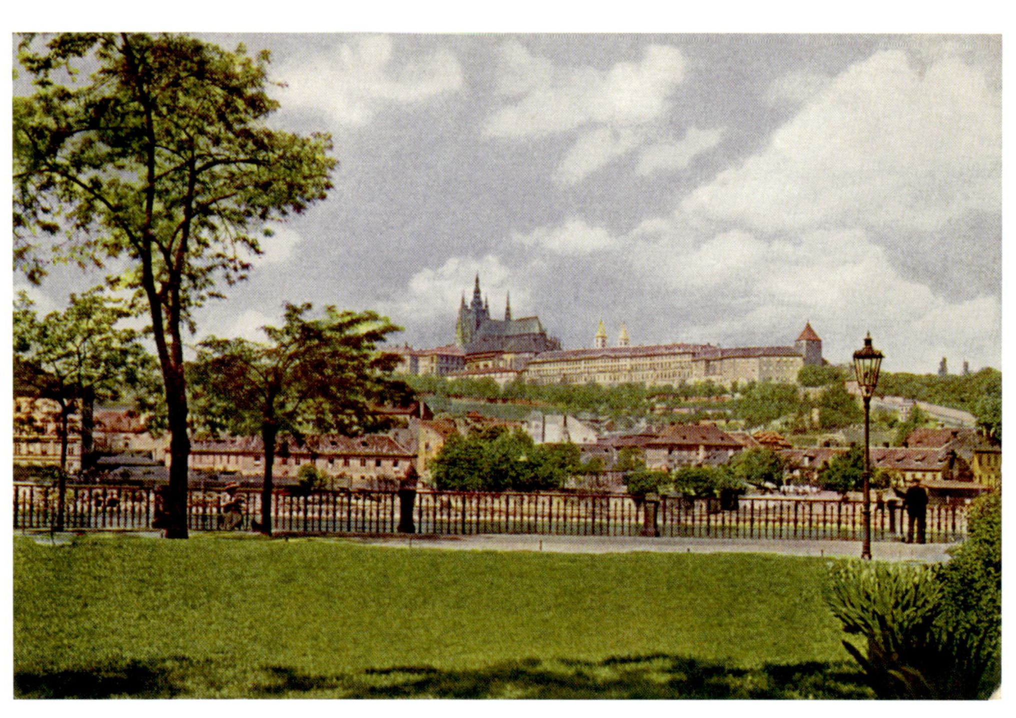

 From the Prague series / Ze souboru Praha 1910

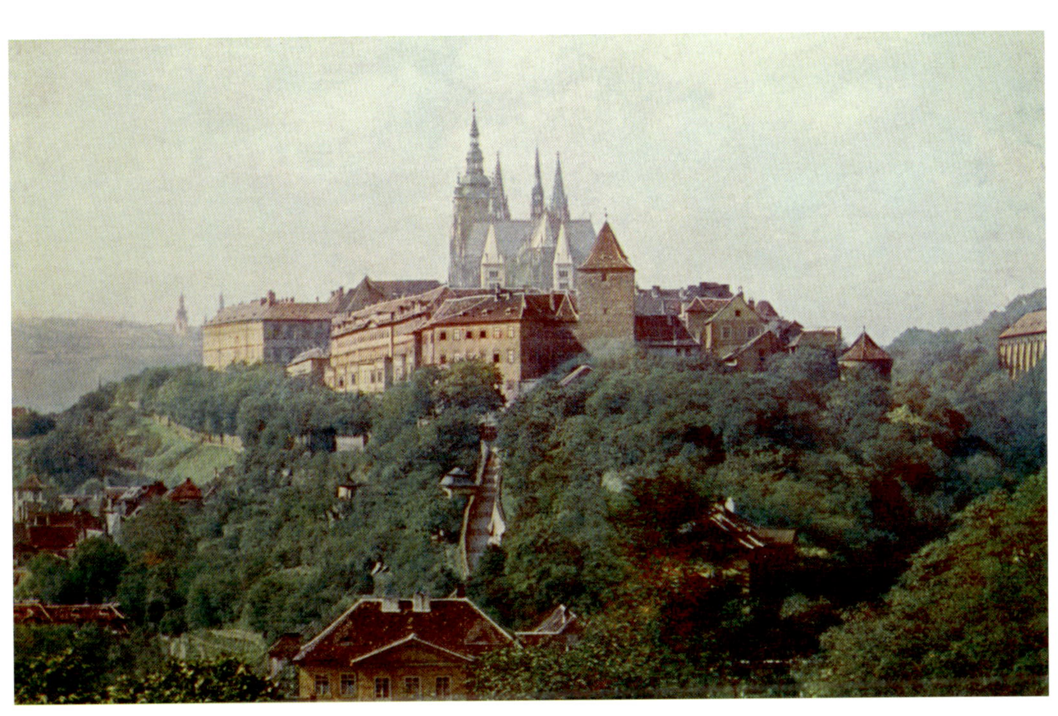

69 **From the Prague series / Ze souboru Praha** 1910

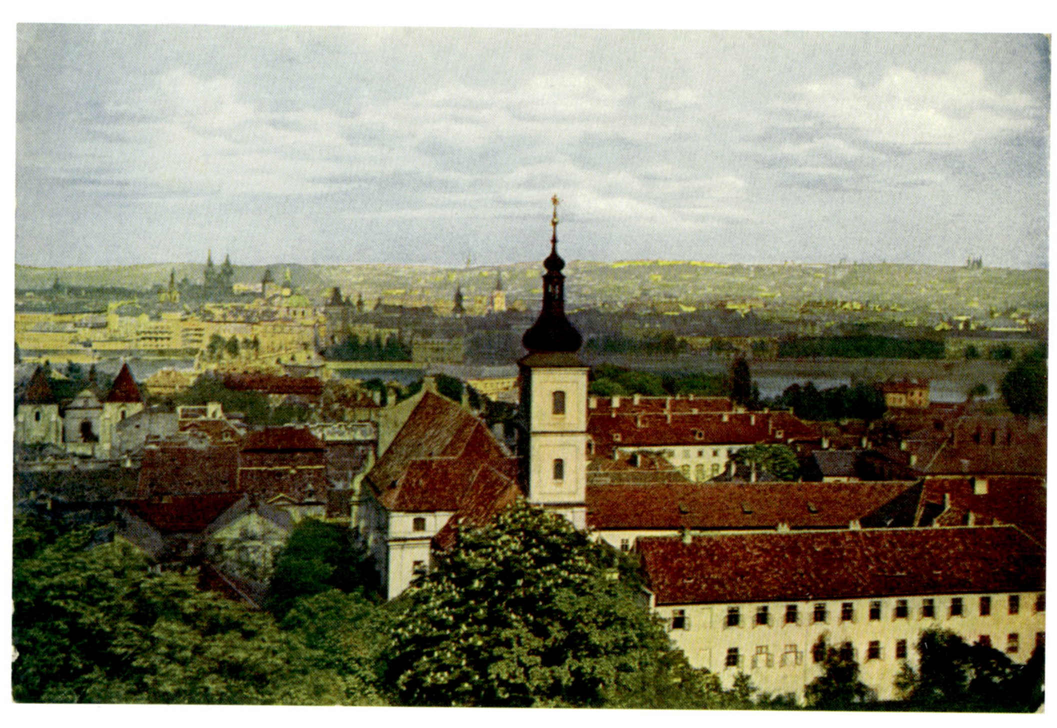

70 **From the Prague series / Ze souboru Praha** 1910

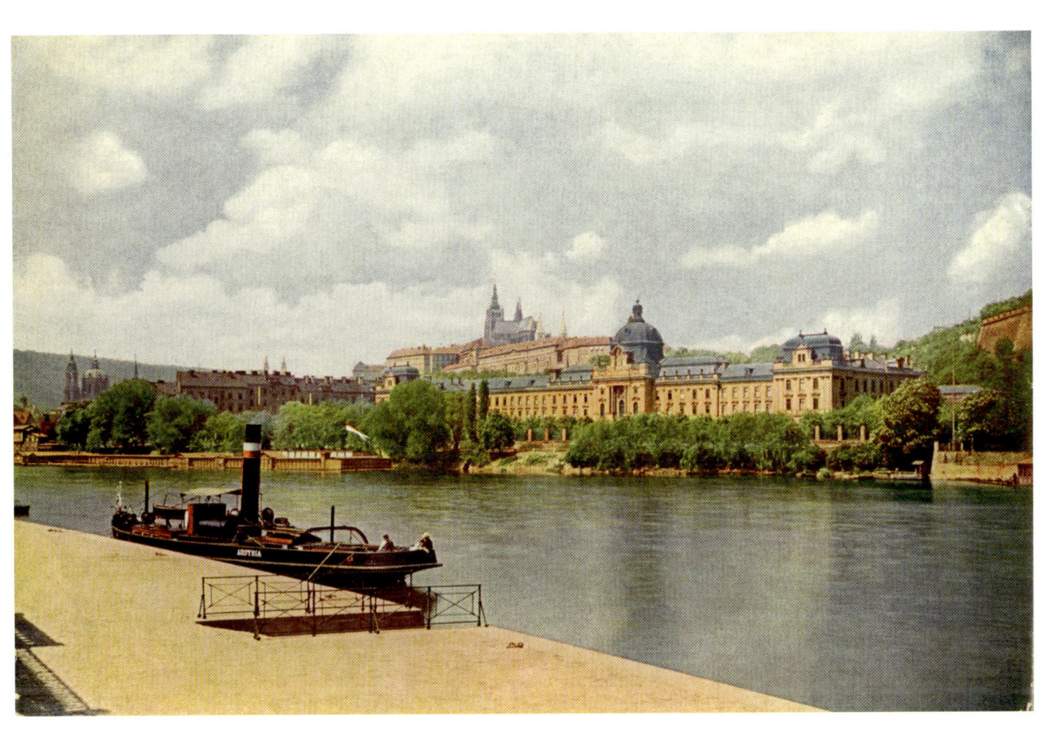

71 **From the Prague series / Ze souboru Praha** 1910

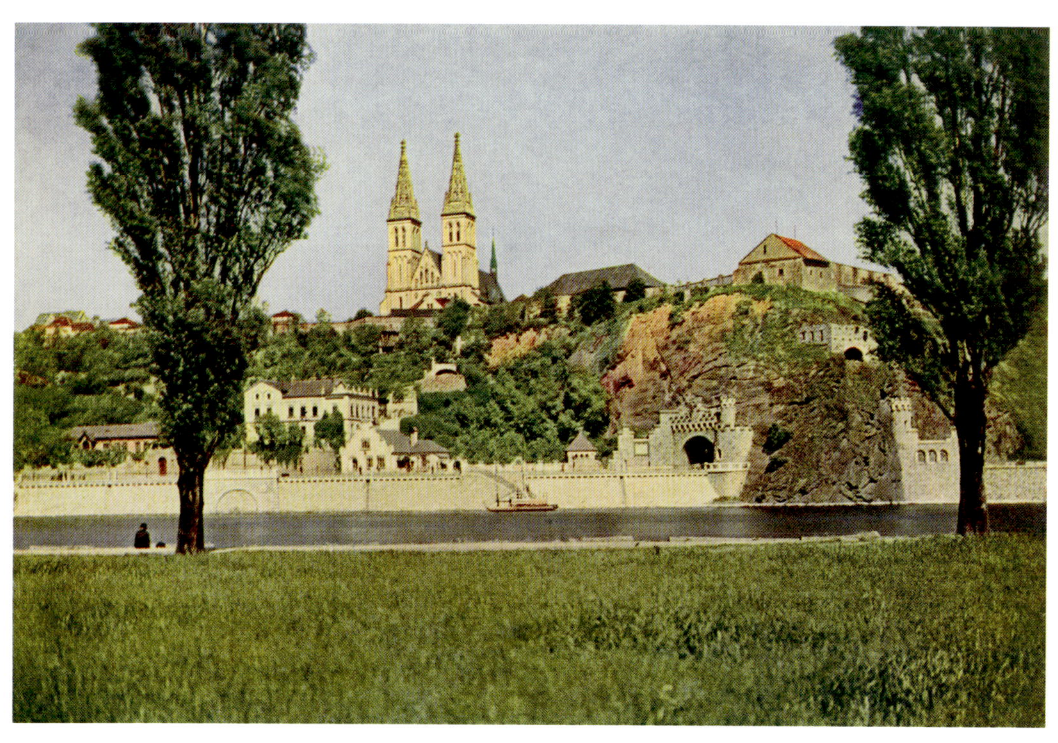

72 **From the Prague series / Ze souboru Praha** 1910

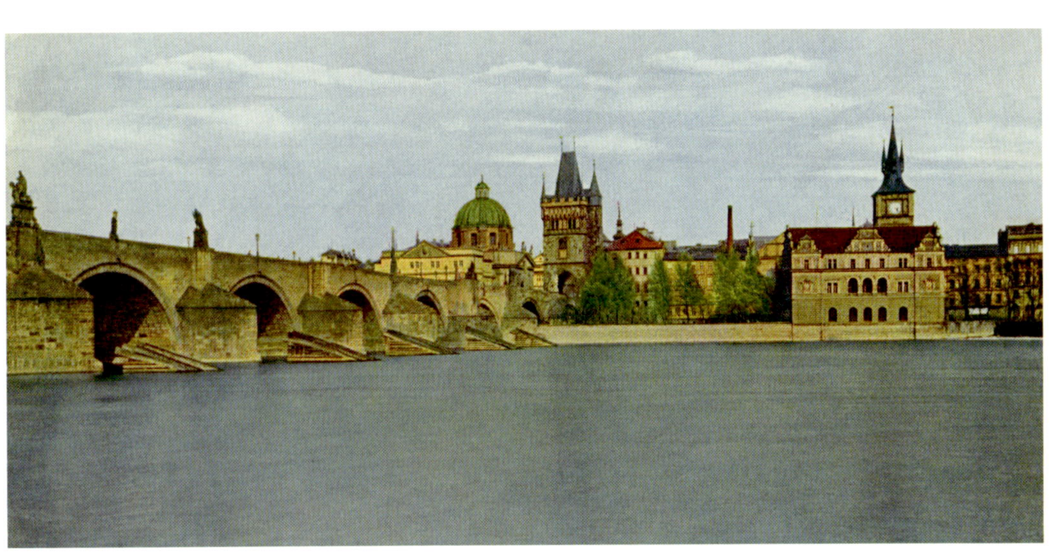

73 **From the Prague series / Ze souboru Praha** 1910

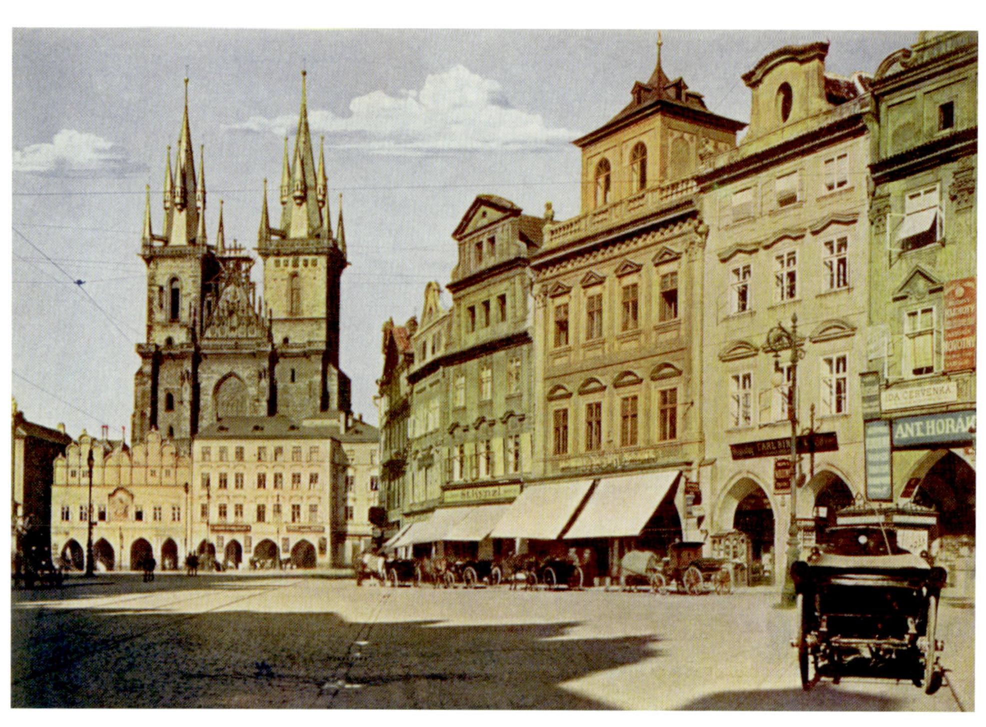

74 **From the Prague series / Ze souboru Praha** 1910

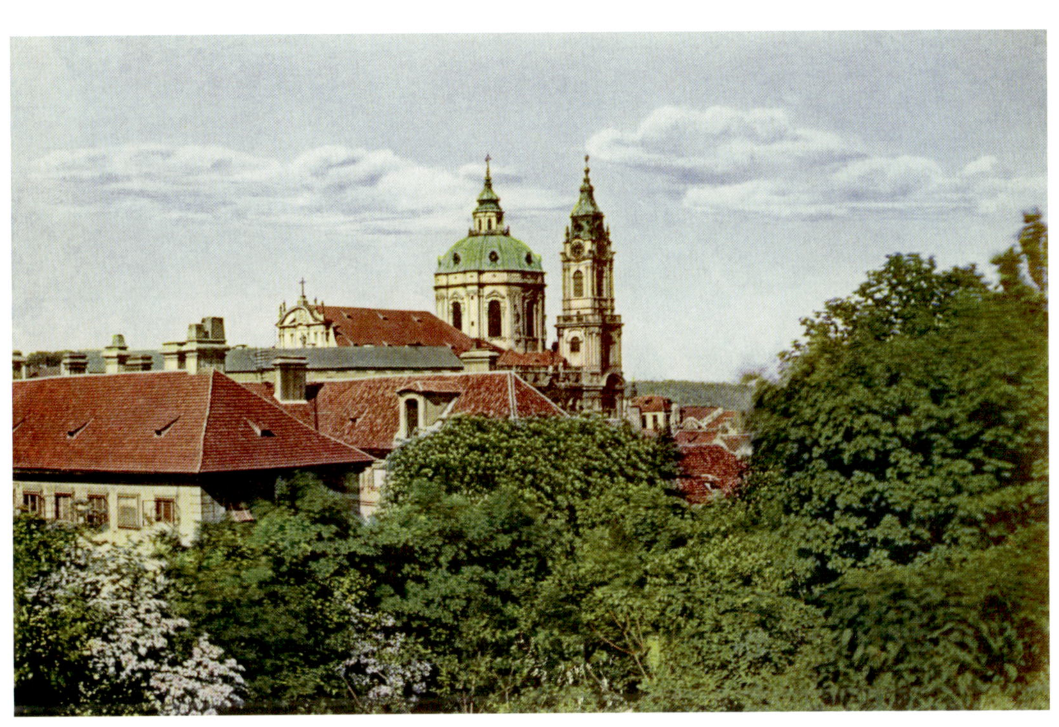

75 **From the Prague series / Ze souboru Praha** 1910

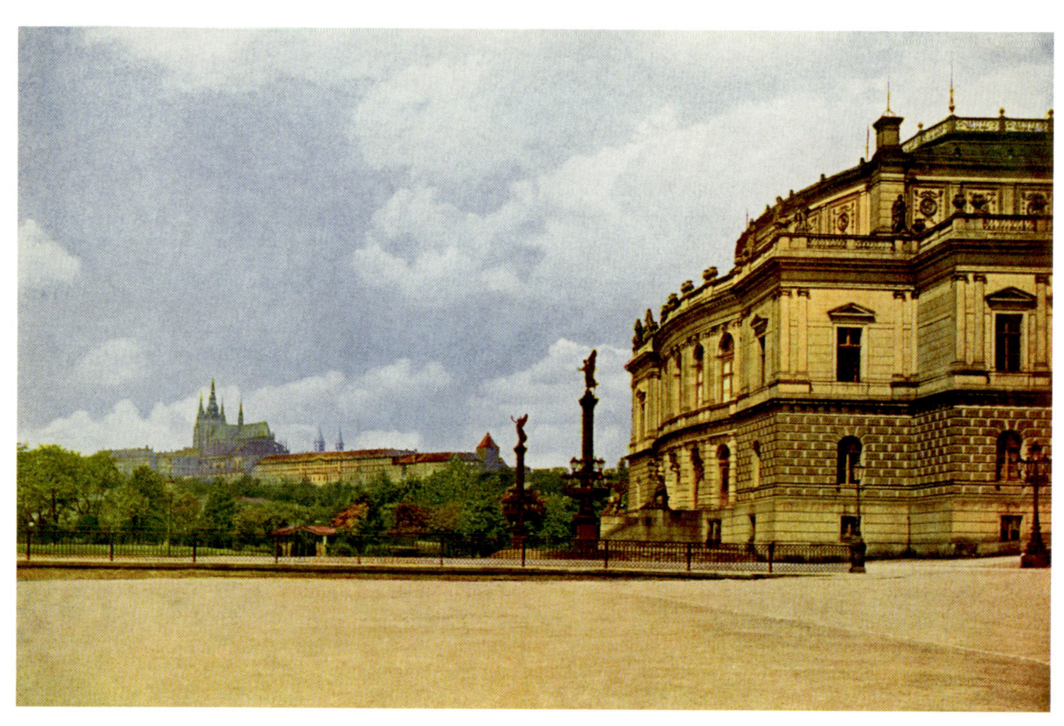

76 **From the Prague series / Ze souboru Praha** 1910

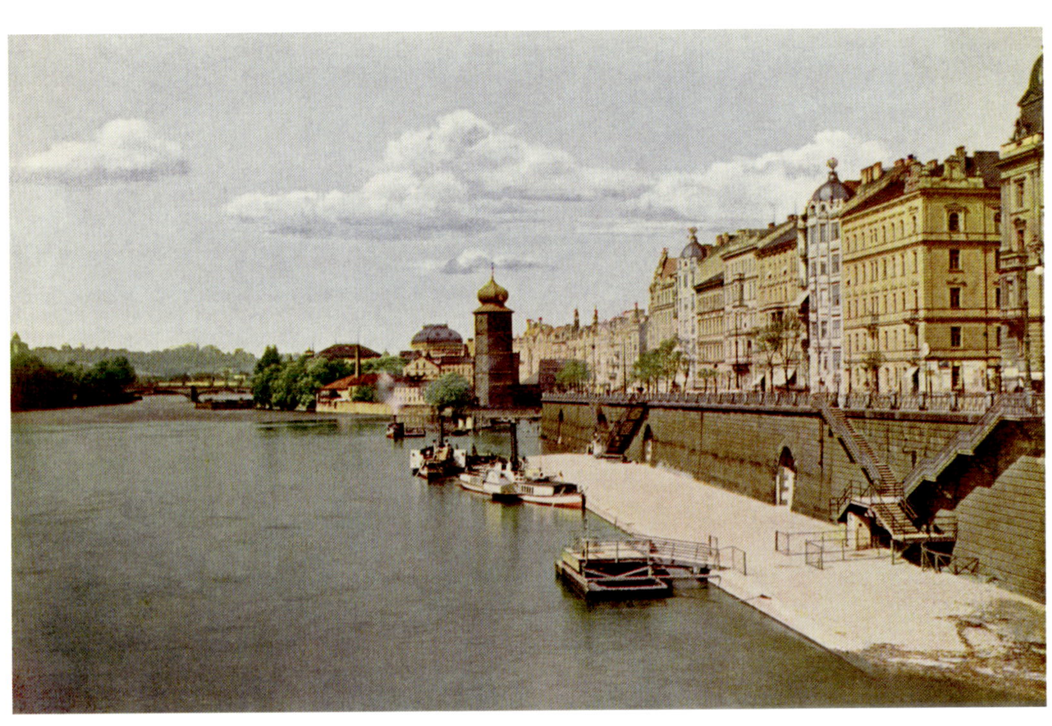

77 **From the Prague series / Ze souboru Praha** 1910

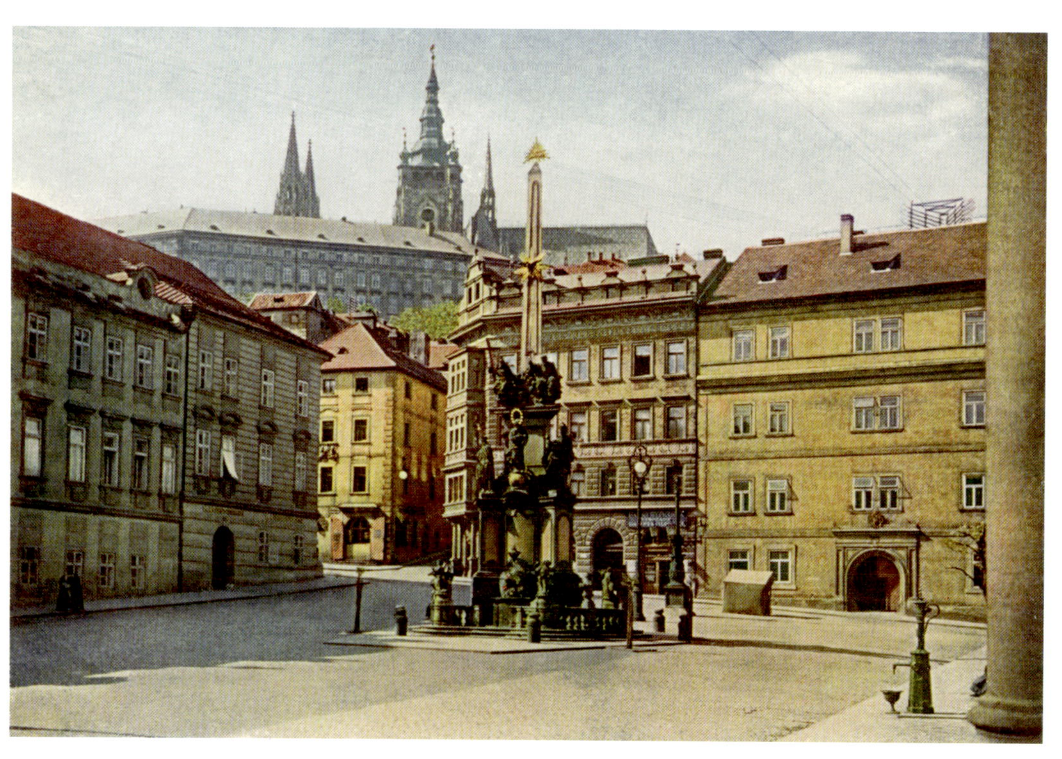

78 **From the Prague series / Ze souboru Praha** 1910

Biographical Chronology

1887	Registered as born in Pavlovice near Kojetín, Moravia, on 16 July, Vladimír Jindřich Bufka was the only child of the second marriage of Karla Wanklová (1855–1941) and the bank clerk Eduard Bufka (1854–1921) in Olomouc (where Eduard also performed in the theatre) and Prague. Karla was one of four daughters of the renowned Blansko physician, archeologist, and speleologist, "the father of Moravian archeology," Jindřich Wankel (1821–1897) and Eliška, née Šímová (1832–1903). The son from Karla's first marriage, to Vilibald Absolon (1843–1882), Karel Absolon (1877–1960), a renowned archeologist and superb photographer, was Bufka's half-brother. Karla Bufková-Wanklová wrote several books and plays, as well as articles for women's magazines and specialist periodicals. Her portrait (in the photography collection of the Moravian Gallery in Brno) is so far the only autochrome that has with certainty been attributed to Bufka. Bufka also made other portraits of his mother and her sister, Lucie Bakešová, but they are published anonymously on pp. 36 and 24 of Berthold Kladivo (ed.), *Zlatá rodina.* Blansko: Masarykova měšťanská škola, 1936. An important ethnographer and social worker, Lucie Bakešová was the mother of Jaroslav Bakeš, a physician of the Moravian Hospital, who, in 1909, was put in charge of the surgical wing, and, in 1920, was made head of the institute in Žlutý kopec (today, called the Bakeš Pavilion), Brno . In 1928, he and his mother founded the Dům útěchy (House of Hope), a society supported by President Tomáš G. Masaryk. Only in 1935, after Bakeš's death, did the society complete the building that was designed for the treatment of malignant tumors (today called the Masaryk Memorial Cancer Institute). Apart from Lucie, Karla Bufková-Wanklová had two other sisters: Vlasta married the founder of the Olomouc Museum, Professor Jan Havelka, and Madléna, like Lucie, devoted herself to ethnographic research. Bufka clearly had an extraordinarily cultivated and patriotic family background.
1903	Bufka lived in house no. 617 of the Lesser Town, Prague (Prague Municipal Archive, local registry, 1830–1910, Foreigners. Bufka Eduard, Bufka Vladimír; quoted in Hrubeš, p. 34, n. 13). His father moved to Prague the year Vladimír Jindřich was born or the year before. Vladimír Jindřich Bufka therefore probably grew up in Prague. Bufka's listed place of birth in Pavlovice probably means little; it is likely that one of his parents simply had property there. The family lived in Prague and all Bufka's other places of residence were in Prague (Hrubeš, p. 20). Eduard Bufka's address in 1897, for example, was Sázavská ulice, No. 14, Královské Vinohrady.
1903–07	Bufka began to make photographs and to study chemistry at the Prague Polytechnic (though we have no evidence that he graduated).
1907–09	Bufka took detailed photographs of the "house of the workers" in Hybernská ulice, Prague, which was bought by the Workers' Printing and Building Cooperative in 1907 for the purposes of the Social Democratic Party. He wrote and photographed for *Rudé květy* (Red Flowers), their monthly. It was about then that he was taking photographs of workers and miners in the Kladno area (– ec. [Rudolf Skopec], "Mistři světové fotografie: Vladimír Jindřich Bufka," *Československá fotografie* 12 [1961], no. 4, p. 59). Photographs of this kind,

among the precursors of socially concerned documentary photography, definitely merit more attention.

1908   "The Jubilee Exhibition of the Chamber of Trade and Commerce in Prague" presented several dozen of Bufka's photographs with Prague subject matter (Hrubeš, p. 11).
The exhibition was held to mark the sixtieth year of the reign of Emperor Francis Joseph.

1909   Bufka became a contributing member of the Czech Amateur Photographers' Club in Prague.
On 5 May, after the Extraordinary General Meeting of the Czech Amateur Photographers' Club in Prague, Bufka gave a talk called "Taking Night and Atmospheric Photographs." The talk was soon published as "Fotografie za noci", in *Fotografický obzor*. "At the end of the talk, Bufka's own magnificent autochromes were projected. It was the first talk in our club given by this skilled professional [...]" (F.M. [František Mrskoš], "Mimořádná valná hromada dne 5. května 1909," *Fotografický obzor* 17 [1909], no. 6, p. 99).
The monumental "Internationale Photographische Ausstellung in Dresden" presented two photographers from the Bohemian Lands: one professional, Jan Langhans, and one amateur, V. J. Bufka (represented by the work *Praga Caput Regni*). Another photographer with work in the exhibition was the Vienna-based Karel Prokop, who considered himself a representative of the Czechs. The participation of the Bohemian Germans (for example, the Klub deutscher Amateurphotographen, Prag) was even more important. The exhibition ended on 10 October. Bufka gave a written report about another Dresden event, the First International Photographic Congress, published in *Fotografický obzor* 17 (1909), no. 7, p. 145. At the congress he made the acquaintance of a representative of the Lumière brothers' company, the chemist Alphonse Seyewetz, who paved the way to Lyon for him. Beginning in 1907, plates for autochromes were made there and sold all over the world. Autochromes were the first widespread color photographs, diapositives, usually on 13 x 18 cm glass plates. It was in Lyon that Bufka became acquainted with autochromes.
"In order to perfect the making of autochromes in every respect, I undertook a journey to the factory of the Brothers Lumière in Lyon. I was given a warm welcome, on the recommendation of the General Consul of France, to whom I am much obliged. I owe an equal debt of gratitude to the renowned workers in the field of color photography, Messrs August and Louis Lumière and to Professor Seyewetz, the head of the institutes [*sic*] of chemistry at the University of Lyon, for their very warm welcome and the attention that they paid me during my stay" (*O fotografii v barvách pomocí desky autochromové*, Prague: E. Weinfurter, 1910). A talk by Bufka, "From the Foot of Monte Rosa and the Foot of the Matterhorn," was announced for 12 October, at which autochromes were to be publicly projected "for the first time in Prague" (fifty autochromes and fifty other diapositives were announced). "Mr. Bufka has presented the editors with most of the autochromes, some of which are 13 x 18 cm, and we can confirm that we have never before seen such beautiful, transparent, and naturally colored ones, even at the Dresden exhibition." (F. Dvořák, "Přednášky ČKFA," *Fotografický obzor* 17 [1909], no. 9, pp. 160–61.) The talk in the Winter Garden of the National House, Vinohrady (which became a Prague district after the war), "made a pleasantly lasting impression on the people present, though this time the projection was not of the flawless quality

126

to which we have been accustomed in our talks. [...] The arc lamp, which we had hitherto always found satisfactory in the Winter Garden, this time frequently failed and was unable to penetrate the dense grain of the excellent autochromes [...]." The glamour of the evening was increased, however, by the presence of the amiable General Consul of France, M. G[eorges] Colomiès, who is just now departing Prague for Smyrna, and is a personal patron of the gentleman who delivered the talk" (Anonymous, "Projekční přednášky," *Fotografický obzor* 17 [1909], no. 11, p. 177). The following year, the weekly *Světozor* published Bufka's photographs from this same trip. On 7 November, Bufka gave a talk at the Prague Polytechnic, where he was studying or had been studying chemistry, and later in other places as well.

In a report on an Italian periodical written in French, Bufka manifested his patriotic, anti-German orientation: "it will be more to the liking of us Czechs than German periodicals are" ("La fotografia artistica," *Fotografický obzor* 17 [1909], no. 10, p. 163).

An advertisement in the last issue of *Fotografický obzor* for the year states: "A practical course in making color photographs (autochromes, using the Lumière system) will be taught in the very near future by Mr. V. J. Bufka on the premises of the Amateur Photographers' Club, Královské Vinohrady. A modest fee will be charged. Further information is available on request from Mr. V. J. Bufka, Villa No. 1102, Vinohrady. The following people have so far enrolled [...]" (*Fotografický obzor* 17 [1909], 12, p. 196).

1910   Bufka took photographs on commission and held photography courses in his own home in Moravská ulice, Vinohrady (house no. 1553) (Hrubeš, pp. 6 and 20).

Bufka also worked with the Královské Vinohrady Amateur Photographers' Club, holding a course there on autochromes and participating in the members' exhibition this year and the next.

Fotografický věstník 21 (1910), no. 11, p. 173, reported on one of the talks, which included the projection of slides, some of which were autochromes (though the article misspells Bufka's name).

"New Postcards. The Prague art publisher Minerva has just published a new series of ten color postcards with various scenes of Prague. Interestingly, they are the first postcards to have been made in Prague and to be reproduced from autochromes. Nine of the postcards are made from the autochromes of V. J. Buftka [*sic*] and one (part of Stromovka) is by [Ludvík] Bautz. The printing plates and the printing itself are by Unie, a Czech joint-stock printing company" (*Fotografický obzor* 18 [1910], no. 12, p. 228). The photography collection of the Moravian Gallery includes proof sheets of the series, which was probably reduced in number before publishing. Eleven of the twelve photos are by Bufka.

In the article "Internacionální kongres fotografický v Bruselu," *Fotografický věstník* 21 (1910), no. 10, pp. 145–46, Bufka gave a report on another of his journeys. It was intended, among other things, to publicize Prague as a center of intellectual activity, and is critical of the Brussels Congress.

Jaroslav Petrák praises Bufka's work in his book *Žeň světla a stínu: Problém umělecké fotografie v theorii a praksi s uměleckými přílohami* (A Harvest of Light and Shadow: The Problem of Art Photography in Theory and Practice, with Artistic Plates) (Prague, 1910). Bufka welcomes this book in the article "Konečně!" (Finally!), *Fotografický věstník* 21 (1910), no. 7, pp. 97–99.

1910–11 Bufka completed his training at the leading photography studio in Vienna, that of Hermann Clemens Kosel (1867 Temný důl/Dunkelthal – 1945 Vienna), where he worked as an unpaid intern from autumn 1910 to spring 1911 ("Pan V. J. Bufka […] nastoupil dne 1. list. t.r. jako volontér v at. H. Cl. Kosela ve Vídni" [Mr. V. J. Bufka (…) began work on 1 November of this year as an intern at. H. C. Kosel's studio, Vienna], *Fotografický obzor* 18 [1910], no. 11, p. 201. See also *Fotografický věstník* 21, 1910, p. 175.) In 1905 Kosel had establish his own institute for gum bichromate prints and modern photography (Der Anstalt für Gummidruck und moderne Photographie), where, in 1909, he was still training pupils mainly in simple and three-color gum bichromate prints. Bufka and Kosel also made carbon prints and platinum prints. Kosel, whose photographs were known also to Josef Sudek, probably was favorably inclined toward photographers from his native land. Interesting Czech testimony about him survives to this day. See Jaroslav Petrák, "Fotografické potulky Vídní. I., II. H. C. L. Kosel," *Fotografický obzor* 17 (1909), no. 6, pp. 88–89, 110–11. Perhaps it was this article that led Bufka to Vienna.

1911 In the article "Nový rok!" (New Year!), *Fotografický věstník* 22 (1911), no. 1, pp. 1–4, 31, it says: "Written in Vienna, 1 January 1911." The article ends with Bufka's motto: "Per aspera ad astra!" (Through hardship to the stars!").

After his return from Vienna, Bufka apparently held two courses in his studio in the Lucerna building, Prague, begining on 15 March (in, among other things, the platinum, pigment, oil, and gum bichromate printing processes) (*Fotografický věstník* 22 [1911], no. 1, pp. 15 and 30).

16–23 April, in the Lucerna building, Prague, the springtime "Exhibition of the Czech Amateur Photographers' Club" was held, accompanied by a catalogue in which Bufka's works appear under nos. 25–30. Three of them, nos. 26–28, are published in *Fotografický obzor* 19 (1911), no. 5, p. 105 (*The Sculpture*), no. 7, loose print (*H. C. Kosel, Master Photographer*), and no. 9, loose print (*The Urania Building*). A selection of 150 prints (from a total of more than twice that number) travelled to Pilsen and Kolín.

According to a *Fotografický obzor* article of 10 June (though one must take the date with a grain of salt), "Mr. V. J. Bufka, who has recently returned from his sojourn in Kosel's studio in Vienna, has just left for Russia – St. Petersburg and Warsaw [part of the Russian Empire till 1918] – in order to make color reproductions there. We entertain the hope that Mr. Bufka will succeed in bringing a whole series of interesting photos of the towns and people of Russia, which he will then surely present to us in a talk and slide projection" (*Fotografický obzor* 19 [1911], no. 6, p. 151). It is fair to assume that Bufka left in early June (the periodical could well have come out later, rather than earlier), and that the pictures of the Napoleonic Wars for the Neubert printing house (as we know from the testimony of Bufka's mother) were most likely printed from autochromes. According to Skopec, Bufka photographed in the Louvre as well (- ec. [Skopec, Rudolf], "Mistři světové fotografie: Vladimír Jindřich Bufka," *Československá* fotografie 12 [1961], no. 4, p. 58).

In its regular column, "Zu unseren Bildern," the periodical *Kamera-Kunst* 8 (1911), no. 7, p. 89, comments on the Bufka works it has published here, but without titles: "The photos by Bufka, a Prague resident, who has this time chosen his subject matter in Vienna, are very interesting. The selected cropped prints are highly original and demonstrate a sense of artistry. In terms of technique too, the works are of very high quality." In addition to the five prints by Bufka, this issue includes eight photos by Kosel. Of Bufka's published works (untitled), two apparently no longer survive in the original: the back view of the Urania building and St. Charles's Church with a landau.

Josef Váchal noted: "In October Vladimír Bufka returned from his travels to settle down here for good. He is a photographer with whom I parted on bad terms some years ago. We have now reconciled and become friends again. On the 25th, I carved a tablet with his name in relief for him, for ten crowns" (quoted in Hrubeš, pp. 6–7). For more on the book, see Josef Váchal, *Paměti Josefa Váchala, dřevorytce*, Prague: Prostor, 1995. For Bufka, pp. 104, 113, 185, 203, 206, 207, 208, 218, 249, 251, 300; for the photographers, Jindra Imlauf, 303; Jaroslav Petrák, 229, 260, 267, 284, 285, 303; Jan Srp, 220, 258; and Karel Šmirous, 259, 295.

Probably at the end of the year, after his return from Russia (including what was soon again Poland), Bufka opened a studio in the Lucerna building, Prague, which became a center of art activity. The studio emblem, a lantern, is a wood engraving by Váchal. There was also a print version for the cardboard mounts.

On 8 November, Bufka married Marie Bezděková (b. 1888) in the Church of St. Ludmila, Prague. (After Bufka's death, five years later, she married a gentleman farmer named Budínský.) (According to *Paměti Josefa Váchala, dřevorytce*; see Hrubeš, p. 34, n. 8.)

In the new Royal Bohemian Museum of Technology, Prague, thanks to Jaroslav Husník, a graphic arts department was opened, including photography, techniques of print-making, book-printing, and book-making. It was either this year or the next that Bufka completed the permanent exhibition of amateur photography, probably one of the first permanent exhibitions of amateur art photography in the world, even if in the context of photographic technology.

1912   Bufka moved his studio from the Lucerna building (where he had been very briefly) to Palackého ulice no. 740, in Královské Vinohrady (Hrubeš, p. 21, according to *Chytilův adresář* for 1912).

On 23 April, Bufka was granted a license to operate a photography business (Prague Municipal Archive, companies registry for 1912, no. 316. Quoted in Hrubeš, p. 21). Until 1911 photography was an unregulated occupation, but in 1911 portrait photography became classified as a trade. (Owners of photography businesses did not manage to get photography as a whole fully recognized as a trade until 1926.)

1913   Bufka moved his studio to Jindřišská ulice no. 898. His stamp (in Czech) says: "A Studio for Art Photography and All Kinds of Photography / (V. J. Bufka, Proprietor) / Jindřišská ulice no. 13, Prague II / Opposite the Main Branch of the Imperial and Royal Post Office." Bufka's wife, Marie, became a member of the Czech Amateur Photographers' Club in Prague (according to the regular column, "Klubový oznamovatel" [Club Announcements], *Fotografický obzor* 21 [1913], no. 4, p. 15).

1914   On 26 February, Bufka gave a talk (including a slide show), called "From the Starry Spheres," at the Czech Amateur Photographers' Club in Prague, thus making his motto, "Per aspera ad astra!," a reality (*Fotografický obzor* 22 [1914] nos. 5 and 6, p. 96). In addition to astrophotography, Bufka was also interested in microphotography.

1914–15 An anniversary "Exhibition of Photography" was organized by the Decorative Arts Museum of the Chamber of Trade and Commerce in Prague. Held at the Rudolfinum in late 1914 and early 1915, to mark the 75th anniversary of the public announcement of the daguerreotype, the exhibition presented commercial photography with works by some of the most important professionals. One large set was Bufka's, comprising twenty-two photographs. The exhibition was accompanied by a slender catalogue with an introduction by F. X. Jiřík, a prominent art historian.

1916 On 23 May, Bufka died of severe anemia in the Královské Vinohrady District Hospital. He was buried in the Vinohrady Cemetery. (According to the records of deaths, which are kept at the Church of the Sacred Heart. Quoted in Hrubeš, p. 7.) According to Skopec, Bufka died of tuberculosis, but according to Věra Lesná-Bakešová he died of leukemia. The information that he died in the First World War also appears in several places in the literature. After the death of her husband, Marie Bufková took over the photography studio in Jindřišská ulice, keeping the business until 24 April 1928 (Prague Municipal Archive, companies registry from 1916, trades, no. 231. Hrubeš, p. 34, n. 15). Even as a professional, Marie Bufková was able to remain a member of the Czech Amateur Photographers' Club in Prague. According to Pavla Vrbová, the only evidence of her photographic work in the club, which she joined in 1913, is several photos mentioned in a list of the club collection for the art photography exhibition in Pilsen in 1921. She still appears in the membership list of 1925. We do not know when Marie Bufková married Budínský.

Information taken from Pavel Scheufler appears here without references. The works of Martin Hrubeš (from 1988) and Pavla Vrbová (from 2010) are cited in abbreviated form. See the Bibliography.

Životopisná data

1887	16. 7. se v Pavlovicích u Kojetína na Moravě narodil Vladimír Jindřich Bufka, jediné dítě z druhého manželství Karly Bufkové-Absolonové, rozené Wanklové (1855–1941) a Eduarda Bufky (1854–1921), bankovního úředníka v Olomouci (1872–1886, kde také hrál divadlo) a v Praze. Karla byla jednou ze čtyř dcer slavného lékaře, archeologa a speleologa v Blansku, „otce moravské archeologie" Jindřicha Wankela (1821 Praha – 1897 Olomouc) a Elišky, rozené Šímové (1832–1903). Syn z jejího prvního manželství s MUDr. Vilibaldem Absolonem (1843–1882), slavný archeolog a skvělý fotograf prof. Karel Absolon (1877–1960), byl nevlastním bratrem Vladimíra J. Bufky. Karla Bufková-Wanklová napsala několik knih a divadelních her a psala též do ženských a odborných časopisů. Portrét Karly Wanklové je dosud jediným zjištěným autochromem V. J. Bufky (fotografická sbírka Moravské galerie v Brně). Bufka je také autorem portrétů Karly Bufkové (s. 36) a její sestry Lucie Bakešové (s. 24) v knize Bertholda Kladiva (ed.) *Zlatá rodina* (Blansko, Masarykova měšťanská škola 1936, autorství fotografií neuvedeno). Významná etnografka a sociální pracovnice Lucie Bakešová (1853–1935) byla matkou primáře Doc. MUDr. Jaroslava Bakeše (1871–1930), který roku 1909 převzal chirurgický pavilon v Zemské nemocnici v Brně a roku 1922 ústav na Žlutém kopci v Brně (dnes Bakešův pavilon). Společně s matkou byl protagonistou spolku Dům útěchy (1928), který po Bakešově smrti dobudoval budovu pro léčení zhoubných nádorů (1935, dnes Masarykův onkologický ústav). Karla Bufková měla kromě Lucie ještě dvě další sestry. Vlasta se stala manželkou zakladatele olomouckého muzea prof. Jana Havelky, Madléna se podobně jako Lucie věnovala etnografickému výzkumu. Rodinné zázemí V. J. Bufky bylo mimořádně kultivované a vlastenecké.
1903	V. J. Bufka bydlí na Malé Straně č. p. 617. (Archiv hlavního města Prahy, konskripce pražských obyvatel 1830–1910, Cizinci – popisní arch. Bufka Eduard, Bufka Vladimír; Hrubeš, s. 34, pozn. 13). Jeho otec přesídlil do Prahy v roce jeho narození nebo již o rok dříve (adresa Eduarda Bufky v roce 1897 byla Královské Vinohrady, Sázavská ul. č. 14 n., viz http://www.historie.hranet.cz/heraldika/cspsc/cspsc1896-4.pdf), takže V. J. Bufka pravděpodobně vyrůstal od narození v Praze. Místu narození V. J. Bufky patrně nemůžeme připisovat zvláštní důležitost, v Pavlovicích měl snad majetek některý z rodičů. Rodina žila v Praze a všechna další Bufkova bydliště jsou pražská (Hrubeš, s. 20). Adresa roku 1897: Ed. Bufka, t. č. pokladník, Král. Vinohrady, Sázavská ul. č. 14n.
1903–07	V průběhu těchto let V. J. Bufka začíná fotografovat a studovat chemii na VUT v Praze (nevíme, zda studium dokončil).
1907–09	Bufka detailně fotografoval „dělnický dům" v Hybernské ulici v Praze, který roku 1907 zakoupilo Tiskové a stavební družstvo dělnické pro účely sociálně demokratické strany. Psal a fotografoval pro měsíčník sociální demokracie Rudé květy. Přibližně v této době fotografoval dělníky a hutníky na Kladensku (-ec. [Rudolf Skopec]: Mistři světové fotografie. Vladimír Jindřich Bufka, *Československá fotografie* 12, 1961, č. 4, s. 59). Takové fotografie byly tehdy jedny z prvních vlaštovek sociálně dokumentární fotografie a zasloužily by si zvláštní pozornost.

1908   Jubilejní výstava obchodní a živnostenské komory v Praze předkládá veřejnosti několik
desítek Bufkových fotografií s pražskými náměty (Hrubeš, s. 11). Výstava uctila šedesáté
výročí vlády císaře Franze Josefa.

1909   V. J. Bufka vstupuje do Českého klubu fotografů amatérů v Praze jako přispívající člen.
5. 5. na schůzi Českého klubu fotografů amatérů v Praze následující po Mimořádné
valné hromadě V. J. Bufka přednáší o fotografování nočních a náladových snímků. Obsah
přednášky přináší zanedlouho *Fotografický obzor* (Fotografie za noci). „[...] nakonec
promítány byly nádherné jeho vlastní autochromy. – Byla to v klubu našem prvá přednáška
tohoto rutinovaného odborníka [...]" (F. M. [František Mrskoš]: Mimořádná valná hromada
dne 5. května 1909, *Fotografický obzor* 17, 1909, č. 6, s. 99).
Monumentální Internationale Photographische Ausstellung in Dresden představuje
z českých zemí profesionála Jana Langhanse a amatéra V. J. Bufku, který je zastoupen
dílem Praga caput regni. Výstavy se zúčastní také vídenský vlastenec Karel Prokop, který se
považuje za reprezentanta Čechů. Významnější je účast českých Němců (například Klub
deutscher Amateurphotographen, Prag). Výstava končí 10. října. O další drážďanské akci
podává Bufka písemnou zprávu: 1. internacionální kongres fotografický v Drážďanech
(*Fotografický obzor* 17, 1909, č. 9, 10. 9., s. 145). Na tomto kongresu se Bufka seznamuje
s reprezentantem firmy Lumière profesorem A. Seyewetzem, který mu otevírá cestu do
Lyonu. Zde se od roku 1907 vyrábějí a po celém světě prodávají desky pro autochromy.
Autochromy byly první široce rozšířené barevné fotografie, diapozitivy obvykle na
skleněných deskách 13 x 18 cm. Vyrábějí se průmyslově v závodě jejich vynálezců bratří
Lumièrů v Lyonu. Bufka se s autochromy seznámil přímo v Lyonu. „Abych se v každém
ohledu zdokonalil v praxi autochromové, podnikl jsem cestu do Lyonu, do továrny bratří
Lumièrů, kde se mi dostalo laskavého přijetí zvláště na přímluvu generálního konzula
francouzského, jemuž jsem velmi zavázán. Nemenšími pak díky jsem povinen slavným
pracovníkům na poli barevné fotografie, pánům Augustovi a Louisovi Lumière-ûm a panu
prof. Seywetzovi [sic], šéfu chemických ústavů university lyonské, za jejich velmi srdečné
přijetí a pozornosti, jimiž jsem byl za svého pobytu vyznamenáván" (*O fotografii v barvách
pomocí desky autochromové*, Praha, E. Weinfurter 1910).
Na 12. 10. je ohlášena přednáška V. J. Bufky Od úpatí Monte Rosy a Matterhornu, při
které se promítají „poprvé v Praze" veřejně autochromy (ohlášeno je 50 autochromů a 50
dalších diapozitivů). „Pan Bufka předložil redakci většinu autochromů, některé rozměrů
13 x 18, a můžeme potvrditi, že tak krásných, tak průhledných a tak přírodně zbarvených
neviděli jsme ani na drážďanské výstavě." (F. Dvořák: Přednášky ČKFA, *Fotografický obzor* 17,
1909, č. 9, 10. 9., s. 160–161.) Přednáška v Zimní zahradě Vinohradského Národního domu
„zůstavila pěkný dojem mezi přítomnými, ačkoli nebyla tentokrát projekce tak bezvadnou,
jako býváme u svých přednášek zvyklí. [...] světlo obloukové, které nás vždy ještě v Zimní
zahradě uspokojovalo, selhávalo častěji a nebylo s to prorazit husté zrno dokonalých
autochromů [...]. K lesku večera však přispívala přítomnost roztomilého, do Smyrny právě
z Prahy odcházejícího francouzského generálního konsula pana G[eorgese] Colomiése,
jenž jest osobním příznivcem pana přednášejícího" (anonym: Projekční přednášky,
Fotografický obzor 17, 1909, s. 177). V následujícím roce jsou publikovány fotografie ze

stejné Bufkovy cesty v týdeníku Světozor. 7. 11. se uskutečnila přednáška na vysoké škole technické v Praze, kde Bufka studoval chemii, a poté na dalších místech.

Ve zprávě o francouzsky psaném italském časopisu manifestuje Bufka svou vlasteneckou protiněmeckou orientaci: „[...] bude nám Čechům bližší než časopisy německé" (La fotografia artistica, *Fotografický obzor* 17, 1909, s. 163).

Inzerce v posledním čísle *Fotografického obzoru*: „Cvičný kurs pro fotografování v barvách (autochromii dle systému Lumière) vyučovati bude v nejbližší době pan V. J. Bufka v místnostech Klubu fotografů amatérů na Král. Vinohradech. Honorář mírný. Bližší podmínky sdělí na požádání pan V. J. Bufka, Vinohrady, Villa č. 1102. Dosud se přihlásili [...]" (*Fotografický obzor* 17, 1909, č. 12, s. 196).

1910	V. J. Bufka fotografuje na zakázku a pořádá fotografické kurzy ve svém domě v Moravské ulici na Vinohradech (č. p. 1553) (Hrubeš, s. 6, 20).

V. J. Bufka spolupracuje také s Klubem fotografů amatérů na Královských Vinohradech, pořádá zde kurs o autochromech a účastní se v tomto a následujícím roce členských výstav. O jedné z přednášek s promítáním diapozitivů, zčásti autochromů, referuje *Fotografický věstník* 21, 1910, s. 173. Bufkovo jméno je zde zkomoleno.

„*Nové dopisnice.* Pražské umělecké nakladatelství Minerva vydalo právě novou sérii krátce deseti barevných dopisnic s různými pražskými pohledy. Zajímavo jest, že jsou to první v Praze zhotovené pohlednice dle autochromů reprodukované. Devět dopisnic zhotoveno jest dle autochromů V. J. Buftky [sic] a jedna (partie ze Stromovky) od Bautze. Klišé a tisk provedla Česká grafická akc. společnost Unie." (*Fotografický obzor* 18, 1910, č. 12, s. 228).
Ve fotografické sbírce Moravské galerie jsou nátisky série, která byla zřejmě před vydáním zredukována. Bufkových záběrů je jedenáct z celkem dvanácti.

O další ze svých cest, mimo jiné zviditelňujících i Prahu jako intelektuální centrum, referuje Bufka v textu Internacionální kongres fotografický v Bruselu (*Fotografický věstník* 21, 1910, s. 145–146). Kongres si vysloužil jeho kritiku.

Jaroslav Petrák oceňuje Bufkovo dílo ve své knize *Žeň světla a stínu. Problém umělecké fotografie v theorii a praksi s uměleckými přílohami*, Praha, B. Kočí 1910. Bufka vítá jeho knihu článkem Konečně! (*Fotografický věstník* 21, 1910, s. 97–99).

1910–11	Své fotografické vzdělání dokončil v prominentním ateliéru Hermanna Clemense Kosela

(1867 Temný důl / Dunkelthal v Krkonoších – 1945 Vídeň) ve Vídni, kde pracoval jako volontér od podzimu 1910 do jara 1911. („Pan V. J. Bufka ... nastoupil dne 1. list. t. r. jako volontér v at. H. Cl. Kosela ve Vídni", *Fotografický obzor* 1910, s. 201. Též *Fotografický věstník* 21, 1910, s. 175.) Kosel roku 1905 zřídil vlastní Ústav pro gumotisk a moderní fotografii (Der Anstalt für Gummidruck und moderne Photographie), v kterém ještě roku 1909 prováděl výhradně výcvik v jednoduchém a trojbarevném gumotisku. Bufka i Kosel však praktikovali uhlotisk a platinotisk. Kosel, jehož fotografie znal i Josef Sudek, byl pravděpodobně fotografům z rodné země nakloněn, dochovalo se o něm zajímavé české svědectví – Jaroslav Petrák: Fotografické potulky Vídní. I., II. H. C. L. Kosel (*Fotografický obzor* 17, 1909, s. 88–89 a 110–111). Nasměroval pávě tento text Bufku do Vídně?

1911	U textu Nový rok! (*Fotografický věstník* 22, 1911, s. 1–4 a 31) je uvedeno: „Psáno ve Vídni 1. 1.1911. Článek ukončuje Bufkovo heslo: Per aspera ad astra! [Přes překážky ke hvězdám!]).

Po návratu z Vídně měl Bufka již 15. 3. dávat kursy (mj. platinotisk, pigmentový tisk, olejotisk a gumotisk) ve svém ateliéru Lucerna v Praze (*Fotografický věstník* 22, 1911, s. 15, s. 30).

16.–23. 4. se v pražské Lucerně koná památná (jarní) Výstava Českého klubu fotografů amatérů v Praze, provázená katalogem, v němž Bufkovy práce figurují pod č. k. 25–30 (Bufka V. J., Král. Vinohrady). Tři z nich (č. k. 26–28) jsou reprodukovány ve *Fotografickém obzoru* 1911, č. 7, s. 9. Výběr 150 pozitivů (z více než dvojnásobného množství) putuje do Plzně a Kolína.

Podle *Fotografického obzoru* z 10. 6. (datum je nutno brát s rezervou) „Pan V. J. Bufka, který se nedávno vrátil ze svého pobytu v ateliéru Koselově ve Vídni, odcestoval tyto dny do Ruska, Petrohradu a Varšavy [do roku 1918 patřila k Ruské říší], aby tam zhotovoval barevné reprodukce. Můžeme se těšiti nadějí, že se podaří p. Bufkovi přivésti [sic] celou řadu zajímavých snímků na města i lid ruský, což nám pak jistě v projekční přednášce ukáže“ (*Fotografický obzor* 19, 1911, s. 151). Můžeme předpokládat, že Bufka odjel počátkem června (časopis mohl mít spíš zpoždění, než vyjít předčasně), a že obrazy napoleonských válek pro tiskařskou firmu Neubert (jak víme ze svědectví jeho matky) reprodukoval se vší pravděpodobností na autochromy. Podle Rudolfa Skopce fotografoval i v Louvru (-ec. [Rudolf Skopec]: Mistři světové fotografie. Vladimír Jindřich Bufka, *Československá fotografie* 12, 1961, č. 4, s. 58).

Časopis *Kamera-Kunst* 8, 1911, č. 7, s. 89, komentuje reprodukované Bufkovy práce bez názvu v pravidelné rubrice K našim obrazům: „Velmi zajímavé jsou snímky Pražana Bufky, který si tentokrát své motivy vybral ve Vídni. Vybrané výřezy jsou velmi originální a prokazují umělecký cit. Také technicky stojí práce velmi vysoko.“ (přel. A. D.) Číslo přináší na příloze kromě pěti Bufkových fotografií také osm snímků Hermanna C. Kosela. Z reprodukovaných Bufkových prací (bez názvu) se dvě zřejmě nedochovaly v originálech: zadní pohled na Uranii a fiakr u Karlskirche.

Josef Váchal si zaznamenal: „ V říjnu navrátil se z cest k trvalému usídlení Vladimír Bufka, umělec-fotograf, se kterým jsem se před léty nedobře rozešel. Nyní jsme se usmířili a stali opět přáteli. Dne 25. vyřezal jsem mu tabulku s jeho jménem co reliéf, za 10 korun“ (cit. dle Hrubeš, s. 6–7). (Další informace k tématu této publikace in: Josef Váchal: *Paměti Josefa Váchala, dřevorytce*, Praha, Prostor 1995 – Vladimír Jindřich Bufka, fotograf: s. 104, 113, 185, 203, 206, 207, 208, 218, 249, 251, 300; Jindra Imlauf, fotograf, 303; Jaroslav Petrák, fotograf: 229, 260, 267, 284, 285, 303; Jan Srp, fotograf: 220, 258; Karel Šmirous, fotograf: 259, 295.)

Až koncem roku po návratu z Ruska (?) otevírá Bufka v pražské Lucerně ateliér, který se stal uměleckým centrem. Autorem značky (dřevoryt) s motivem svítilny je Josef Váchal. Značka měla ještě tiskovou verzi pro podkladové kartony.

8. 11. se V. J. Bufka žení v kostele sv. Ludmily na Královských Vinohradech. Jeho manželka Marie, rozená Bezděková (* 1888) se po Bufkově smrti provdá za statkáře Budínského (dle *Pamětí Josefa Váchala, dřevorytce*, viz Hrubeš, s. 34, pozn. 8).

V novém „Technickém muzeu v Království českém“ v Praze je zásluhou Jaroslava Husníka zpřístupněno tzv. grafické oddělení, jehož součástí byly fotografie, grafické techniky, knihtisk a knihařství. V. J. Bufka zde tohoto nebo následujícího roku dokončuje expozici amatérské fotografie. Je to zřejmě jedna z prvních stálých expozic amatérské – tedy umělecké – fotografie na světě, byť v kontextu techniky.

1912   Bufka stěhuje ateliér z Lucerny, kde byl velmi krátce, do Palackého ulice č. p. 740 na Vinohradech (viz Hrubeš, s. 21, dle *Chytilova adresáře 1912*).
23. 4. tohoto roku získává Bufka živnostenský list pro fotografii (Archiv hlavního města Prahy, živnostenský rejstřík z roku 1912, č. 316; Hrubeš, s. 21). Až do roku 1911 byla fotografie svobodnou živností, roku 1911 byla zřemeslněna portrétní fotografie. Živnostníkům se tehdy ještě nepodařilo dosáhnout zřemeslnění fotografie v plném rozsahu (k tomu došlo až v roce 1926).

1913   Bufka stěhuje ateliér do Jindřišské ulice č. p. 898. Razítko: „Atelier pro uměleckou a veškerou fotografii / (maj. V. J. Bufka) / Praha II., Jindřišská ul. č. 13. / Proti c. k. hlavní poště.“
Členkou Českého klubu fotografů amatérů v Praze se stává Marie Bufková, manželka V. J. Bufky (dle Klubového oznamovatele *Fotografického obzoru* 21, 1913; Hrubeš, s. 13).

1914   Diapozitivní přednáška V. J. Bufky Z hvězdnatých oblastí je doslovnou realizací výzvy Per aspera ad astra! Koná se v Českém klubu fotografů amatérů v Praze 26. 2. 1914 (*Fotografický obzor* 22, 1914, s. 96). Kromě astrofotografie se Bufka zabýval též mikrofotografií.

1914–15   „Jubilejní“ Výstava fotografií, uspořádaná Uměleckoprůmyslovým muzeem obchodní a živnostenské komory v Praze v pražském Rudolfinu na přelomu let 1914–15 při příležitosti 75. výročí zveřejnění daguerrotypie, představuje živnostenskou fotografii včetně jejích nejvýznamnějších představitelů. Bufka je zastoupen jednou z nejpočetnějších kolekcí 22 děl. Výstavu provází útlý katalog s úvodním textem prominentního historika umění F. X. Jiříka.

1916   23. 5. V. J. Bufka umírá v okresní nemocnici na Královských Vinohradech na anemii, pohřben je na Vinohradském hřbitově (podle matriky zemřelých kostela Nejsvětějšího srdce Páně, viz Hrubeš, s. 7). Podle Rudolfa Skopce V. J. Bufka zemřel na tuberkulózu, podle Věry Lesné-Bakešové na leukémii, několikrát se objevil též údaj, že padl v první světové válce.
Po smrti manžela přebírá jeho fotografický ateliér v Jindřišské ulici Marie Bufková, živnosti se vzdala až 24. 4. 1928 (Archiv hlavního města Prahy, živnostenský rejstřík z roku 1916, živnosti řemeslné, č. 231; Hrubeš, s. 34, pozn. 15.) Je zajímavé, že jako profesionálka mohla zůstat Marie Bufková členkou Českého klubu fotografů amatérů v Praze. Podle Pavly Vrbové jediným dokladem o její fotografické činnosti v Českém klubu fotografů amatérů, do něhož vstoupila v roce 1913, je několik snímků uvedených na seznamu klubové kolekce pro výstavu umělecké fotografie v Plzni v roce 1921. V členské evidenci byla vedena ještě v roce 1925. Nevíme, kdy se Marie Bufková provdala za statkáře Budínského.

Údaje bez citací jsou zčásti převzaty od Pavla Scheuflera. Zkráceně jsou označeny práce Martina Hrubeše (1988) a Pavly Vrbové (2010) – viz seznam literatury.

Solo Exhibitions / Samostatné výstavy

1988   *Vladimír J. Bufka*, Moravská galerie v Brně, Brno
2010–11 *Vladimír Jindřich Bufka, Camera*, Uměleckoprůmyslové muzeum Moravské galerie v Brně, Brno

Selected Group Exhibitions / Účast na skupinových výstavách (výběr)

1908   *Jubilejní výstava obchodní a živnostenské komory*, expozice Klubu Za starou Prahu, Praha
1909   *Internationale Photographische Ausstellung in Dresden*, Dresden
1911   *Výstava Českého klubu fotografů amatérů v Praze*, Lucerna, Praha
1914–15 *Výstava fotografií*, Rudolfinum, Praha
1961   *Dějiny fotografie II*, Dům umění města Brna, kabinet fotografie Jaromíra Funka v Domě pánů z Kunštátu, Brno
1986   *Fotografie v Praze 1839–1914*, Muzeum hlavního města Prahy, Praha
1987   *Člověk a technika v české fotografii do roku 1914*, Středočeské muzeum, Roztoky u Prahy
1989   *Co je fotografie?*, Mánes, Praha
1989   *Česká fotografická moderna (V. J. Bufka, F. Drtikol, K. Novák, J. A. Trčka)*, Uměleckoprůmyslové muzeum, Praha
1989   *Fotografie na Kladensku*, OKS Kladno, Kladno
1989–90 *Czech Modernism 1900–1945*, Museum of Fine Arts, Houston. Reprízy výstavy: Akron Art Museum, Akron; Brooklyn Museum, International Center of Photography, Anthology Film Archives, New York
1990   *Fotografie v Čechách*, Galerie hlavního města Prahy, Zámek Trója, Praha
1991–92 *Photographie der Moderne in Prag 1900–1925. Vladimír Jindřich Bufka, František Drtikol, Karel Němec, Karel Novák, Josef Sudek, Josef Anton Trčka, Alois Zych*, Neue Galerie der Stadt Linz, Wolfgang Gurlitt-Museum, Linz; Österreichische Fotoarchiv im Museum moderner Kunst, Wien; Frankfurter Kunstverein, Frankfurt am Main
1992   *Mittel Europa, fin de siècle*, La grande halle, Paris
1995   *Bratislava – Budapest – Praha – Wien 1856–1918*, Zichyho palác, Bratislava
1997   *Prague 1900–1938. Capitale secrète des avant-gardes*, Musée des Beaux-Arts, Dijon
1998   *Skulptur im Licht*, Museum moderner Kunst, Wien
1999–2000 *Český piktorialismus 1895–1928*, České centrum fotografie, Praha
2003   *Ejhle světlo*, Moravská galerie v Brně, Brno; Jízdárna Pražského hradu, Praha
2005   *Vídeňská secese a moderna 1900–1925. Užité umění a fotografie v českých zemích*, Moravská galerie v Brně, Brno; Obecní dům, Praha
2005   *La photographie pictorialiste en Europe 1888–1918*, Musée des Beaux-arts de Rennes, Rennes
2006   *Impressionist Camera. Pictorial Photography in Europe, 1888–1918*, Saint Louis Art Museum, Saint Louis
2006–07 *Pražský hrad ve fotografii / 1900–1939*, Pražský hrad, Starý královský palác, Tereziánské křídlo, Praha

Represented in Galleries / Zastoupení ve sbírkách

Moravská galerie v Brně, Brno
Národní technické muzeum, Praha
Uměleckoprůmyslové museum, Praha

Bibliography / Literatura

As Author / Vlastní publikace

Fotografie za noci, *Fotografický obzor* 17, 1909, s. 133–137.
1. internacionální kongres fotografický v Drážďanech, *Fotografický obzor* 17, 1909, s. 145.
La fotografia artistica, *Fotografický obzor* 17, 1909, s. 163. [Referát o italském časopisu.]
Příspěvek k rozpoznání solarizace a odrazu v praxi, *Fotografický obzor* 17, 1909, s. 185–188.
Zimní večer, in: Jaroslav Petrák, *Žeň světla a stínu*, Praha, B. Kočí 1910, s. 87. [Komentář
    k vlastní fotografii pořízené pro knihu, Tab. I.]
Konečně!, *Fotografický věstník* 21, 1910, s. 97–99. [Referát o knize Jaroslav Petrák: *Žeň světla
    a stínu*, Praha, B. Kočí 1910.]
Internacionální kongres fotografický v Bruselu, *Fotografický věstník* 21, 1910, s. 145–146.
Fotografický věstník 21, 1910, s. 173. [O přednášce V. J. Bufky, zkomoleno jeho jméno.]
 O fotografii v barvách pomocí desky autochromové, Praha, E. Weinfurter 1910.
Stručný návod k nejdůležitějším pracím s deskami fotografickými a vyvolacími papíry, Praha,
    E. Weinfurter 1910, 2. vydání 1913.
Od úpatí Monte Rosy a Matterhornu, *Světozor* 10, 1910, s. 179–180 a 205–208.
Nový rok!, *Fotografický věstník* 22, 1911, s. 1–4 a 31.
Moderní fotografie stylová, *Český svět* 7, 1911, 14. 4., č. 31.
 O vývoji moderní fotografie, *Veraikon*, 1912, s. 67–69.
Češí grafikové I, Prof. Jakub Husník, *Fotografický obzor* 20, 1912, s. 213–214.
Češí grafikové II, PhDr. Jaroslav Husník, *Fotografický obzor* 20, 1912, s. 237–238.
Letošní zatmění slunce, *Fotografický obzor* 20, 1912, s. 112–113.
Nejnovější výzkumy ve fotografii, *Fotografický věstník* 23, 1912, s. 161–163 a 177–179.
Katechismus fotografie, Praha, Hejda a Tuček 1913.
Moderní fotografie odvětvím uměleckého průmyslu grafického, *Dílo* 12, 1913, s. 73–75.
Za světy hvězdné říše, Několik kapitol z astrofysiky a pokroků hvězdářské fotografie,
    Světozor 14, 1914, 20. 3., č. 5.
Praha, Praha, Klub Za starou Prahu 1924. [Roku 1925 s francouzským textem.]

Books / Knihy

Petrák, Jaroslav: *Žeň světla a stínu. Problém umělecké fotografie v theorii a praksi s uměleckými přílohami*, Praha, B. Kočí 1910.

Bufková-Wanklová, Karla: Vzpomínky, in: Berthold Kladivo (ed.): *Zlatá rodina*, Blansko, Masarykova měšťanská škola 1936, s. 35–42.

Skopec, Rudolf: *Dějiny fotografie v obrazech od nejstarších dob k dnešku*, Praha, Orbis 1963.

Skopec, Rudolf: *Photographie im Wandel der Zeiten*, Praha, Artia 1964.

Wittlich, Petr: *Česká secese*, Praha, Odeon 1982.

Mrázková, Daniela & Remeš, Vladimír: *Tschechoslowakische Fotografen 1900–1940*, Leipzig, Fotokinoverlag 1983.

Scheufler, Pavel: *Praha 1848–1914. Čtení nad dobovými fotografiemi*, Praha, Panorama 1984, 1986.

Scheufler, Pavel: *Pražské fotografické ateliéry 1839–1918. II. 1889–1918*, Praha, Muzeum hlavního města Prahy 1989.

Scheufler, Pavel: *Přehled vývoje fotografie v Praze v letech 1839–1918. II. 1889–1918*, Učební texty FAMU, Praha, Státní pedagogické nakladatelství 1987.

Mrázková, Daniela & Remeš, Vladimír: *Cesty československé fotografie*, Praha, Mladá fronta 1989.

Scheufler, Pavel: *Fotografické album Čech*, Praha, Odeon 1989.

Birgus, Vladimír: *Vývoj československé fotografie v datech*, Učební texty FAMU, Praha, Státní pedagogické nakladatelství 1990.

Dufek, Antonín: V. J. Bufka, in: Petr Balajka (ed.): *Encyklopedie českých a slovenských fotografů*, Praha, Asco 1993, s. 45.

Hrubeš, Martin: *Vladimír Jindřich Bufka*, Bakalářská teoretická práce, Praha, FAMU 1994.

Dufek, Antonín: V. J. Bufka, in: *Nová encyklopedie českého výtvarného umění*, Praha, Academia 1995, s. 95.

Váchal, Josef: *Paměti Josefa Váchala, dřevorytce*, Praha, Prostor 1995.

Hrubeš, Martin: *Vladimír Jindřich Bufka*, Magisterská teoretická práce, Praha, FAMU 1998.

Dufek, Antonín: Fotografie 1890–1918, in: *Dějiny českého výtvarného umění 1890–1938, IV / 1*, Praha, Academia 1998, s. 195–207.

Birgus, Vladimír & Scheufler, Pavel: *Fotografie v českých zemích 1839–1999*, Praha, Grada Publishing a Kant 1999.

Scheufler, Pavel: Galerie c. k. fotografů, Praha, Grada Publishing 2001, s. 218–221 a 243–244.

Dufek, Antonín: Vladimír Jindřich Bufka, in: Hana Rousová (ed.): *Vademecum neboli rukověť moderního výtvarného umění v Čechách a na Moravě 1890– 1938*, Praha, Gallery 2002, s. 61–63.

Vogelová, Pavlína: *České fotografické sbírky*, Praha, Asociace muzeí a galerií 2005.

Dufek, Antonín: Rudolf Skopec in Relation to Helmut Gernsheim, in: Anna Auer and Alistair Crawford ed.): *Helmut Gernsheim Reconsidered, The proceedings of the Mannheim symposium*, Passau, Dietmar Klinger 2004, s. 53–56.

Čejka, Jiří: *Pohled do minulosti Masarykova onkologického ústavu v Brně*, Brno, Masarykův onkologický ústav v Brně 2004.

Kontra, Gabriela: *Fotografky v českých zemích 1839–1918*, Praha, Diplomová teoretická práce FAMU 2005.

Clegg, Elizabeth: *Art, Design and Architecture in Central Europe 1890–1920*, New Haven and
    London, Yale University Press 2006.
Scheufler, Pavel et al: *Pražský hrad ve fotografii / Prague Castle in Photographs 1900–1939*, Praha,
    Správa Pražského hradu a Kant 2006.
Trnková, Petra: *Technický obraz na malířských štaflích. Česko-němečtí fotoamatéři a umělecká
    fotografie, 1890–1914*, Brno, Společnost pro odbornou literaturu Barrister & Principal
    a Masarykova univerzita 2009.
Trnková, Petra: Světlopis ve službách vědy, in: Kostrhun, Petr & Oliva, Martin (eds.):
    Dr. Karel Absolon – Fotografie z evropských jeskyní a krasů, Brno, Moravské zemské muzeum
    2010, s. 26–30.
Mühldorf, Josef & Vrbová, Pavla: *Od sportu fotografického k umělecké fotografii. Historie prvního
    klubu fotografů amatérů v Čechách a Svazu československých klubů fotografů amatérů, 1889–1945*,
    Praha, Národní informační a poradenské středisko pro kulturu 2010.
Birgus, Vladimír & Mlčoch, Jan: *Tschechische Fotografie des 20. Jahrhunderts*, Bonn a Praha,
    Kunst-und Ausstellunghalle der Bundesrepubik Detschland, Uměleckoprůmyslové mu-
    seum a Kant 2009.
Birgus, Vladimír & Mlčoch, Jan: *Česká fotografie 20. století*, Praha, Kant 2010.
Birgus, Vladimír & Mlčoch, Jan: *Czech Photography of the 20th Century*, Praha, Kant 2010.

Exhibition Catalogues / Katalogy výstav

Jiřík, F. X.: Fotografie, in: Katalog výstavy fotografií, Praha, Rudolfinum 1914–15,
    nestránkováno.
Skopec, Rudolf: *Dějiny fotografie II*, Brno, Dům umění města Brna 1961.
Scheufler, Pavel: *Fotografie v Praze 1839–1914*, Praha, Muzeum hlavního města Prahy 1986.
Scheufler, Pavel & Hozák, Jan: *Člověk a technika v české fotografii do roku 1914*, Roztoky u Prahy,
    Středočeské muzeum 1987.
Dufek, Antonín: *Vladimír Jindřich Bufka*, Brno, Moravská galerie v Brně 1988.
Kirschner, Zdeněk & Kroutvor, Josef: *Česká fotografická moderna (V. J. Bufka, F. Drtikol,
    K. Novák, J. A. Trčka)*, Praha, Uměleckoprůmyslové muzeum v Praze 1989.
Scheufler, Pavel: *Pražské fotografické ateliéry 1839–1918. II. 1889–1918*, Praha, Muzeum
    hlavního města Prahy 1989.
Mrázková, Daniela: *Co je fotografie? / What is Photography?*, Praha, Videopress a Credit Praha
    1989.
Scheufler, Pavel: *Fotografie na Kladensku*, Kladno, OKS Kladno 1989.
Anděl, Jaroslav: Modernism, the Avant-garde, and Photography, in: Jaroslav Anděl & Anne
    Tucker (ed.): *Czech Modernism 1900–1945*, Boston, Toronto and London, Bulfinch Press
    1989.
Scheufler, Pavel: *Fotografie v Čechách 1839–1914*, Praha, Galerie hlavního města Prahy 1990.
Faber, Monika: Portraits zwischen Versunkenheit und Pose, in: Monika Faber (ed.):
    Photographie der Moderne in Prag 1900–1925, Wien, Österreichisches Fotoarchiv im
    Museum moderner Kunst Wien 1991, s. 89–104.

Kroutvor, Josef: Die tschechische Moderne, in: Monika Faber (ed.): *Photographie der Moderne in Prag 1900–1925*, Wien, Österreichisches Fotoarchiv im Museum moderner Kunst Wien 1991, s. 6–13.

Gay-Bellile, Christian & Sayag, Alain & de Gouvion Saint-Cyr, Agnès & Müller, Heiner & Wisniewski, Jana: *Mittel Europa, fin de siècle*, Paris, Paris Audiovisuel, Commission Nationale de la Photographie, Ministère de l'Education Nationale et de la Culture 1992.

Scheufler, Pavel: Počátky autochromu v Čechách / The Beginnings of the Autochrome in the Czech Lands, in: Číp, Jiří & Jung, Rudolf & Scheufler, Pavel: *Karel Šmirous – výběr barevných fotografií z rastrových diapozitivů z let 1908–1955 / selection of color photographs from the screened positives from 1908–1955*, Praha, Národní technické muzeum 1993, s. 33–44.

Anděl, Jaroslav & Starcky, Emmanuel (ed.): *Prague 1900–1938, Capitale secrète des avant-gardes*, Dijon, Musée des Beaux-Arts 1997.

Mlčoch, Jan & Scheufler, Pavel: *Český piktorialismus 1895–1928*, Praha, České centrum fotografie 1999–2000.

Dufek, Antonín: Hry světel a stínů, hry o skutečnost / Lightplays and Shadowplays, Plays for Reality, in: Jiří Zemánek (ed.): *Ejhle světlo / Look Light*, Praha a Brno, Kant a Moravská galerie v Brně 2003, s. 180–203 a 361–364.

Dufek, Antonín: Fotografie mezi internacionálním stylem a regionálními inspiracemi, in: Ambroz, Vladimír (ed.): *Vídeňská secese a moderna 1900–1925. Užité umění a fotografie v českých zemích*, Brno, Moravská galerie v Brně 2005, s. 238–245. [German version on CD / Německá verze na CD.]

Trnková, Petra: Umělecké ambice amatérské fotografie, in: Ambroz, Vladimír (ed.): *Vídeňská secese a moderna 1900–1925. Užité umění a fotografie v českých zemích*, Brno, Moravská galerie v Brně 2005, s. 238–245. [German version on CD / Německá verze na CD.]

Dufek, Antonín: Vladimír Jindřich Bufka, in: Ribemont, Francis & Daum, Patrick (ed.): *La photographie pictorialiste en Europe 1888–1918*, Rennes, Musée des Beaux-arts de Rennes 2005, s. 315.

Dufek, Antonín: Vladimír Jindřich Bufka, in: Ribemont, Francis & Daum, Patrick (ed.): *Impressionist Camera, Pictorial Photography in Europe, 1888–1918*, Sant Louis Art Museum 2006, s. 287.

Kostrhun, Petr & Oliva, Martin (ed.): *Dr. Karel Absolon – Fotografie z evropských jeskyní a krasů*, Brno, Moravské zemské muzeum 2010.

Trnková, Petra: Světlopis ve službách vědy, in: Kostrhun, Petr & Oliva, Martin (eds.): *Dr. Karel Absolon – Fotografie z evropských jeskyní a krasů*, Brno, Moravské zemské muzeum 2010, s. 26–30.

Radio Programme / Rozhlasový pořad

Vykoupil, Libor: *Ecce homo, Vladimír Jindřich Bufka*, Český rozhlas Brno, 16. 7. 2007.

Articles / Články

anonym: Zemřel V. J. Bufka, *Fotografický obzor* 24, 1916, s. 23–24.

anonym: [nekrolog], *Fotografický věstník* 27, 1916, s. 70.

Lauschmann, Jan: Vývoj naší fotografie od let devadesátých, *Fotografický obzor* 36, 1928, s. 73–74.

-ec. [Skopec, Rudolf]: Mistři světové fotografie, Vladimír Jindřich Bufka [7 reprodukcí], *Československá fotografie* 12, 1961, č. 4, s. 58–59.

Dufek, Antonín: Fotografická sbírka MG v Brně 14 – Vladimír Jindřich Bufka, *Československá fotografie* 28, 1977, č. 3, s. 125.

Dufek, Antonín: Z historie české fotografie (od roku 1890 do roku 1918), *Revue fotografie* 28, 1984, č. 4, s. 36–43.

Scheufler, Pavel: Vladimír Jindřich Bufka, *Dobré světlo*, 1987, č. 2, nestránkováno.

Scheufler, Pavel: Fotografie v Čechách a na Slovensku 1889–1919, *Revue fotografie* 21, 1989, č. 2, s. 2–9.

Kroutvor, Josef: Česká fotografická moderna, *Revue fotografie* 24, 1990, č. 3, s. 68–73.

Scheufler, Pavel: V. J. Bufka, *Antique* 4, 1997, č. 7, s. 30–31.

Scheufler, Pavel: Pražský hrad na fotografiích Vladimíra Jindřicha Bufky, in: *Pražský hrad*, 2002, č. 3, s. 15–18.

Dufek, Antonín: Rudolf Skopec, předseda poradního sboru fotografické sbírky Moravské galerie v Brně, 62. *Bulletin Moravské galerie v Brně* / 2006, s. 29–32.

List of Published Photographs

Titles given on the original photographs or in the secondary sources are written in quotation marks. If the photographic process is not mentioned, the print is a gelatin silver print, sometimes toned. MG = Moravská galerie v Brně (the Moravian Gallery in Brno), UPM = Uměleckoprůmyslové museum v Praze (the Museum of Decorative Arts in Prague), NTM = Národní technické muzeum v Praze (the National Technical Museum in Prague).

21   Untitled (Prague?), c. 1911 (UPM GF 44.934)
22   The Urania building, Vienna, 1910–11 (platinum print, NTM 63922_4)
23   The Urania building, from the river, Vienna, 1910–11 (published 1911)
24   The Town Hall and The Votive Church, Vienna, 1910–11 (published 1911)
25   Untitled (At the Votive Church, Vienna), 1910 (platinum print, MG6822)
26   A Landau at St. Charles's Church, Vienna, 1910–11 (published 1911)
27   "The Sculpture" (Kunsthistorisches Museum, Vienna), 1910 (gum bichromate print, MG6804)
28   The Opera House, Vienna, 1910 (platinum print, NTM 63922_2)
29   The Town Hall, Vienna, 1910 (platinum print, NTM 63922d_6a)
30   From Prague, 1911 (gum bichromate print, MG6805)
31   Untitled (poplars in the light of the full moon, Vršovice), 1915 (color gum bichromate print, MG6816)
32   Untitled (steamboat), 1909 (gum bichromate print, MG6802)
33   At Chuchle, 1913 (gum bichromate print, MG6812)
34   Untitled (landscape), c. 1914 (gum bichromate print, MG6820)
35   "Evening Train, January–February 1911" (hand-colored gum bichromate print, MG6806)
36   "At the Wonderful Old Smíchov Cemetery," 1914 (gum bichromate print, MG6815)
37   "At the Chuchle Cemetery," 1912 (color gum bichromate print, MG6810)
38   "From a Košíře Garden," c. 1914 (color gum bichromate print, MG6811)
39   Birches, 1913 (color gum bichromate print, MG6808)
40   "A Wood at Říčany," 1911/1913 (combined gum bichromate print, MG6809)
41   Untitled (birches at the edge of a wood), 1912 (gum bichromate print, MG7336)
42   Untitled (blue still life), 1915 (color gum bichromate print, MG6817)
43   Untitled (sunflowers in a blue vase), c. 1914 (color gum bichromate print, MG6829)
44   Untitled (Marie Bufková in a Sioux headdress), c. 1912 (MG6819)
45   Untitled (Marie Bufková), c. 1912 (MG6784)
46   Lucie Bakešová in the Bakeš villa, Brno, c. 1912–15 (MG13324)
47   Untitled (a woman on a sofa), c. 1912 (MGA27)
48   Untitled (Marie Bufková), 1909–10 (published 1910)
49   "The Artist's Wife," 1909–10 (published 1913)
50   "The Bufka Studio, 1914," Marie Bufková (MG6786)
51   Self-portrait, Marie Bufková, c. 1919 (MG6785)
52   Marie Bufková, by V. J. Bufka?, c. 1912 (MG6783)
53   Untitled (Eleonora Schwarzenberg), before 1914 (MG6794)
54   Untitled (Karl Schwarzenberg [V] with his son, Karl [VI]), 1914 (MG6797)
55   Untitled (Eleonora Schwarzenberg with her son Franz), 1914 (MG6796)
56   Lucie Bakešová, 1915 (MG13327)
57   Portrait (Lucie Bakešová), 1913 (MG13328)
58   "Josef Váchal, 24 December 1911" (Archive of the Library of the National Museum in Prague)
59   Alberto Vojtěch Frič, c. 1909 (private collection, Prague)
60   Professor Jakub Husník, 1911–12 (platinum print?, NTM)
61   Jaroslav Husník, 1911 (MG6458)

62   "Portrait of F. H., Writer" (František Herites), c. 1911 (published 1912)

63   Jan Kotěra, c. 1912 (UPM GF 9756)

64   Anna Sedláčková in Robert de Flers's La Belle Aventure, by Marie Bufková, c. 1927 (MG6793)

65   Jan Kubelík, c. 1911–13 (private collection)

66   Leopolda Dostalová, by Marie Bufková, c. 1920 (private collection, Prague)

67   Míla Pačová, 1914 (private collection, Prague)

68   From the Prague series, 1910 (MGA42)

69   From the Prague series, 1910 (MGA42)

70   From the Prague series, 1910 (MGA42)

71   From the Prague series, 1910 (MGA42)

72   From the Prague series, 1910 (MGA42)

73   From the Prague series, 1910 (MGA42)

74   From the Prague series, 1910 (MGA42)

75   From the Prague series, 1910 (MGA42)

76   From the Prague series, 1910 (MGA42)

77   From the Prague series, 1910 (MGA42)

78   From the Prague series, 1910 (MGA42)

Soupis publikovaných fotografií

Názvy uvedené na předlohách nebo v literatuře jsou psány v uvozovkách. Není-li uvedena technika zhotovení díla, jedná se o želatinostříbrné pozitivy, v některých případech tónované. MG = Moravská galerie v Brně, UPM = Uměleckoprůmyslové museum v Praze, NTM = Národní technické muzeum v Praze.

s. 2	V. J. Bufka (autoportrét?), asi 1911 (MG7545)
s. 9	V. J. Bufka u klavíru, asi 1911 (MGA26)
s. 9	V. J. Bufka při práci v ateliéru, asi 1911 (MGA37)
s. 14	Josef Váchal: Značka ateliéru V. J. Bufky v Lucerně, dřevoryt, 1912 (MGA3067)
s. 15	Inzerce ateliéru V. J. Bufky
s. 18	Karla Bufková-Wanklová, matka V. J. Bufky, autochrom, asi 1915 (MG6560)
s. 18	„Mistr H. C. Kosel" (publikováno 1910)
s. 25	„Tabulka ke článku p. Vl. J. Bufky: Letošní zatmění slunce." (publikováno 1912)
s. 34	V. J. Bufka (?): Marie Bufková, asi 1914 (MG6790)
s. 34	V. J. Bufka: Marie Bufková, asi 1910 (MG6789)
s. 35	Marie Bufková (autoportrét?), asi 1914 (MG6787)
s. 35	V. J. Bufka: Marie Bufková, asi 1910 (MG6791)

1	Praha, 1914 (barevný gumotisk, MG6814)
2	„Z Kladenska", 1908 (MG6831)
3	„Po západu slunce", 1908 (platinotisk, MG7335)
4	Bez názvu (nokturno), 1908 (barevný gumotisk, MG6798)
5	Západ slunce nad jezerem, asi 1908 (pigmentový tisk, UPM GF 26603)
6	„Františkovo nábřeží", z alba Večerní Praha, 1909 (MG7546)
7	„Praga Caput Regni", 1909 (tónovaný platinotisk, MG7337)
8	„Bruncvík", z alba Večerní Praha, 1909 (soukromá sbírka)
9	„Zimní večer" (Praha), asi 1909
10	„Sníh a led v Praze", z alba Večerní Praha, 1909 (soukromá sbírka)
11	„Na Kampě", z alba Večerní Praha, 1909 (soukromá sbírka)
12	Bez názvu (pomník Františka I. na Smetanově nábřeží v Praze), asi 1909 (MG6821)
13	Bez názvu (Praha, Staroměstské náměstí s Mariánským sloupem a částí radnice), asi 1909 (MG6826)
14	„Karlův most", z alba Večerní Praha, 1909 (soukromá sbírka)
15	„Západ slunce na Petříně", z alba Večerní Praha, 1909 (soukromá sbírka)
16	„Pod Emauzy", Praha, 1909/1914 (MG6799)
17	„Pražské Benátky", z alba Večerní Praha, 1909 (soukromá sbírka)
18	Bez názvu (trh), 1914 (olejotisk, MG6813)
19	Bez názvu (modlitba), asi 1911 (MG6828)
20	„Zelený trh v dešti", 1912 (publikováno 1912)
21	Bez názvu (Praha?), asi 1911 (UPM GF 44.934)

22   Vídeň, Urania, 1910–11 (platinotisk, NTM 63922_4)

23   Vídeň, Urania od řeky, 1910–11 (publikováno 1911)

24   Vídeň, Radnice a Votivkirche, 1910–11 (publikováno 1911)

25   Bez názvu (Vídeň, U Votivkirche), 1910 (platinotisk, MG6822)

26   Vídeň, Fiakr u Karlskirche, 1910–11 (publikováno 1911)

27   „The Sculpture" (Kunsthistorisches Museum, Vídeň), 1910 (gumotisk, MG6804)

28   Vídeň, Opera, 1910 (platinotisk, NTM 63922_2)

29   Vídeň, Radnice, 1910 (platinotisk, NTM 63922d_6a)

30   Z Prahy, 1911 (gumotisk, MG6805)

31   Bez názvu (topoly při úplňku ve Vršovicích), 1915 (barevný gumotisk, MG6816)

32   Bez názvu (parník), 1909 (gumotisk, MG6802)

33   U Chuchle, 1913 (gumotisk, MG6812)

34   Bez názvu (krajina), asi 1914 (gumotisk, MG6820)

35   „Večerní vlak, leden–únor 1911" (kolorovaný gumotisk, MG6806)

36   „Na starém a báječném hřbitově smíchovském", 1914 (gumotisk, MG6815)

37   „Na chuchelském hřbitově", 1912 (barevný gumotisk, MG6810)

38   „Z košířské zahrady", asi 1914 (barevný gumotisk, MG6811)

39   Břízy, 1913 (barevný gumotisk, MG6808)

40   „Les u Říčan", 1911/1913 (kombinovaný gumotisk, MG6809)

41   Bez názvu (břízy na kraji lesa), 1912 (gumotisk, MG7336)

42   Bez názvu (modré zátiší), 1915 (barevný gumotisk, MG6817)

43   Bez názvu (slunečnice v modré váze), asi 1914 (barevný gumotisk, MG6829)

44   Bez názvu (Marie Bufková v čelence Siouxů), asi 1912 (MG6819)

45   Bez názvu (Marie Bufková), asi 1912 (MG6784)

46   Lucie Bakešová v Bakešově vile, Brno, asi 1912–15 (MG13324)

47   Bez názvu (žena na pohovce), asi 1912 (MGA27)

48   Bez názvu (Marie Bufková), 1909–10 (publikováno 1910)

49   „Choť umělcova", 1909–10 (publikováno 1913)

50   „Atelier Bufka, 1914": Marie Bufková (MG6786)

51   Marie Bufková: Autoportrét, asi 1919 (MG6785)

52   V. J. Bufka?: Marie Bufková, asi 1912 (MG6783)

53   Bez názvu (Eleonora Schwarzenbergová), před 1914 (MG6794)

54   Bez názvu (Karel V. Schwarzenberg se synem Karlem VI.), 1914 (MG6797)

55   Bez názvu (Eleonora Schwarzenbergová se synem Františkem), 1914 (MG6796)

56   Lucie Bakešová, 1915 (MG13327)

57   Portrét (Lucie Bakešová), 1913 (MG13328)

58   „Josef Váchal, 24. 12. 1911" (Archiv knihovny Národního muzea v Praze)

59   Alberto Vojtěch Frič, asi 1909 (soukromá sbírka, Praha)

60   prof. Jakub Husník, 1911–12 (platinotisk?, NTM)

61   Jaroslav Husník, 1911 (MG6458)

62   „Portrét spisovatele F. H." (Františka Heritese), asi 1911 (publikováno 1912)

63   Jan Kotěra, asi 1912 (UPM GF 9756)

64 Marie Bufková: Anna Sedláčková ve hře Rozkošná příhoda od Roberta de Flers, asi 1927 (MG6793)
65 Jan Kubelík, 1911–13 (soukromá sbírka)
66 Marie Bufková: Leopolda Dostalová, asi 1920 (soukromá sbírka, Praha)
67 Míla Pačová, 1914 (soukromá sbírka, Praha)
68 Ze souboru Praha, 1910 (MGA42)
69 Ze souboru Praha, 1910 (MGA42)
70 Ze souboru Praha, 1910 (MGA42)
71 Ze souboru Praha, 1910 (MGA42)
72 Ze souboru Praha, 1910 (MGA42)
73 Ze souboru Praha, 1910 (MGA42)
74 Ze souboru Praha, 1910 (MGA42)
75 Ze souboru Praha, 1910 (MGA42)
76 Ze souboru Praha, 1910 (MGA42)
77 Ze souboru Praha, 1910 (MGA42)
78 Ze souboru Praha, 1910 (MGA42)

Vladimír Jindřich Bufka

by Antonín Dufek
Translation: Derek & Marzia Paton
Graphic concept: Studio Najbrt, Prague
Graphic design: Pavel Lev & Klára Hájková, Studio Najbrt
Lithography: Art D, Prague
Printed by Trico, Prague
Copy editors: Jan Šulc & Derek Paton
Published by TORST
Address: Opatovická 24, Prague 1
CZ-110 00, Czech Republic
www.fototorst.com
First edition, 2010

Also available through D. A. P. /Distributed Art Publishers
155 Sixth Avenue, 2nd Floor, New York, N.Y. 10013, USA
Tel: ++1 (212) 627-1999 Fax: ++1 (212) 627-9484
www.artbook.com